ORIGINAL
INSTRUCTIONS

"Melissa Nelson, in collaboration with Bioneers, has produced an invaluable resource of Indigenous wisdom. This book is a must-read for every socially conscious political leader, member of the clergy, educator, activist, community worker, and entrepreneur interested in participating in the creation of a new and more ecologically sound worldview, one that will be capable of sustaining society in an era of significant global climate change."

GREGORY CAJETE, FOUNDING DIRECTOR OF
THE INSTITUTE OF AMERICAN INDIAN ARTS,
SANTA FE, NEW MEXICO, AND ASSOCIATE PROFESSOR OF
EDUCATION AT THE UNIVERSITY OF NEW MEXICO

ORIGINAL
INSTRUCTIONS

Indigenous Teachings
for a Sustainable Future

Edited by Melissa K. Nelson

PROPERTY OF
ALPINE PUBLIC LIBRARY
805 W. AVE E
ALPINE, TX 79830

Bear & Company
Rochester, Vermont

Bear & Company
One Park Street
Rochester, Vermont 05767
www.BearandCompanyBooks.com

Bear & Company is a division of Inner Traditions International

Copyright © 2008 by Collective Heritage Institute, Inc., d/b/a Bioneers

All rights reserved. No part of this book may be reproduced or utilized in any form or by any means, electronic or mechanical, including photocopying, recording, or by any information storage and retrieval system, without permission in writing from the publisher.

LIBRARY OF CONGRESS CATALOGING-IN-PUBLICATION DATA
Original instructions : indigenous teachings for a sustainable future / edited by Melissa K. Nelson ; with contributions by Rebecca Adamson . . . [et al.].
     p. cm.
  Summary: "Indigenous leaders and other visionaries suggest solutions to today's global crisis"—Provided by publisher.
  ISBN-13: 978-1-59143-079-7
  ISBN-10: 1-59143-079-8
  1. Indigenous peoples—Ecology. 2. Human ecology—Philosophy. 3. Philosophy of nature. I. Nelson, Melissa K.

  GF50.O74 2008
  304.2—dc22

                                                            2007041337

Printed and bound in the United States by Lake Book Manufacturing

10 9 8 7 6 5 4 3

Text design and layout by Virginia L. Scott Bowman
This book was typeset in Sabon with Agenda Condensed and Parchment as display typefaces

Excerpts from *Snake Poems* by Francisco X. Alarcón © 1992 by Francisco X. Alarcón. Published by Chronicle Books. Reprinted with the kind permission of Francisco X. Alarcón.

DEDICATED TO JOHN MOHAWK (1945–2006)
VISIONARY, TEACHER, FARMER, FRIEND

A Seneca Greeting—Relationship Requires Us to Be Thankful

John Mohawk

It is right when people come together that the first thing they do is greet one another. It's also true that we depend on our fraternity and sorority together, our friendships together. We acknowledge that we need one another, we who walk about on the earth. We extend greetings and thanksgiving to each other, so be it our minds.

We walk about on the earth, she supports our feet, and we have been instructed that we will call her our Mother, the earth. It is good when we come together that we remember her, and we think about what we owe her. We extend greetings and thanksgiving to our Mother, the earth, so be it our minds.

We look about us and we see growing from the earth also the small grass life and herb life, thrush life. We know that from these things we get many things that we need. We get fiber to make things with, medicines, and even food. We need to put our minds to thinking about all the herbs and thinking about all the grasses, to think about all the low-growing vegetable life that comes to us, and extend to them, the grass people, as we extend to people, our greetings and thanksgiving, so be it our minds.

There are others, too, as we walk about and see the waters. We see many different kinds of water. The waters that flow in small streams and the ones in great rivers and the ones in great oceans, and we also see that water is very central to our life. About the first thing we do in the morning when we get up is we use water to wash ourselves with, we use it to cook with. We need the water. Within our veins flows that water. We want to extend greetings and thanksgiving to the waters and all the water life, so be it our minds.

There is another: As you look about, what grows within our sight is the new tree life. The tree life also provides us with medicines, wood that keeps us warm, things we use to build our houses, but it does more than that. It also provides us with beauty, things that we can see and appreciate about the world we live in. Among those, there's a leader; in the world I come from it is the maple syrup tree. We want to think about that tree, too. We put our minds together as one mind and extend greetings and thanksgiving to all of the tree life and all of the spirit of the tree life in all of the world, so be it our minds.

And there's another. As we look up higher into the sky, we see those ones that fly about around us. When they come north in the springtime, they bring us a good song and cheer. They always lift up our spirits. As we look at them too, they know that they bring us knowledge and intelligence about the world that they have inhabited for so long. Let us think about all the bird life, especially that of the greatest birds—the eagles and the high-flying birds, too, the migratory birds. We extend greetings and thanksgiving to all the bird life, so be it our minds.

As we walk upon the earth, we see that there are others: four-legged beings that are related to us, and these four-legged beings also exist in a way in the world that brings us delight and brings us good cheer of our minds. To all of the four-legged beasts and all of the animals that walk about on the earth, we extend greetings and thanksgiving in the same spirit that we extend the greetings and thanksgiving to others.

And there's another. As we look up higher into the sky we see, also, that there is the one that walks across the sky in the daytime and brings light. That's the one that we call our elder brother, the sun. Let us think about that sun. It is the one that represents the power of the universe. We put our minds together as one mind and extend greetings and thanksgiving to our brother, the sun.

There's a nighttime sun, that's the grandmother moon, the one that also regulates the birth of everything on the earth, and we want to extend greetings and thanksgiving to our grandmother, the moon, so be it our minds.

There's another that each year comes from the West, what we call the thunder voices, and the thunder voices are the ones that bring the winds and the weather that changes and cleanses the earth. We want to acknowledge that those spirits change and cleanse the earth. We put our minds together as one mind and extend greetings and thanksgiving to the thunder voices.

There are the others. When we look up high in the sky, we can see that there are the stars that represent the face of the universe, unknowable to us, with knowledge that we've already forgotten. We want to extend greetings and thanksgiving to all of that, to all of the universe, to all the life of the universe, so be it our minds.

Finally, there's another. There's a mystery about the universe, a plan that brought us and made all of this coherent, the intelligence that created everything. We want to think about that. We want to extend greetings and thanksgiving to what they call the Great Creator, so be it our minds.

This is the talk that our people give at the beginning and at the end of every group gathering, so that we remember our relationships. The point of the talk is to remember that we are related to one another, related to the earth, and related to all the things that support life—and we are related to the universe, too. I've always thought it a very useful thing to remember that relationship requires us to be thankful.

This presentation took place at the Bioneers Conference in 1998.

Contents

Acknowledgments   xv

About Bioneers   xvii

Bioneers and Editor's Statement on Indigenous Knowledge
and Intellectual Property Rights   xix

Preface: Remembering the Original Instructions
Kenny Ausubel   xxi

Introduction: Lighting the Sun of Our Future—How These
Teachings Can Provide Illumination
Melissa K. Nelson   1

Part One
UNCOVERING THE ECO-SPIRITUAL
VALUES OF THE ORIGINAL INSTRUCTIONS

1   Listening to Natural Law
    Chief Oren Lyons   22

2   First Nations Survival and the Future of the Earth
    Rebecca Adamson   27

3   Acoma Coexistence and Continuance
    Petuuche Gilbert   36

4   Ethics from the Land: Traditional Protocols and
    the Maintenance of Peace
    Marlowe Sam   39

5   Indigenous Knowledge as the Basis for Our Future
    Priscilla Settee   42

6   Clear Thinking: A Positive Solitary View of Nature
    John Mohawk   48

Part Two
INDIGENOUS DEMOCRACIES

7   The Iroquois Confederacy
    John Mohawk   54

8   A Democracy Based on Peace
    Chief Oren Lyons   59

9   An Okanagan Worldview of Society
    Jeannette Armstrong   66

10 Peace Technologies from the San Bushmen of Africa
    Megan Biesele, Kxao =Oma., and l'Angn!ao l'Un   75

Part Three
THE ART AND SCIENCE OF KINSHIP

11 Where Is the Holy Land?
    Leslie Gray   86

12 Restoring Indigenous History and Culture to Nature
    Dennis Martinez, Enrique Salmón, and Melissa K. Nelson   88

13 Protecting Water Quality and Religious Freedom
at the Isleta Pueblo

Verna Williamson-Teller   116

14 The Art of Thriving in Place

John Mohawk   126

Part Four

INDIGENOUS FEMININE POWER: IN HONOR OF SKY WOMAN

15 She Is Us: Thought Woman and the Sustainability of Worship

Paula Gunn Allen   138

16 Ethiopian Women: From Passive Resources to Active Citizens

Bogaletch Gebre   145

17 Powerful Like a River: Reweaving the Web of Our Lives in
Defense of Environmental and Reproductive Justice

Katsi Cook   154

Part Five

YOU ARE WHERE YOU EAT: NATIVE FOODS AND TRADITIONAL AGRICULTURE

18 From the First to the Last Bite: Learning from the
Food Knowledge of Our Ancestors

John Mohawk   170

19 Re-Indigenizing Our Bodies and Minds through
Native Foods

Melissa K. Nelson   180

20 Dancing for the Apus: Andean Food and Farming
    Julio Valladolid Rivera   196

21 On the Importance of Our Connection to Food
    Jacquelyn Ross   201

22 Protecting the Culture and Genetics of Wild Rice
    Winona LaDuke   206

23 Cultural Change, Climate Change, and the Future
    of Civilization
    John Mohawk   215

Part Six

DECOLONIZATION AND GLOBAL INDIGENOUS STRUGGLES FOR JUSTICE

24 Protecting the Web of Life: Indigenous Knowledge
    and Biojustice
    Tom Goldtooth   220

25 Return of the Ancient Council Ways: Indigenous Survival
    in Chiapas
    Ohki Siminé Forest   229

26 Front Line of Resistance: Indigenous Peoples and Energy
    Development
    Clayton Thomas-Muller   239

27 Speaking for the Voiceless
    Richard DeerTrack   247

Part Seven
RE-INDIGENIZATION

28 Re-Indigenization Defined
    Greg Cajete, John Mohawk, and Julio Valladolid Rivera   252

29 *El Poder de la Palabra/* The Power of the Word:
    Toward a Nahuatl/Mestizo Consciousness
    Francisco X. Alarcón   265

30 Mending the Split-Head Society with Trickster
    Consciousness
    Melissa K. Nelson   288

31 Re-Nativization in North and South America
    Tirso Gonzales   298

32 Taro Roots Run Deep: Hawaiian Restoration of Sacred
    Foods and Communities
    Mark Paikuli-Stride, Eric Enos, and Nalani Minton   304

33 The Power of Being a Human Being
    John Trudell   318

Indigenous Resources   324

Notes   338

Bibliography   343

Contributors   347

Acknowledgments

This book would not have been possible without the visionary leadership and lifetime commitments of the Indigenous Peoples who graciously share their knowledge in these teachings of cultural survival and ecological renewal. I thank each and every one of them for their courage and compassion. I also acknowledge their families, their nations, and their ancestors for making them who they are. I am grateful to know many of these contributors as teachers, colleagues, and friends.

I acknowledge the foresight and dedication of Kenny Ausubel and Nina Simons for recognizing and honoring the wisdom of Indigenous Peoples, and the urgency of Indigenous issues, by always making a fertile space for cross-cultural education at the annual Bioneers Conference. Kenny's inspiration and passion for positive cultural change has been infused with his steadfast recognition of the Original Instructions, which catalyzed the creation of this special book.

The late Seneca teacher, scholar, and leader John Mohawk, to whom this book is dedicated, was an integral part of the Bioneers movement. His profound words are spread throughout these pages as seeds of insight, wisdom, and hope. I bow to the lives of John and his late wife, Yvonne Dion-Buffalo, and their extended family. Although we all miss John and Yvonne very much, we are blessed to have been enriched by their lives and continue to be inspired by their vision and spirit.

I want to acknowledge and express my deep appreciation for Clayton

Thomas-Muller, Tom Goldtooth, and J. P. Harpignies. With thoughtful feedback, guidance, humor, and friendship their assistance has made this book as good as it can be.

I want to recognize the Institute of American Cultures and the American Indian Studies Center (AISC) at the University of California, Los Angeles, for providing me with a wonderful place to work and for supporting my time to do oral history research and to write, which includes essential work on this book. The AISC staff and my oral history colleagues were very helpful in my editing and writing process.

The dedicated staff at the Collective Heritage Institute/Bioneers offices in Lamy, New Mexico, and beyond assisted me with the details of editing this book. It was a joy to work with every one of them. A special thank you goes to Marita Prandoni for all of her attention to detail and her good spirit and humor. Much gratitude also goes to Kelli Webster and Arty Mangan.

Last, I recognize and honor my closest kin: my Anishinaabeg ancestors and all of my foremothers and forefathers; my spirit brother, Mike; my parents, Teresa Davis Nelson and Carlyle Nelson; and my loving partner, Colin Farish. I am forever grateful for your unconditional love and support.

Chi-miigwech! (many thanks, in Ojibwe).

MELISSA K. NELSON,
EDITOR

About Bioneers

In 1990, Kenny Ausubel and Nina Simons created Bioneers to disseminate breakthrough solutions in response to the urgent call from leading scientists: Humanity needed to change our way of living on earth to avert global environmental catastrophe. By 2006, the landmark UN Millennium Ecosystem Report warned: "Human activity is putting such strain on the natural functions of earth that the ability of the planet's ecosystems to sustain future generations can no longer be taken for granted."

For the last eighteen years, the annual Bioneers Conference has acted as a dynamic, leading-edge forum. Bioneers celebrates people and nature—"human ingenuity wedded to the wisdom of the wild." It brings together the most innovative and effective leaders from the grassroots to the canopy, leaders who are focused on nature-based solutions and social strategies for restoring the earth's imperiled ecosystems and healing our human communities. The Bioneers' framework of interdependence brings together all the parts—and diverse voices—to build connections among many communities across boundaries of gender, race, culture, class, and age.

The time to act is now. By illuminating the interdependence of life on earth, Bioneers fosters a culture of solutions grounded in four billion years of evolutionary intelligence. The solutions in nature consistently surpass our concept of what is even possible. Together the Bioneers are changing the story—from separation to connection, from fear to hope, from destruction to restoration. Bioneers reflects a "reverence move-ment" devoted to creating conditions conducive to life. It's part of a large global movement to create a world that's healthy, equitable, demo-cratic, and diverse, beautiful and fun.

Learn more about Bioneers and its many programs, including the Bioneers Conference, Beaming Bioneers satellite conferences, radio series, book series, women's leadership program, youth initiative, and food and farming programs. Become a member and connect locally and globally with the Bioneers Community Network!

Visit www.bioneers.org or call 1-877-BIONEER.

Bioneers and Editor's Statement on Indigenous Knowledge and Intellectual Property Rights

Bioneers is aware of and sensitive to the national and international controversy and debate on the commodification of the sacred and on the intellectual and cultural property rights of Indigenous Peoples. Bioneers is aware of the conflicts between Western and traditional Indigenous concepts of ownership and intellectual property. This publication is a collection of talks by, and panel discussions with, Indigenous speakers who have participated in Bioneers Conferences. The collection addresses the intersection of traditional and modern expressions of Indigenous Knowledge and life experiences. Approval to print the oral presentations contained in this publication has been duly received.

Bioneers has chosen to express our gratitude to our Indigenous brothers and sisters by directing any potential royalties from the distribution and/or subsequent sales of this publication to support Indigenous Peoples' further participation at Bioneers annual conferences.

All Indigenous Knowledge held by Bioneers is always available and accessible to the Indigenous individuals, organizations, societies, and communities who shared their valuable knowledge with Bioneers in connection with the preparation of this publication, and access thereto will be provided, upon request, at a cost that is equivalent to Bioneers' costs to provide such access.

Bioneers will never knowingly use the knowledge of Indigenous Peoples in a way that creates harm, that is exploitative, or that violates Indigenous protocols. Bioneers will continue to maintain and strengthen its relationship with its Indigenous allies and networks that provide needed advice and guidance.

Bioneers will strive to understand and support Indigenous efforts to protect Indigenous traditional knowledge and uphold the sacredness of life. Bioneers does not condone or support ideas, systems, and practices, including patent laws, that define the natural world, its life-forms and the knowledge of Indigenous Peoples as property or commodities. We stand in solidarity with Indigenous Peoples to protect the sacredness of Mother Earth and their collective and inherent rights. Bioneers supports the UN Declaration on the Rights of Indigenous Peoples.

Bioneers is committed to continuously finding new and innovative ways of sharing our archives of audio and video content with Indigenous nations, communities, grassroots organizations, and networks. We are further committed to finding, developing, and supporting ongoing initiatives that build the capacity of Indigenous nations, communities, organizations, and networks to organize and to speak for themselves on the critical issues profiled in this book.

MELISSA K. NELSON,
TURTLE MOUNTAIN CHIPPEWA,
EDITOR AND PAST BIONEERS BOARD MEMBER

CLAYTON THOMAS-MULLER,
CREE NATION,
BIONEERS BOARD MEMBER

KENNY AUSUBEL,
BIONEERS FOUNDER
AND CO-EXECUTIVE DIRECTOR

PREFACE

Remembering the Original Instructions

I wept repeatedly at the beauty and wisdom painted by the voices and visions of the First Peoples and their allies in these numinous pages. They reveal a "house made of stories," in N. Scott Momaday's phrase. They embody some of the most ancient wisdom on earth from the world's "old-growth cultures." It's precisely what humanity most needs now to slip through this epochal keyhole of history where the stakes are the very survival of our species and countless other beings in the web of life. It's a journey to retrieve the Original Instructions for how to live on earth in a good way, in a way that lasts. It's a journey to recover the sacred.

As we enter the turbulent onset of global environmental collapse, these teachings remind us that what we do to the earth, we do to ourselves. Of equal importance, what we do to each other, we do to the earth. We'll have peace with the earth only when we have peace with each other, as Chief Oren Lyons says. And we'll have peace with each other only when we have justice.

Part of the Original Instructions resides in Traditional Ecological Knowledge (TEK). For millennia, Indigenous Peoples have acted as guardians of the biological diversity of the planet. They've successfully managed complex reciprocal relationships between diverse biological and human cultures, with their eyes on the time horizon of seven generations to come. This is high-TEK that has already solved many of the environmental challenges threatening humanity today. It shows how human beings can actually play a richly positive role in the web of life as a keystone species that creates conditions conducive to life for *all* beings.

As Native American restoration ecologist Dennis Martinez observes, humanity has never faced global ecological collapse before. To get through this keyhole, we're going to need the enduring knowledge of Indigenous science, as well as the best of leading edge Western science. It's high-tech meets high-TEK, and in many cases modern science is affirming what the keen empiricism of First Peoples has long known. These are the original bioneers.

This is the sacred geography of a world where all life is revered and animated by spirit. There is no separation between the technical and spiritual. It's a world of kinship where all life is related. Its instructions seem so simple: to be grateful—to practice reverence for community and creation—and to enjoy life.

The Original Instructions remind us that it's not people who are smart. The real intelligence dwells throughout the natural world and in the vast mystery of the universe that's beyond our human comprehension. Humility is our constant companion.

The Original Instructions celebrate our interdependence and interconnection with the diversity of life and one other. They help us remember who we are, that we were all Indigenous to a place not so many generations ago. They invite us to re-indigenize ourselves to our common home, Mother Earth. That is the keyhole we must slip through. It's very small, and we'll have to make ourselves very small to pass through it.

In these pages, you will hear the heartbeat of people whose spirits refused to be conquered in the murderous face of genocide. People who refused to forsake their culture and values even through the trauma of violent, racist colonization. People who refused to close their hearts even when they were up against unimaginable suffering, loss, and disrespect. In spite of all this, their instructions are to be thankful, to be kind, to love and take care of one another.

But make no mistake: These are heartbreaking stories of survival and cultural persistence in a brutal history whose legacy of oppression and atrocity rages to this day. As native peoples continue to wage frontline struggles to protect their lives, their lands, their rights, their cultures, and their sovereignty, they embrace allies dedicated to standing with them in their unending quest for justice and self-determination. The voices of some of their devoted allies are also reflected in these pages.

These chapters, with the exception of two, are drawn from talks given at the annual Bioneers Conferences from 1990 to 2006. From its origin, Bioneers has been indelibly imprinted with Indigenous Knowledge and perspectives, for which we give our most profound thanks, a thanks that is beyond the ability of words to express. It's an enormous honor and gift to publish these luminous stories of survival and transcendence. We do so with the generous permission of the contributors, to whom we offer our deepest gratitude and respect.

In many Indigenous traditions, seeds are considered sacred. For Six Nations people, this is known as the Law of the Seed, an honoring of the natural cycles of continuous creation and regeneration. Seeds carry life from generation to generation without end. Through the seeds speak the voices of the ancestors. Each time we plant a seed, we become ancestors for the generations to come. If we follow the instructions, life will be everlasting.

These stories are seeds. It's our deepest wish that they land in fertile ground to sprout and spread. Nurture them well, spread them, and give thanks, so that once again we may all live with each other on earth in a good way that lasts.

To invoke my beloved teacher and friend, the late John Mohawk, in whose memory we lovingly dedicate this book:

"So be it our minds."

KENNY AUSUBEL, FOUNDER, BIONEERS,
CAÑADA DE LOS ALAMOS, NEW MEXICO
JULY 16, 2007

Kenny Ausubel is an award-winning social entrepreneur, journalist, and filmmaker. He is the founder and copresident of Bioneers, with his partner and wife, cofounder Nina Simons. Bioneers is a national nonprofit educational organization seeding practical solutions for people and planet. Together they have received several awards, including the Global Green award for Community Environmental Leadership and Rainforest Action Network's World Rainforest award. Kenny cofounded Seeds of Change, a leading national biodiversity organic seed company that received widespread recognition for its innovative market partnership with backyard gardeners to create backyard biodiversity as a conservation strategy. His feature documentary *Hoxsey: How Healing Becomes a Crime* won the Best Censored Stories award and played in movie theaters as well as on HBO. He founded and operates Inner Tan Productions, a visionary feature film development company. He acted as a central advisor to Leonardo DiCaprio's feature documentary *The 11th Hour,* half of whose interviewees came through Bioneers, and he is featured in the film. His books include *Seeds of Change: The Living Treasure, The Bioneers: Declarations of Interdependence,* and *When Healing Becomes a Crime: The Amazing Story of the Hoxsey Cancer Clinics and the Return of Alternative Therapies.* He has also served as executive editor and editor of the Bioneers anthology books series and executive producer and cowriter of the award-winning radio series: *Bioneers: Revolution from the Heart of Nature.*

Lighting the Sun of Our Future— How These Teachings Can Provide Illumination

Melissa K. Nelson

On the cover of this book is an image from a painting entitled "Nanabozhoo Lights Up the Sun" by Ojibwe artist Rabbett Strickland. *Nanabozhoo* is the Anishinaabeg culture hero and trickster figure who uses primal fire to ignite the Sun. Nanabozhoo is part human, part spirit. He is often depicted as a man or a rabbit or both. He is a shape-shifter, a mover and a shaker, and a creator and destroyer. He is our first human being. He was born of the Creator through a woman and the North Wind. He illuminates and then, at times, he conceals. He enlightens but can also complicate matters. He has many names; one of them means "he who walks the shoreline forever," and another means "he who makes good laws." Ultimately, Nanabozhoo teaches, he instructs. For Ojibwe people, he is our first teacher of the Original Instructions given to us by our Creator, *Gitche Manitou*, the Great Mystery. Nanabozhoo travels the lands and waters and shows us the full spectrum of being human—the good, the bad, and everything in between. Ojibwe elder Tobasonakwut Kinew calls him the "Forrest Gump" of the Ojibwe.*

Nanabozhoo has an enormous appetite for the sensual pleasures of life. He would love Slow Food† dinners but would probably eat them too fast. He can be extremely selfish in pursuit of his desires but he is also compassionately wise and gives us what we need to survive and thrive on this earth. After all, he did light up the sun. As an *Anishinaabe-ikwe,* (Ojibwe woman) he is one of my spiritual references and orients me to a moral compass.

In this particular image and story, Nanabozhoo provides sunshine and heat, light and illumination. In other stories he steals fish, eats too much, falls asleep, gets burned, and laughs at his own antics. He is a creator and survivor of floods, storms, droughts, lightning, and, equally disastrous (and often humorous), his own human foibles. His *miss takes* show us what *not* to do. In this way, Indigenous education is more about observing things in action, understanding things in their context, and listening to the reflective rhythms and inherent wisdom that spiral through a story.

This book is focused on illuminating the Indigenous Knowledge intrinsic within the Original Instructions and oral traditions of the first nations Indigenous Peoples of the world. No matter where you go on the planet, Indigenous and traditional cultures regularly refer to the "Original Instructions" or "First Teachings" given to them by their Creator(s)/Earth-Maker/Life-Giver/Great Spirit/Great Mystery/Spirit Guides. Original Instructions refer to the many diverse teachings, lessons, and ethics expressed in the origin stories and oral traditions

---

*Like the character in the film *Forrest Gump,* Nanabozhoo travels around the world and has heroic adventures with others. He almost haphazardly finds himself meeting historic figures, influencing everything from politics to popular culture, and setting in motion "the way things are." He does all of this through a fumbling, comic style, often unaware of the impacts of his actions.

†Slow Food refers to an international organization, movement, and philosophy committed to "good, clean, and fair food." It is a response to the Fast Food epidemic. Slow Food encourages slowing down and taking the time to grow, cook, eat, and enjoy healthy foods and the pleasure of eating. See www.slowfood.com/ and www.slowfoodusa.org

of Indigenous Peoples. They are the literal and metaphorical instructions, passed on orally from generation to generation, for how to be a good human being living in reciprocal relation with all of our seen and unseen relatives. They are natural laws that, when ignored, have natural consequences.

OVERVIEW OF GLOBAL INDIGENOUS PEOPLES AND ISSUES

There are at least 350 million people on the Earth who identify themselves as Indigenous Peoples.[1] This is approximately 6–8 percent of the world population. According to the last U.S. Census Bureau reports, there are 4.1 million American Indians living in the United States. We make up 1.5 percent of the total U.S. population.[2] We may be minorities in terms of population, but we certainly are not minorities in terms of knowledge, culture, and diversity. As Native American law professor David Wilkins puts it, "Indian peoples are nations, not minorities."[3]

Today in the United State alone there are over 550 Native American nations speaking over 175 distinct languages. We have clearly demonstrated our powers of survival and adaptation. We have not vanished and we are "back from extinction" as the San Francisco Bay Area-based Muwekma Ohlone assert.[4] Not only are Indigenous Peoples reasserting our presence and demanding our rights, but we are "re-writing history and re-righting history" as Maori scholar Linda Tuhiwai Smith recommends in her book *Decolonizing Methodologies—Research and Indigenous Peoples*.

This book, *Original Instructions*, attempts to do that also, by sharing profound teachings from diverse Indigenous individuals coming from distinct lands, cultures, languages, worldviews, philosophies, and ways of life. It gives native "insider" perspectives on a wide range of Indigenous concerns: land rights, governance, religious freedom, conflict resolution, politics, health, women's rights, food and agriculture, sustainability, science, art, activism, justice, identity, and healing. Because there is such a multiplicity of Native American nations, communities, and individuals, you will find information in these pages that may appear to contradict other information from other chapters. Within diverse Indigenous ways of knowing, there is ultimately no conflict with this. In fact, it points to two very important insights generally practiced by Indigenous Peoples: for humans to get along with each other and to respect our relations on the earth, we must embrace and practice cognitive and cultural pluralism (value diverse ways of thinking and being). We need to not only *tolerate* difference but respect and celebrate cultural diversity as an essential part of engendering peace.*

ORAL TRADITIONS AND INDIGENOUS PEDAGOGY

The oral tradition is alive and well in Indian Country today as witnessed by these essays, which are based on live, oral presentations with all of the added benefits of eye contact, body language, gesture, timing, audience response, and the magic of storytelling and performance in the moment, with elements that are improvised, spontaneous, and participatory. I have done my best to maintain the feel and dynamic quality of the oral tradition in these edited talks while making them accessible and stimulating for the general reader. You didn't have to "be there" to gain deeply from the knowledge and teachings shared in this book. The words and stories speak for themselves.

Since most Indigenous cultures were, historically, oral/aural cultures, meaning that they relied on voice, speech, story, listening, and memory rather than written text on a page for gaining and transmitting knowledge, Indigenous forms of education are usually based on storytelling. This dynamic oral tradition—although severely threatened by waves of colonial disruption, forced assimilation, and cultural homogenization—is being maintained and restored by persistent language keepers and culture bearers throughout the world. As the late great Lakota scholar Vine Deloria Jr. has written, "Every human society maintains its sense

---

*Of course this cultural relativity argument does not mean we do not stand up against violations of human or indigenous rights, such as land theft or female genital mutilation.

of identity with a set of stories that explain, at least to its satisfaction, how things came to be. A good many societies begin at a creation and carry forward a tenuous link of events which they consider to be historical—which is to say actual experiences of the group which often serve as precedents for determining present and future actions."[5]

As the Inland Northwest Tribes of America say, "stories make the world."[6] Native stories include origin legends and history, famous speeches and epic poems, songs, the teachings of spirit mentors, instructions for ceremony and ritual, observations of worlds, and storehouses of ethno-ecological knowledge. Stories often live in many dimensions, with meanings that reach from the ordinary to the divine, from the "before worlds" to the present. Stories are possessed with such power that they have survived for generations despite attempts at repression and assimilation. Native American storytelling is an invaluable cross-cultural continuum that has no beginning and no end. All cultures can learn and be enriched by Native storytelling.

Different "bundles" of stories represent different aspects of life teachings: women's knowledge, healer's knowledge, children's knowledge, hunter's knowledge, and so on. "In the Indigenous world a 'bundle' is made by the bringing together of spiritual and material objects, elements, allies and energies that will be needed to sustain the spiritual life and secular outcomes of a ceremony or gathering that is being undertaken."[7] These teaching bundles are the "curriculum" for indigenous educators. But teaching bundles are only part of the story. The other part is the *learning* bundles. In Indigenous pedagogy there is a great emphasis on learning. Chickasaw law professor James Sakej Henderson often refers to the "learning spirit" within each person. He earnestly asks us, "How do we awaken and sustain the learning spirit?"

Put another way, the eminent Tewa Indian educator Gregory Cajete asks us to "ignite the sparkle" of our own learning; follow our passion and listen to the deeper meanings within a story or watch for the hidden pattern that connects seemingly disparate things.[8] Examining our own learning process requires a self-inquiry process to assess the strengths and weaknesses of what Cajete calls the "rational mind" and the "metaphoric mind." He suggests that the metaphoric mind is the first foundation of native science.[9]

This Indigenous way of learning through observing and listening to stories and teachings and recognizing and valuing our learning spirits is quite different from contemporary forms of mainstream education where an authority figure usually shares abstracted, so-called "objective" information in a more linear, pedantic way. In this book, you will not necessarily find teachings laid out for you as 1, 2, 3, or A, B, C. The native leaders, Elders, teachers, artists, and activists offer you here a bundle of teachings in the form of heartfelt personal stories of struggle, resistance, survival, and transformation. As you read these teachings, imagine yourself listening to stories of Nanabozhoo walking through maple forests or canoeing down the Mississippi River. These contributors are postcolonial Native leaders sharing an urgent message of cultural recovery, renewal, and survivance.*

PROPHECY AND THE URGENCY
OF THESE TEACHINGS

Urgent messages are needed for urgent times. Humanity and life on this planet currently face an unprecedented ecological crisis. Climate change, biodiversity extinction, food and water scarcity, overpopulation, the threat of nuclear war, pollution, and toxicity . . . sadly, the list goes on and on. Additionally, we face a greater social divide between the rich and the poor, with fewer people controlling more power and resources. We live in a world where a billion people are starving to death, and a billion people are obese. This economic disparity combined with ecological breakdown and unresolved social issues such as racism and sexism fuels wars and genocides and poses serious threats to the quality and continued existence

---

*This word "survivance" was coined by Ojibwe scholar/writer Gerald Vizenor to differentiate normal "survival" from what Native Americans have had to do, which is continue to exist after five hundred years of conquest and attempted genocide and do so through a highly adaptive process that is not simply a matter of continuing past practices but combining and creating new ones.

of life on Earth, including our own species. Is this process of ecological and social disintegration a massive collective mistake? Did humanity take a wrong turn? Does humanity learn from its mistakes? Are we facing an evolutionary dead-end? Or is this disorder subsumed under a larger order? Has the destruction of the earth been prophesized? Will the human species go extinct? Part 1 addresses these weighty questions and uncovers the ecological and spiritual values of the Original Instructions.

Deep within the teachings of the Original Instructions and millenna-old oral/verbal art forms are certain story bundles that serve as important warning signs and guideposts. These are often called prophecies. They are another type of instruction. There are countless examples of prophetic traditions from all of the world's cultures. Within Indigenous traditions there are numerous stories (recorded and unrecorded) regarding the consequences of our decisions, collective actions, and the future of humanity and the earth. In discussing prophecy with my Lakota/Dakota friend and colleague Woableza (Robert LaBatte), he commented, "It is my understanding from my Elders that once a prophecy has been told it must not be changed and that it has a code or sacred process embedded in the words or translation."

Unlike many classical Western and Eastern prophecies, Indigenous prophecies do not necessarily revolve around a prophet. Maybe a prophet brought the teaching, but the emphasis is on the message, and the collective tribal body or community that holds that message, not the messenger. Prophecies are a way to both remember and look forward. They orally record the events of the past and provide lessons and warning signs for potential changes in the future. Prophecies do not *predict* the future but they outline the probable consequences of violating natural laws, of not heeding the Original Instructions. In this book, you will find several references to prophecies from many different Indigenous traditions. The Hopi of the American Southwest and the Iroquois of the American Northeast are two tribal groups who have been actively sharing their prophecies with the world.

In 1948 traditional Hopi Elders selected Hopi tribal member Thomas Banyacya to be the translator and messenger for their Fourth World prophecy and bring their message to the world, including the United Nations. This prophecy describes how we are currently living in the Fourth World, after three previous worlds were destroyed by natural disasters due to humans not listening to the Original Instructions and letting greed, selfishness, and materialism dominate. After decades of trying to give the Hopi message to the United Nations, Banyacya was finally able to formally address the world's nations in 1992 (John Mohawk refers to this historic event in chapter 14 of this book). Referring to the Creator on this historic occasion, Banyacya shared the Hopi ancient prophecy with the United Nations intergovernmental political body.

> We made a sacred covenant to follow his life plan at all times, which includes the responsibility of taking care of this land and life for his divine purpose. We have never made treaties with any foreign nation, including the United States, but for many centuries we have honored this sacred agreement. Our goals are not to gain political control, monetary wealth nor military power, but rather to pray and to promote the welfare of all living beings and to preserve the world in a natural way.[10]

Banyacya describes how and why the previous three worlds perished—the last one by a large flood—a common symbol of purification in many cultures. He then states that a line running around the Hopi ceremonial rattle represents Mother Earth. "The line is a time line and indicates that we are in the final days of the prophecy. What have you, as individuals, as nations and as the world body been doing to take care of this Earth?"

He summarizes some of the serious problems occurring today, from the poisoning of our foods to starving children. He describes the warning signs from nature, such as beaching whales. Banyacya then stresses, "If we humans do not wake up to the warnings, the great purification will come to destroy this world just as the previous worlds were destroyed."

In a statement to humanity, 105-year-old Hopi Snake Priest Evehema echoed the following Hopi warning:

We are now faced with great problems, not only here but through-out the land. Ancient cultures are being annihilated. Our people's lands are being taken from them. Why is this happening? It is hap-pening because many have given up or manipulated their original spiritual teachings. The way of life that the Great Spirit has given to all people of the world, whatever your Original Instructions, are not being honored. It is because of this great sickness called greed, which infects every land and country.[11]

The great Haudenosaunee or Six Nations Iroquois Confederacy also has many prophecies regarding the earth and peace. Over one thousand years ago their prophet, the Great Peacemaker, united warring tribes and brought the Great Law of Peace. This profound process, historical event, and model is described in detail in chapters 7 and 8 by John Mohawk and Chief Oren Lyons respectively.

Other Indigenous prophecies discussed in oral and mainstream lit-erature, media, and academia are the Mayan calendar and its predictions for the year 2012; the prophecy of the Eagle and the Condor, which says that the Indigenous peoples of North and South America will be united in peace; the Kogi Warning from the Heart of the World, and numerous other warning teachings from nations, tribes, communities, and individu-als. I am not here to promote or dismiss any of these as valid or invalid but to point to the fact that story, prophecy, and oral literature are some of the most important ways to transmit cultural knowledge and collec-tive memory. They serve as important touchstones for human behavior, ethics, and lifeways. They help us reassess our relationship to time and to place, and remind us to ask ourselves, "What have we, as individuals, as nations, and as the world body, been doing to take care of this earth?"

ADDRESSING THE ECOLOGICAL INDIAN AND ROMANCING THE STONE AGE

As the late Western Shoshone spiritual leader Corbin Harney used to say, "native people are not separate from the environment. We *are* the environment!" With every bite of food we eat, every drop of water we drink, every breath of air we inhale, we are on the fluid edge of "inside" and "outside," "me" and the "environment," the person and the planet, and the individual and humanity. As the late physicist and philosopher David Bohm has said, "The consciousness of humanity manifests in each individual, each individual manifests the consciousness of humankind."*

In this sense, our biological and psychological space is a communal ground, a commons. As much as human thought and Eurocentric conditioning tries to divide and fragment us, we are ultimately part of an undivided wholeness. With this profound philosophical and ethical understanding, Indigenous Peoples have taken it upon themselves to be the caretakers of the last remaining healthy, sacred, biodiverse places on earth because they are us, we cannot be separated from these places. The bones and blood of our ancestors have become the soil, the soil grows our food, the food nourishes our bodies, and we become one, literally and metaphorically, with our homelands and territories. This profound inter-relationship of nature and culture is further elaborated in part 3, "The Art and Science of Kinship."

Due to imposed economic and colonial regimes, many native lands have been mined, bombed, stripped, deforested, and polluted with the worst chemicals and toxic waste known to humanity. So not only are indigenous peoples caretakers of some of the last healthy, diverse natural lands and waters of the planet, they are also caretakers of some of the most decimated (strip-mined, bombed, dammed, and polluted) places on Earth. Part 6 of this book, "Decolonization and Global Indigenous Struggles for Justice," directly addresses the native resistance to mining and toxic colonialism of Indigenous lands and peoples.

Many Native Peoples believe that the center of the universe or the heart of the world is in their backyard, literally. And there is no conflict over this as the Wintu of California can perceive Mount Shasta

---

*I heard David Bohm use this phrase repeatedly at his Dialogues in Ojai, California, in 1989 and 1990.

in northern California as the center of their universe while the Kogi of Colombia can understand that they are from the "heart of the world" in the Sierra Nevada de Santa Marta of Colombia. Place-based spiritual responsibility and cognitive pluralism are imbedded in most Original Teachings. It is good that each nation, each tribe, each community perceives their ancestral lands as the center of the universe, as their holy land, as Leslie Gray's chapter 11 provocatively discusses. It is when people think there is only "one place" that is holy or only "one way" that is right that hegemony rears its ugly head and societies get into trouble with conflict and war.

All cultures have this challenge and Indigenous Peoples have gone to war with each other since the beginning. Many Indigenous groups, such as the Hopi, Iroquois, and Tibetans, have a profound commitment to peace and live their lives with the least amount of conflict as possible. Yet other tribes and groups have had many wars with their neighbors. For example, my own tribe, the Ojibwe, have been traditional enemies with the Lakota or Sioux nation and both nations remember many brutal battles with each other. Intertribal conflicts and alliances have existed since before contact with European powers and certainly continued afterward.

It is important to note that many of these historical intertribal conflicts were also a result of or escalated by the U.S. government's military strategy of "divide and conquer" to prevent intertribal alliances that presented more of a threat to the United States. These histories of conflict and war not only divide tribes but actually connect them in many deep ways. The Ojibwe and Lakota, for example, often tease each other about these old confrontations but do so with great mutual respect regarding their entwined history. As the old saying goes, "keep your friends close and your enemies closer." Many tribes learned, shared, and coevolved with each other through complex rituals and cycles of traditional warfare and peace.

Native Peoples, like all peoples, strive for positive and peaceful lives yet sometimes find themselves amidst conflict and war. It often ends up being a profound personal ethical question, both historically and for today, about the best way to deal with conflict. Many tribes and native individuals are committed to nonviolent, peaceful responses while others feel it is sometimes necessary to take up arms. Part 2 on "Indigenous Democracies" looks directly at this question and provides four different Indigenous groups' perspectives regarding collective decision-making, social organization, conflict resolution, and peacemaking.

Indigenous Peoples have millennia-old Indigenous Knowledge Systems (IKS) that are tribally and geographically specific. Within these knowledge systems or teaching bundles of Indigenous Knowledge is Traditional Ecological Knowledge (TEK). This "TEK" or native science holds the memories, observations, stories, understandings, insights, and practices for how to follow the natural laws of a particular place. TEK is often encoded in the stories and songs of the oral tradition and within particular rituals and daily practices. The Coast Miwok of Marin and Sonoma Counties in northern California hold the traditional knowledge for how to live in dynamic equilibrium with the oak woodlands, redwood forests, grasslands, creeks, wetlands, and coastal prairies of their rich landscape. My Ojibwe nation holds the traditional knowledge for navigating the Great Lakes, rivers, and the maple and birch woodlands of the Minnesota, Ontario, and Wisconsin area.

Knowing, remembering, practicing, and implementing these place–based native sciences and laws comes with a great responsibility. Greg Cajete has called this a practice of sacred ecology or sacred science. It is not for everyone. Unfortunately, much of this knowledge and its associated practices were systematically erased, taken away, and forbidden by colonial powers. Many fluent language keepers and Elders still hold this knowledge. Today, those of us who are younger and of mixed-blood heritage are doing many things to recover and restore these essential ethics and practices of sustainability in a modern context.

Because of these diverse knowledge systems and teaching bundles within Indigenous communities, there has been much debate and discussion about the stereotype of the "ecologically noble savage," as well as concerns over a romanticization of the past. What is interesting is that these questions do not often concern Indigenous Peoples themselves. The issues of romanticization and exotification seem to be more of a concern and practice from outside, from Euro-American academia and the New Age movement respectively. Certainly Native Peoples are concerned and upset when they are stereotyped and romanticized; this form of racism needs to change. But the question of whether Indigenous Peoples were, historically, environmentalists or not, is almost irrelevant. To say that American Indians were the "first ecologists" fragments environmental matters from other issues of daily life and imposes a modern postcolonial concept onto a historical, precolonial context.

On one hand, given the rich philosophical worldviews and life practices of land and kin, it is absurd for Indigenous Peoples (or others) to question whether they were or are environmentalists or not. Dennis Martinez and Enrique Salmón address this issue in chapter 12 by pointing out that TEK is first and foremost *practical* knowledge for survival, not some mystical training for transcendence. Just the fact that so many Indigenous Peoples are still here indicates they have profound ecological knowledge and skills of survival and adaptation. As Southern Paiute elder Vivienne Jake says, "Whether we know it or not, there could come a time when we have to go through hardship again, and the Paiute survival arts are what is going to save my people, as long as we know what those survival arts are and how to live through hardship."[12]

On the other hand, many Indigenous groups, tribes, and villages made and make ecological mistakes, whether it's letting a prescribed fire get out of hand, overharvesting an animal, or more recently, allowing toxic waste on their lands. Additionally, due to the trauma of colonization, assimilation, and extreme poverty amid a capitalistic landscape, many Native Peoples have become "Americanized" with the same materialism and greed as any one else and have been conditioned to forget the earth and our nonhuman relatives. The fact that many Native American tribal councils are prioritizing casinos, golf courses, and resorts over traditional agriculture, sustainable land use, and cultural centers makes this point.

Indigenous Peoples, like all peoples, are far from perfect and make mistakes. And yes, native groups have historically made ecological mistakes; that is natural. Yet the question then becomes, how do we learn from these mistakes? Embedded within most Indigenous Knowledge systems, languages, and worldviews are profound teachings for an entirely different reality of our relationship to the land, water, and other elements of the earth and universe. These teachings are based on long-held cultural memories that recount historic mistakes to remind us not to make them again. These mistakes have been transformed into lessons inculcated into Indigenous cultures and spiritual teachings. The Original Instructions provide a form of moral checks and balances on the collective consciousness of a people. How well we listen to these memories and instructions will determine our future.

Because local TEK is so foreign to the mindset of modern, western science and the Eurocentric paradigm, it is often difficult for non-native outsiders to understand these realities and teachings. As Edward Said, the late Palestinian-American scholar and writer articulated so well (and many others have said since), when people do not understand things, it is easy to denigrate, romanticize, or exoticize different ways and peoples—to dehumanize the "Other."

CULTURAL RECOVERY AND REVITALIZING INDIGENOUS LIFEWAYS

For many of us, the process of re-indigenization means we have to decolonize our minds, hearts, bodies, and spirits and revitalize healthy cultural traditions. We also have to create new traditions, new ways to thrive in this complex world during these intense times. As John Mohawk states in chapter 28 of this book, "We're in recovery from the effects of more than five centuries of what only can be described as cultural madness." After suffering from conquest and surviving attempted genocide, many Indigenous Peoples are affected by what Ojibwe scholar Lawrence Gross calls, "Post-Apocalyptic Stress Disorder."[13] Gross goes on to define his meaning by saying that today's

Native Peoples are in a "post-apocalyptic" time because after conquest our worlds came to an end. He then argues that "although the traditional world of the Anishinaabe (or any tribe) may have come to an end, the worldview that informed that life still survives."[14]

Today's Native Americans are descendants of survivors of a holocaust. "The historical losses of Native peoples meet the United Nations definition of genocide."[15] Genocide, foreign disease, and colonial violence have affected every aspect of Indian life. "A violation of this nature occurs at the physical, psychological and spiritual levels and therefore, the issue must be addressed at all of these levels. Healing of the body, mind and spirit is further compounded by the fact that the trauma occurs at the personal, community and collective level."[16]

Historical trauma is a result of governmental policies of genocide, removal and relocation, assimilation and termination that have affected Native Americans for five hundred years. Such extreme experiences of violence, cultural disruption, forced assimilation through mission and boarding schools and other means, and economic marginalization and poverty has created a systemic problem of psychological disempowerment and trauma for American Indians. Socially unacknowledged and individually untreated, these traumas are inherited intergenerationally. "Personal traumas lead to collective traumatization, and in turn, collective traumatization (oppression, repression, etc.) impacts personal trauma."[17] This trauma manifests as internalized oppression that perpetuates a negative cycle of mental health disorders within native individuals, families, and the community at large. This negative cycle is directly related to the horrific statistics that show that Native Americans are disproportionately represented in high rates of suicide, incarceration, and death row sentencing.

Internalized oppression is a result of the socioeconomic and psychospiritual domination of oppressive political systems that seeks to colonize and control culturally diverse peoples (their knowledge and practices), usually for economic labor and religious conversion. The political structures of oppression—racism, poverty, sexism, violence, acculturation stress—become so dominant in the minds of the oppressed peoples that they begin to believe these dominant narratives and internalize this oppression. As the well-known South African social justice activist Steven Biko stated, "the most potent weapon in the hands of the oppressor is the mind of the oppressed."

Many diverse thinkers, writers, and native Elders have asserted that the collective consciousness of Native American communities and of the dominant American society will be not be at peace until modern Americans acknowledge the past treatment of American Indians and the fact that this country was built on genocide and slavery. There must be an acknowledgment of the truth, an apology, a reconciliation, restitution, and a healing.

The health of American Indians is directly tied to the historical, social context of America. In many ways, for American Indians, political justice and psychological healing are connected. It is native women who are often at the forefront of making these links and leading cutting-edge movements. We hear from powerful native women throughout this book and dedicate part 4 to "Indigenous Feminine Power: In Honor of Sky Woman."

Today, this legacy of pain is being addressed through the Native American wellness movement, traditional and integrative medicine, a renewal of native practices such as traditional foods and ceremonies, and through contemporary arts and media. This book shows how resilient Indigenous communities are and provides contemporary examples of recovery. For example, the native foods revitalization movement is flourishing in North America; part 5, "You Are Where You Eat: Native Foods and Traditional Agriculture," shares heartbreaking stories of loss of foods and well-being but also provides excellent models and case studies of native communities restoring their strength through the renewal of Indigenous foods and medicines.

IDENTITY AND INDIGENEITY

Natives and nonnatives alike often ask, "Who is a real Indian?" Full-bloods, mixed-bloods, members of a federally recognized tribes, those who speak their language, those who live on their reservations, those who "look" Indian—are *these* real Indians? They are certainly some of the stereotypes of Indian authenticity. Native American cultural psychologist Joseph Gone has pointed out that due to internalized oppression and other issues, many Indian people suffer from the "More Indian Than Thou" (MITT) syndrome. This is a subtle and often not so subtle measuring up of who is an authentic Indian person. Mixed-raced people like myself, and like most of us these days, are often told, "you don't *look* Indian," or "you must be a half-breed." As Paula Gunn Allen suggests, mixed-race people are not "half and half" but "all and all." The questions of who is Indigenous in the twenty-first century and what is indigeneity are critical questions of our time. This book, particularly the last section on "Re-Indigenization," helps elucidate these concepts and shares important responses. Ultimately, as many of these contributors describe, we must heal the relationship between the colonizer and the colonized, starting within ourselves. Only then can we be authentic human beings who will be able to contribute positively to a more just, compassionate, and sustainable world for Indigenous Peoples and *all* peoples, including our winged, four-legged, and finned relatives in the natural world.

AN OFFERING OF NATIVE VOICES

This book is a collection of edited talks presented at the annual Bioneers Conference in California between 1990 and 2006. These native leaders and eco-visionaries come from North, Central, and South America, Hawaii, and Africa, with the majority of contributors being Native American from the United States and Canada. Over twenty Native nations are represented in this rare collection of over thirty Indigenous intellectuals, farmers, scholars, faithkeepers, poets, educators, activists, writers, ecologists, and healers. These contributors represent four tribes of the great Six Nations Iroquois Confederacy, five of the Southwestern Pueblo nations, and a wide range of Indian nations from throughout Turtle Island.

Some of these contributors, like Paula Gunn Allen, Greg Cajete, and the late John Mohawk, are giants in the field of American Indian/Native American/Indigenous Studies. Others like Chief Oren Lyons, Richard DeerTrack, and Katsi Cook are tradition keepers and cultural healers. Some, like Winona LaDuke and Rebecca Adamson, are known as international Indigenous leaders making significant changes in policies, laws, and economics. Others like Tom Goldtooth, Ohki Siminé Forest, and Clayton Thomas-Muller are frontline activists working on the ground with grassroots communities. And yet others, like John Trudell, Jeannette Armstrong, and Francisco X. Alarcón are known as eloquent writers, poets, and cultural revolutionaries. Every contributor fits into one of these categories and most fit into all of them. Every one, known and unknown, are making significant and important changes in their communities and around the world. We are all working to maintain and create a more sustainable future for "all of our relations."

I have been participating in the annual Bioneers Conference since 1994, first as a participant, then, after 1997 as a speaker and moderator of Indigenous workshops. I served on the Bioneers/CHI board of directors for four years and worked as an associate producer for three years, assisting with including local California Indian and national Native American leaders in the conference as participants and for presentations, workshops, and opening blessings. I have been present, either as a co-presenter, moderator, or participant at the majority of the Bioneers presentations that most of these chapters derived from. There are a few chapters included that are based on interviews by Bioneers staff and contributions by like-minded native activists and scholars.

Those of us included in this book are interested in maintaining and renewing native teachings that are fundamental, primal, and essential to the maintenance of life on earth. These are natural laws. No matter how hard our mischievous human species tries to change them or transcend them, they are beyond our control. And yet many of us have forgotten that. Our technologies, sciences, and Eurocentric conditionings have given us the illusion that we are in control. Some tribal leaders accuse scientists, especially nuclear physicists and geneticists of "playing God."

These primal teachings and instructions are profound ethical and moral teachers that remind us of our smallness in the universe. If we listen and act, perhaps we can help humanity and our extended relatives in the web of life survive and be sustained well into the future. As the Haudenosaunee say, we are interested in maintaining "cycles of regeneration" and "cycles of continuous creation." Please join us in this unfolding journey.

To *Mino-bimaadiziwin* and *Miyo-wicehtowin*—"to good life and well-being for all our relatives" in Ojibwe and Cree languages, respectively.

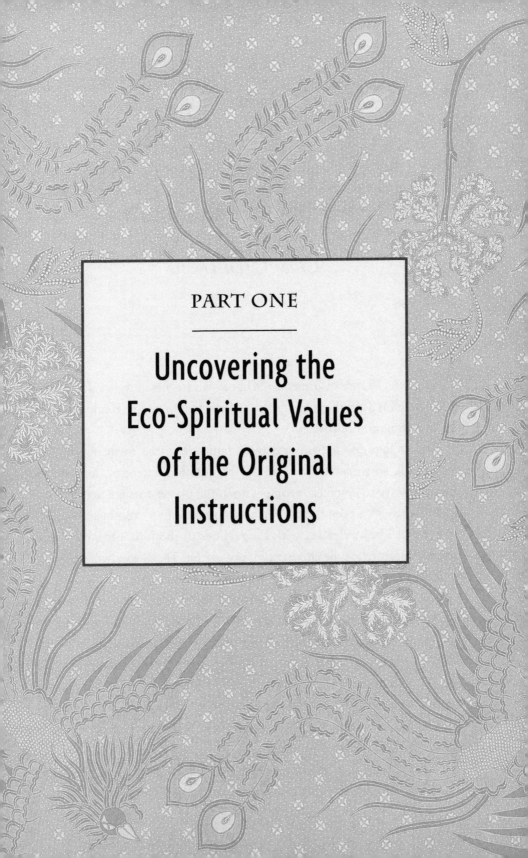

PART ONE

Uncovering the Eco-Spiritual Values of the Original Instructions

1

Listening to Natural Law

Chief Oren Lyons

Neyawenha Skannoh. It means "Thank you for being well." The greeting in itself is something of an idea of how Indian people think and how their communities operate.

What happens to you and what happens to the earth happens to us as well, so we have, as I said before, common interests. We have to somehow try to convince people who are in power to change the direction that they've been taking. We need to take a more responsible direction and to begin dealing with the realities of the future to insure that there *is* a future for the children, for the nation. That's what we're about. It is to our advantage as well as yours to be doing that.

In the concern and in the fights that we face as a common people, as human beings, as a species, we have to get together and we have to do things like we're doing now—meeting, sharing, learning. It all comes down to the will, what is in your heart. Indian people have survived up to this time because we have a strong will. We do not agree that we should be assimilated. We do not agree that we should give up our way of life. And that same will should be in your heart—the will that you do not agree that there be no future.

I don't believe, personally, that we have reached a point of no return in this situation that we're in, but we are approaching it. The farther you're away from a point of no return, the more options you have. As we move each day closer to a point of no return, we lose that day's option. And there will come a point where we won't have an option. There will be no more options. At that point, people will cry and people will carry on and so forth. But as Chief Shenandoah said to me, "I don't know what the big problem is. It's too late anyway." I said, "Uncle, what do you mean by that?" "Well," he says, "they've done a lot of damage. They're going to suffer." Kind of a simple observation, but true enough. There is a lot of damage done and people are going to suffer but he didn't carry out the thought that we were told a long time ago in the prophecies; the prophecies that said there was going to be a degradation of the earth. We were told that you could tell the extent of the degradation of the earth because there would be two very important systems to warn you.

One would be the acceleration of the winds. We were told that the winds would accelerate and continue to accelerate. When you see that the acceleration of the winds are growing, then you are in dangerous times. They said the other way to tell that the earth was in degradation was how people treated their children. They said it will be very important to note how people treat their children, and that will tell you how the earth is degrading. So when you open up the newspapers today they talk about exploitive sex and children, they talk about homeless children, and you can count homeless children by the millions. To us, it's a severe indication of the degradation. Society doesn't care.

So we have to take those signposts seriously and begin to organize ourselves and do the best we can. We must gather ourselves together, give ourselves some moral support, enough to go home and start over and do it again, because everything starts at home. It starts right there with you. It starts with you and then your family. Then from your family it goes out and that's how you do it, that's how you have to do it. It's grassroots. You go back and you begin to inform and you get a little more excited and you get a little more severe in your positions and you begin to insist that people hear and listen. There's a lot of information and that's one of the good things about this Bioneers coalition that comes together. There's a lot of exchange and support and important information conveyed. Education is important and how you educate people as to what we need is fundamentally important.

The spiritual side of the natural world is absolute. The laws are absolute. Our instructions, and I'm talking about for all human beings, our instructions are to get along. Understand what these laws are. Get along with laws, and support them and work with them. We were told a long time ago that if you do that, life is endless. It just continues on and on in great cycles of regeneration, great powerful cycles of life regenerating and regenerating and regenerating.

If you want to tinker with that regeneration, if you want to interrupt it, that's your choice, but the results that come back can be very severe because again, the laws are absolute. There's no habeas corpus in natural law. You either do or you don't. If you don't, you pay. It's quite simple. So what we have to do is get our leaders to change, and if our leaders don't do it we've got to raise better leaders, newer leaders. Raise your own leaders. Get them up there. It's your responsibility to raise good leaders. Get them up there where they can be effective and change the direction of the way things are headed.

I come from Onondaga and from our country I remember when everybody planted. I stood behind one of those plows that you hooked behind a horse. And at my age, if you hit a rock, you flew right over the plow handle. It was hard to hold that plow. I remember that. It was hard work. Planting and agriculture is hard work. You have to get up early. You've got to do stuff, but it's great training for character. It's great training for becoming adult and becoming responsible, the best training, really. But getting back to agriculture is hard to do these days. There will come a time, however, when only those that know how to plant will be eating.

That's not far off. So all of those Indian Nations that built whole civilizations around food and around thanksgiving and around spiritual law, those Indian nations have to resurge and have to remind one another how important that is. All communities talk about prayer.

We just don't call it prayer but we do it all the time. We sing songs, dawn songs, morning ceremonies, thanksgiving-coming-up-soon songs. Thanksgiving all summer, all spring. All of our ceremonies are thanksgiving. We have thanksgiving twelve months a year.

In the spring when the sap runs through the trees we have ceremonies, thanksgiving. For the maple, chief of the trees, leader of all the trees, thanksgiving. Thanksgiving for all the trees. Planting thanksgiving. Thanksgiving for the strawberries, first fruit. Thanksgiving for the bees, the corn, green corn, thanksgiving. Harvest thanksgiving. Community, process, chiefs, clan mothers, everybody is there. Families are there. How do you inspire respect for something? By giving thanks, by doing it.

We have to do that. We have to be thankful. That's what we said. Two things were told to us: to be thankful, so those are our ceremonies, ceremonies of thanksgiving. We built nations around it, and you can do that, too. And the other thing they said was enjoy life. That's a rule, a law—enjoy life—you're supposed to. I know you can only do as much as you can do and then when you do that, you're supposed to get outside and enjoy life. Don't take yourself so seriously. Do the best you can but get at it. That's the way you and I have community. I'll be down in the mouth and be moping and dragging around but by meeting with people and sitting and talking and listening to all of the positive energy and the intentions at Bioneers, for instance, and other gatherings, it's renewable. I can go home and I can say, hey, there is a good bunch of people over there and they're working hard, trying to help us out. Tell our own people to get off their lazy asses and do something. It's true. People are lazy today. They don't know how to work anymore.

That's the way it is and that's what it's going to take. Hard work will do anything. It used to be common, common law. So I would say that in the ideas of renewing yourself and the ideas of finding peace in our community, you should tell your leaders and you should tell everybody that there can never be world peace as long as you make war against Mother Earth. To make war against Mother Earth is to destroy and to corrupt, to kill, to poison. When we do that, we will not have peace. The first peace comes with your mother, Mother Earth.

Dahnayto (Now I am finished).

This presentation took place at the Bioneers Conference in 1996.

2

First Nations Survival and the Future of the Earth

Rebecca Adamson

My mom passed away several years ago. In the traditional Cherokee way of parenting, you didn't necessarily tell your child what to do but you guided. One of the key things my mom used to say over and over to me, particularly during my adolescent years was, "Rebecca Lee, if you don't change directions, you're going to end up where you're headed." Okay, Mom. We have got to change directions. It's crucial to understand that, as a society, we can reorganize. We can reorganize socially, politically, and economically, and we can reorganize according to our values.

Just within my own heritage, within the Cherokee Nation, we always had a white council, which was the women's council, which ruled during times of peace. And then we had a red council, which was the men's council, which ruled during times of war. The goal was the balance, the harmony, the bringing together of both wisdoms and both energies for the good of the Nation. We absolutely have to begin that journey on a grand scale because we are running out of time.

I'd like to share with you several stories starting with one about the San people in Botswana and Namibia, in South Africa. I'm sure many people have seen *The Gods Must Be Crazy*. It's an incredibly popular film. If you listen to that film, you hear the most amazing language. You hear pops and clicks, and there is a voice-over over a lot of it. But when you hear a strange language being spoken in the film, that is the San people.

Up until 1963, it used to be legal to hunt the San people. You could go to the government in Botswana and Namibia and get a hunting permit and hunt them down as if they were trophy animals. We began working with them in 1997. We met with them in the Kalahari Desert, which was essentially the very last of their ancestral territories. They had been driven and driven into what was one of harshest environments imaginable and yet they had adapted and were surviving. While we were there, they were notified by the government of Botswana that they were going to be removed at the end of the rainy season, and once again displaced from now what was the remaining little bit of their territorial lands.

We sat that night under a full moon and by a campfire, and in their generosity of spirit they gifted us with a trance dance. A trance dance is a very ancient calling for guidance and understanding and a universal form of what was to take place. As I listened to that dance and I listened to the singings, I listened to the language, I closed my eyes, and I'd hear the snap of twigs. I'd hear the crack of branches. I'd hear the rustle of grasses. I'd hear the wind, the whirring, as a bird takes flight. I realized what I was hearing were the sounds of nature, that these people were a part of the sacred creation in every expression of their life. Reading later, I discovered that—by most anthropological accounts—this was the most ancient language known to humankind. How else would we have learned to speak if it wasn't through the sheer imitation of nature ? But what's happening to the Sans people is happening to Indigenous Peoples throughout the world.

As Indigenous Peoples, we are three hundred to four hundred million people and we cover over seventy countries. We truly *are* the globalization issue with face, heart, feelings, and soul. What defines an Indigenous person is the fact that we predate any other groups in our territories. But also equally important is our spiritual link to the land, our connection that is deeply embedded with who we are in understanding and in relating to the land.

The next point I want to share is that globally and geographically, Indigenous Peoples' territories and critical habitats overlap. Alaska would be a classic example of the critical habitat story as it unfolds for Indigenous Peoples in North America. They have arboreal forests and the major wetlands. I went up there in 1992 on a fact-finding mission because, at the time, Governor Hinkle had put a ban on the fishing of chum salmon. There are no grocery stores in most Alaskan villages. You basically live off what you gather, hunt, or fish. So the governor's actions were basically a death sentence to many of the village people and, quite simply, it meant they would starve.

We went to nineteen different villages, starting with Port Graham in the southern part where you find the mouth of the Yukon River. We were traveling up the Yukon. At Port Graham, they had already lost their sealing because of the Valdez oil spill back in 1989. We all remember that one, with eleven million gallons of oil absolutely destroying the marine ecosystem. They no longer could hunt caribou. They no longer could hunt moose, no longer hunt mountain goat. And in one single year, sports hunters had killed every single bear in that territory, taking the paws and the heads home as trophies. Two bears will carry a village through the winter.

Now the Indigenous Peoples there were being told they could no longer fish chum salmon. As the story unfolded, we went to the community meeting house for dinner, and I was clearly wondering what we were going to eat at this point. As we walked in, there were tables full of casserole dishes. I asked the people, Well, what do you eat? And they said, dog food. It was essentially the bottom fish that they had always fed their sledding dogs. We had it barbecued, we had it dried, we had it roasted, we had it in casseroles. But with a tremendous generosity of spirit, the people of Port Graham shared every bit of the food they had at that gathering.

One of the points I'd like to make with Alaska though is that as far as the salmon fishing goes, within the State's harvest, it's only 3 percent of the take. So 97 percent of the salmon take really is done by commercial and sports fishing in what is a very fragile and delicate ecosystem.

Another major overlap is between Indigenous territories and the world's biodiversity hot spots. You can see this clearly on a map. You need to understand that however natural it appears in those biodiversity hot spots, absolutely no territorial ecosystem outside of the Antarctic has escaped Indigenous Peoples' bio-engineering. Extensive knowledge of the medicinal properties of plants, fungi, and even insects within their territories has provided a sort of pharmacopoeia for Indigenous Peoples around the world. Many of the early synthetic drugs such as quinine and aspirin were derived from Indigenous Knowledge, and today, this traditional knowledge is one of the principle sources for identifying new molecules and genes in the rapidly growing pharmaceutical and genetic engineering industries.

The covert acquisition and commercial marketing of this knowledge, and we call it bio-piracy, is undertaken by all kinds of different groups and institutions, from obscure university research departments to multinational pharmaceutical corporations. Once patented and trademarked, the knowledge is effectively expropriated from Indigenous Peoples. A clear example of this is the fact that the Winnebago tribe cannot even use their tribal identity in marketing any commercial products because it's trademarked by the Winnebago trailers.*

Once it enters the trademark system, it is completely expropriated. Also occurring throughout these biodiverse regions, especially in Asia and Latin America, is the industrialization of farming. Under this "Green Revolution," large tracts of land are opened up for commercial plantations. The goal of expanded food production is used to justify the wholesale displacement of Indigenous Peoples. This is reported at the very root of ethnic cleansing taking place in Guatemala, Peru, Brazil, Bangladesh, Myanmar, Indonesia, Irian Jaya, Timor, and in Moluccas.

Multinationals have targeted extractive operations through the

---

*The Wisconsin Winnebago Tribe changed its official name to their more original name, the Ho-Chunk Nation of Wisconsin, in 1994.

twenty-first century. The United Nations Multi-National Division clearly shows where corporations have identified their next sites of operation. You cannot understand how the extractive frontier operates without understanding the role that government plays.

I picked up a story in Canada. It's definitely not the worst. If I wanted to use the worst, I'd probably go straight to the oil companies. But this one takes place in the Boreal Forests, which are 230 miles northwest of Edmonton, Alberta, the home of the Lubikon Cree. The Alberta government first opened their territories for oil exploration in the 1970s and the Cree fought an injunction to stop it. While the highest court in Canada ruled that there was clearly "enough evidence to merit a trial," they refused to issue an injunction and nothing was done.

By 1984, four hundred wells were drilled within twenty-five miles of the community and the Cree went to the UN in Geneva, Switzerland, and filed a human rights complaint. Four years later, Deshiwa Maribuni International (DMI) leased eleven thousand square miles of Cree territory from the government to build a half-billion-dollar pulp mill. The Lubikon Cree barricaded the roads. The government offered one hundred square miles and $45 million as a settlement, which roughly breaks down to about $412 a square mile, minus 10,900,000 square miles of traditional territory.

By 1981, one year after DMI had moved in and five years after the complaint had been filed, the UN did declare that the Lubikon Crees' human rights were violated, and nothing was done. The Cree, with an organization called Friends of the Lubikon, organized a consumer boycott of all DMI paper products. By 1995, forty-five thousand retail stores had joined the boycott. At this point, DMI sued the Lubikon Cree. By 1998, two swift years by all these standards, Justice McPherson awarded one million dollars of damage to DMI, but he did allow the picketing to resume, and within two months DMI pulled out from the territories.

A year later the actual legal costs were overturned, so in the end the Lubikon Cree protected their territories, they protected the very sacredness of the forests in which they live and in how they express themselves and in the sense of their survival. But there is example after example of Indigenous Peoples who have no recourse within their own countries. The Broken Hill Property Group out of Australia have joined Papua New Guinea to pass legislation making it a criminal offense for any Indigenous Peoples to research, organize, or challenge any multinational operations in Papua New Guinea. British Petroleum did the very same thing in Dominica.

We, Indigenous Peoples, are the stewards of the last remaining truly sacred territories. They are the critical habitats and the biodiversity hot spots. Indigenous Peoples won't stand a chance of surviving the twenty-first century without everyone's help. The liberalization of trade and its corresponding acceleration of globalized markets threaten our survival more now than ever before.

But I say "our survival," I don't say "Indigenous Peoples' survival." This is not just about Indigenous Peoples. Nor is it just about the right thing to do. This scenario will destroy all of us. It is in gatherings, such as the Bioneers or the Socially Responsible Investment Forum, or the World Trade Organization and IMF demonstrations, that a unity of voice is heard. Now more than ever before Indigenous Peoples need your alliance. First Peoples Worldwide has begun a major Indigenous Peoples' rights campaign.

We have designed a new social investment screen. Its basic screening principles or criteria have been a distillation of all of the international treaties and the rights that have been set forth by these international treaties; and we've come up with about eight principles that go into screening any and every investment. What we have right now, through this investment screen, is the only international advocacy vehicle for Indigenous Peoples. Because with the Sans, with the Cree, when we went to the United Nations, we went to the International Labor Organization. We went to the World Bank. We were always told, sure, we'd really like to help you, but we have to be invited in by your country.

Now, what country is going to say, Come on down. Watch us kill and displace Indigenous Peoples? It doesn't happen. The investment screen gives us a forum we can use to have the market protect our culture, not destroy it. In 1982, Calvert became one of the very first mutual funds to take a stand against apartheid. Back then they said it wouldn't matter. Back then they said it couldn't be done. Yet we all saw an end to apartheid.

The screen can become a powerful tool and I ask you to use it. In addition, together, we need to build an international campaign to stop the genocide of Indigenous Peoples. We can do this by taking lessons from the divestiture of South Africa, taking lessons from the environmental movement's ability to mobilize resources, taking lessons from the networking used to defeat the MIA. We know that we can kill all humankind with a single bomb. We can destroy the ozone. We can blow up the planet. This means the current rules of the game must change. These are not win or lose, power and control scenarios any longer. With the current circumstances, we all lose.

The interdependency of humankind, the relevance for relationship, the sacredness of creation is returning as a fact of life. It is ancient, ancient wisdom. More than any single issue, economic development is the battle line between two competing worldviews. Tribal people's fundamental value was with sustainability and they conducted their livelihoods in ways that sustained resources and limited inequalities in their society. What made traditional economies so radically different and so very fundamentally dangerous to western economies were the traditional principles of prosperity of creation versus scarcity of resources, of sharing and distribution versus accumulation and greed. Of kinship usage rights versus individual exclusive ownership rights. And of sustainability versus growth.

In the field of economic development, economists like to think western economics is value-neutral, but the fact is, it is not. What does the finance system tell us about function and form, about our very values, when the same system pays a merger acquisitionist millions of dollars and a teacher $40,000? The Cartesian reductionist approach defined success according to production units or monetary worth. The contrast with successful Indigenous development is stark.

For example, because the Northern Cheyenne understand the environment to be a living being, they have opposed coal strip mining on their reservation because it kills the water beings. There are no cost measurements of pollution, production, or other elements that can capture this kind of impact. There is an emerging recognition of the need for a spiritual base, not only in our individual lives, but also in our work and in our communities. Perfect harmony and balance with the laws of the universe means that we all know that the way of life is found by protecting the water beings. The Indigenous understanding has its basis of spirituality and recognition of the interconnectedness and interdependence of all living things—a holistic and balanced view of the world. All things are bound together, all things connect.

As the famous quote by Chief Seattle states, "What happens to the earth, happens to the children of the earth. Humankind has not woven the web of life. We are but one thread. Whatever we do to the web, we do to ourselves." The environment is perceived as a sensate, conscious entity suffused with spiritual powers through which the human understanding is only realized in perfect humility before the sacred whole. The Hopi express this concept of being and harmony and balance with the laws of nature as *Novoiti*. The Tlingit refer to it as *Shogan*.

Modern science is just beginning to catch up with such ancient wisdom. Clearly, Bell's theorem of quantum physics, Einstein's theory of relativity, and Heisenberg's uncertainty principle indicates that how and when we look at subatomic particles affects what we see. All particles of matter, property, position, and velocity are influenced by the intention or presence of all other particles. Stated in simpler terms, atoms are aware of other atoms. According to this law of nature, a people rooted in the land over time have exchanged their tears, their breath, their bones, all their elements, oxygen, carbon, nitrogen, hydrogen, phosphorus, sulfur, all of their elements with their habitat many times over.

In the words of Diné traditionalist Ruth Benally, "Our history cannot be told without naming the cliffs and the mountains that have witnessed our people." Here nature knows us. The closest that contemporary philosophy comes to understanding earthbound spirituality is the concept of Gaia. However, tribal people worship the sacredness of creation as a way of life, not as a philosophy or religion. In fact, none of the native languages have words or terms synonymous with religion. The closest expression of belief literally translates to the way you live.

Human consciousness determines what we do and how we do it. Consciousness is given order through a belief system. The reality of any belief system is expressed through ideas. The ideas are realized through values and values permeate human life. They give us practical guidance. Moreover, values do not work alone. Ideas work together with values in a consistent, mutually affirming system, a value system. Ideas such as love, truth, and justice work according to values of caring, honesty, and fairness. The wise, to be wise, must also be just. Every society organizes itself politically, socially, and economically according to its values.

For tribal people who see the world as a whole, the essence of our work is in its entirety. In a society where all are related, simple decisions require the approval of nearly everyone in that society. It is a society as a whole, not merely a part of it, that must survive. This is an Indigenous understanding. It is the understanding in a global sense. Unless there is something I don't know, we are all Indigenous Peoples on this planet, this community. As Indigenous Peoples of this planet, we have to reorganize to get along. I am here because this gathering, the Bioneers, this community of leadership, believes in a sacred vision of humanity; and I was taught that a vision is your life. In this case, it is our survival.

This presentation took place at the Bioneers Conference in 2000.

3

Acoma Coexistence and Continuance

Petuuche Gilbert

The land and people, the natural resources that are on the land and the animal life that exists with the land, have always lived together. We believe it's always been a coexistence of both my people and the humans on the land with the physical things around them. It is a shared spiritual relationship.

As I've been told, even before the Europeans came, the people who came from the West were welcomed. Even today, we still welcome people who have now come from the East. When Europeans did come, we knew there was sustenance for all and there was no such thing as private land ownership. Yet what we saw in the last five hundred years was exploitation and a devastating new way of life that was imposed upon Native Peoples.

Today, at my home, the pueblo of Acoma, we still call ourselves *Aakuume.* We are of Acoma. Our place is called Aakuu. *Aakuu* comes from the Acoma word *Haakuu.* It meant, and still means, "prepared." It was and is the promised land for the people of Acoma. I am an Acoma. I am Petuuche, which is the name my mother's father gave to me. I am of my mother's clan, the Eagle clan, so I am an Eagle. And I am of my father's clan, the Antelope clan, thus I am also part Antelope.

Among the Acoma people, we have these relationships to each other, the clans of people to each other. Even today when our religious people get up in the morning and go to the east end of Acoma with their corn meal and turn to the north and say prayers, they are praying for all things: the rock of Acoma, the land of Acoma, the water, the animal life, the plant life, all people in the world. They are praying for coexistence where we may all survive peacefully and there may be abundance, and there may always be plentiful rains.

As I drive from Acoma, sometimes it rains a slight drizzle all the way to Santa Fe. When it thunders or starts to rain, we say *peh-eh-cha*, "let it rain." Because oftentimes we complain about the storms or the winds or the things that may be irksome to us, bothersome in some way, but all those things fit in a part of our world. I remember an old Acoma man, an Elder that has passed on, and who never went to school, who talked about these changing weather conditions.

He told me, "I never went to school because I had to work, and we had to support each other. Even in my younger days as I was living in the country and herding sheep, when it used to rain, the clouds would come from the west in a gentle rolling way and you could see the clouds bringing the rain and it would just be raining softly. What you see today is scary," he said. "There's a lot of thunder, there's a lot of wind, there's a lot of lightning, and it's almost as if there's an anger. It's very disturbing today." He said that this was prophesied, that storms would occur when the envelope around the earth was torn by man, and people would be beaten up by storms.

Another Acoma man agreed that this is part of our prophecy. Other Indigenous Peoples know this too. It's part of our Indigenous consciousness. We know these changes that we're bringing about are man-induced. In these last years it has increased dramatically at a very rapid pace.

So this is the power of colonization and now we have this new way of life that we're somehow building together. The challenge is going to be our resocialization of each other in producing ourselves as new people. At Acoma I like to say that the next five hundred years are going to produce a new type of Acoma person. We can see, for example, language loss, and we can see the culture change that comes about as a result of not being able to practice our religious ways as completely as before. We are experiencing the loss of other cultural ways because of the inability to talk Acoma any more. And yet, we say that as clans die out, new clans are made. As we lose sacred shrines because of destruction by economic development, coal mines or gas mines, we encourage the revitalization of new areas. We encourage the development of new songs or the revitalizing of old ways and bringing those back into use. That's the way we feel things change and continue. It's always been in the development of our history and in the destiny of a people. We can be self-determining and we should be. We *must* be.

This is the essence of coexistence that we've always espoused—always being in equal relationship. There's a responsibility that comes with being here on the land. There's a responsibility that comes with being here first in trying to make other people understand that we're all part of this phenomena, of this cosmos. We have a duty to maintain this relationship. I have a duty to try to do what my ancestors did for me to survive, for me to be alive at Acoma today.

I see the next five hundred years as not only accepting the responsibility to educate people about love for Mother Earth, but also honoring their personal way, too. Even after five hundred years, in spite of all the bad feelings that have come about, we still welcome people who come to Acoma. We mean it, because we're all coexisting together. We must now survive together. It is our responsibility to do so, in peace and respect, for all things and for all people on the land.

This presentation took place at the Bioneers Conference in 1992.

4

Ethics from the Land: Traditional Protocols and the Maintenance of Peace

Marlowe Sam

Ethics and cultural protocols are part of the Okanagan Four Societies process. This process is a traditional method the Okanagan use for building collaboration, collective decision-making, and consensus-making. It is based on the understanding that every society, group, or organization has four main roles—elders, mothers, fathers, and youth—and these "societies" represent areas of concern: tradition, relationship, action, and vision, respectively. By looking at the concerns of each group, better decisions are made.

As far as ethics and protocol, what I first need to address is the land. We are from a society that had an abundance of natural resources found within our traditional territory and we are obligated and duty-bound to protect and caretake this land that we belong to. My people are not pacifists.

Our histories have been passed down from generation to generation for thousands of years, it is through these oral processes that we ended up having Okanagan names for the mountains and the streams, as well as the sacred and holy places found within our territory. As Okanagan people, we are from the land; we are a part of it; therefore, we have an obligation as *sqilxw* (original people who learned to live together on the land in peace), as we call ourselves, to protect and speak for this land that can't speak for itself. This territory is our home. If we want to look at it in today's modern context, it is our place in space and time. If we want to continue to survive in our homeland, we have an obligation to protect it.

As our society has developed culturally, economically, and socially, we have been taught how to interact with one another. Cultural ethics and protocols were adapted and transformed. Our education system is the natural environment, it becomes the educational tools for our children, and it is our school. As it may be, the adults and Elders became the teachers, because they were the ones who carried the knowledge and sacred teachings of our people.

Our connection to the land has to be the foundation of our society. For untold generations, we evolved from the land and we learned to come to an understanding that this is our basis of teachings. Again, these teachings were passed down orally from generation to generation. It is through the study and interpretation of these origin stories that we were given methods and techniques, frameworks if you will, for how we are to live and interact with this land. It is through these stories that we were shown how to settle disputes and how to get along with one another, and to do this in a manner that makes both sides comfortable, a process whereby each feels that they had an equal say in the resolution process.

The traditional practice in our territory is called the *En'owkinwiwx*. We have adapted and transformed it to fit and accommodate the specific conflict resolution needs of individuals, couples, communities, and Nations. Establishing the ethics and protocols at the start of this process is an important first step, as it gives form and stability to the process. It levels the playing field for everyone involved.

People should totally commit themselves to conflict resolution. From our observations, even when individuals do not totally commit themselves to the En'owkinwiwx process, it becomes such a powerful experience that they end up getting swept up into it anyway. The resistant individuals end up being strong proponents of the process. It is an empowering experience! It reaches down and deals with the unconscious part of their being, the life force of the being: their spirit. There is a healing process that happens in this technology. It's hard to give words to it.

We have seen some minor miracles that have come out of this process, as far as healing a community, healing groups of people, taking people out of dire situations where death was imminent. We have seen situations where people were willing to commit acts of genocide against our people. Yet the Four Societies process (En'owkinwiwx) worked on these individuals without them consciously being a part of it. It definitely changed some hardcore people that were policing our communities. They had fallen head-over-heels into the process and were willing to listen and do anything that we suggested. That's the power of our traditional teachings.

One of the main messages that I want to say about the Four Societies process is that it is from this land. It isn't borrowed from an Eastern philosophy. It is from here! It belongs here! It emanated from this land. It is a powerful tool to be used in this way, it is a peace technology; it is a traditional Okanagan form of conflict resolution.

This presentation took place at the Bioneers Conference in 2006.

5

Indigenous Knowledge as the Basis for Our Future

Priscilla Settee

In educational terms my cultural background today determines the "frame of reference" for my work. I am a northern Canadian Cree woman and I have worked for much of my life as an educator in both community-based and higher education. I have also worked as a community activist, something that is not usually regarded or rewarded within higher learning. This can create a tension that is not always comfortable and is one that is faced by some of my other colleagues who are First Nations.

When I worked as program director for the Engineering Access Program, at the University of Manitoba, I found that none of the curriculum applied to the forty-five or so First Nations and Aboriginal men and women who were studying engineering there. That year I put together a course called the Impact of Western Development on Indigenous Lands. Most First Nations and aboriginal communities have been negatively impacted by development such as mega dams, mines, and deforestation. As an environmental activist I have witnessed similar impacts throughout the world.

During that time I completed a master of education degree that leaned heavily on the engineering course elective that I had developed. My master's degree was called Honouring Indigenous Science Knowledge as a Means of Ensuring Western Scientific Responsibility. This thesis made the case for Indigenous science. It explored the work of Pam Colorado, Oscar Kawagley, Greg Cajete, David Bohm, and others who considered Indigenous Peoples' knowledge as scientific and knowledge that modern science borrows from. This thesis also described some of the nightmares that Indigenous communities have been forced to live with as a result of irresponsible science: the nuclear-bombed islands of the South Pacific and the designation that nuclear dumpsites be on Indigenous Peoples' land— egregious actions that many Indigenous communities are forced to fight. The thesis also included the impact of such development on biodiversity, land, animals, local food sources, and the many plants and medicines that keep communities healthy and fed, and support a way of life.

Shortly thereafter, I became involved in the work of the Convention on Biological Diversity, with colleagues from around the world. This involvement broadened my understanding of the ways that the world's biodiversity was under threat. I met Indigenous groups who were fighting against genocide and biopiracy. Indigenous lands are highly sought after as man's neocolonial greed for money and resources intensifies. Some have called this lust for earth's last precious resources "the new conquistador," a reference to the gold seekers who first colonized and pillaged the so-called New World.

Feeling a great need to document some of the stories of the communities I visited, I decided to record them in the form of a Ph.D. program. This was not my initial intention but I felt paralyzed by the information from my colleagues in the so-called least developed nations, as it reflected the stories from my own community.

This paper describes who Indigenous Peoples are locally and globally. It defines Indigenous Knowledge (IK) and includes a description of Indigenous contributions to the food and medicines of the world and other essential areas of life. It gives examples of IK projects in community development and illustrates how IK is the basis for our future. What I have contributed below is drawn from this paper.

WHO ARE THE
WORLD'S ABORIGINAL PEOPLES?

Aboriginal Peoples in the world currently number in the range of five hundred million. They comprise 8 percent of the global population living in over one hundred countries.[1] They represent thousands of language groups and have developed varied existences based on their natural surroundings. They are as diverse as the lands they live on. Throughout time, tribal groups have developed a unique and harmonious relationship with their natural surroundings. This harmonious existence has developed from a respect, dependence, and spiritual relationship with nature.

Like my people the Cree, *Nahiyawak* or "the exact speaking people," Aboriginal Peoples in all parts of the world have learned to sustain themselves skillfully under very rigorous climate conditions. *Nahiw*, in the Cree language, means one who is skilled in her/his particular performance, whether it is in battle, in hunting, in practicing spirituality, or in speaking. *Wiyaw* means "body" in the sense of having a human body. When put together, the word becomes *Nahiyew.* A Cree person is therefore a person who is skilled or careful in her/ his movements and speech. By living in harmony and developing a respect of all living things Indigenous Peoples developed a symbiotic relationship with nature. Through my various work and visits throughout the world I have noticed a commonalty that exists among Indigenous Peoples with reference to plants, food production, and relationship to natural surroundings. Their knowledge of nature is skillful and precise.

While Aboriginal People did not refer to their knowledge as "science," they knew the requirements for existence with scientific precision, often in harsh climates. People still know which season and what time of the day animals and plants are to be harvested as well as which plants are used in healing illness. People know that each plant and animal has a use as well as a purpose in the natural order of existence. This knowledge of natural surroundings and biodiversity has been developed over millennia and through a careful process of observation, listening, experimentation, and adaptation.

DEFINITION OF INDIGENOUS KNOWLEDGE

Indigenous Knowledge (IK) has many definitions depending on whether one is a scholar or one is community-based. There are probably more questions than answers in relation to IK definitions and because I believe that this definition is ever developing I have included many questions in my definition. As a body of knowledge, IK, albeit with different names, has gained currency in the last twenty years among researchers and governmental agencies, as well as civil society organizations.

Indigenous Peoples view IK as something that has sustained their communities since time immemorial. Dakota Elder Ken Goodwill states that Indigenous Knowledge is valid in its own right and does not need to be validated by other systems. The Canadian International Development Agency uses the following definition, "Indigenous Knowledge represents the accumulated experience, wisdom and know-how unique to cultures, societies, and/or communities of people, living in an intimate relationship of balance and harmony with their local environments. These cultures have roots that extend into history beyond the advent of colonialism. They stand apart as distinctive bodies of knowledge, which have evolved over many generations within their particular ecosystem, and define the social and natural relationships with those environments. They are based within their own philosophic and cognitive system, and serve as the basis for community-level decision-making in areas pertaining to governance, food security, human and animal health, childhood development and education, natural resource management, and other vital socio-economic activities."[2] Some see IK as a last hope in implementation of a sustainable future.

Others have defined IK as local knowledge that is unique to a culture or a society and outside of the formal educational system. IK is that knowledge that allows communities to survive and is the basis for decision-making in the arenas of health, agriculture, food preparation, natural resource management, and education. Communities rather than individuals hold it. It is embedded in community practices, rituals, and relationships and is difficult to codify. IK is part of everyday life. Collectivity is central to Indigenous being and the collectivity of Indigenous Knowledge is reflected in many ceremonies and teachings. Aboriginal scholars and local people have described Indigenous Knowledge with labels that reflect ancient knowledge of community life, well-being, and shared values. In the Cree language, this is called *pimatissiiwan.* A core value is *miyo-wicehtowin,* which means having good relations.

Individually and collectively and since time immemorial, people have been instructed by their teachings to strive and conduct themselves in ways that create positive relationships. My people, the Cree, begin each day by smudging with sage, which helps us to purify our thoughts, actions, and deeds. Smudging ensures that our actions will be done with a good heart and a good mind and with gratitude for the gift of living another day. This ritual also reminds us to perform our duties for the betterment of humanity. Reference is made to the concept of "all my relations," which means that all of humanity and living things are related and must be cared for by one another.

Northern Athabascan values and worldviews are similar and focus on self-sufficiency, hard work, care and provision for the family, good family relations, unity, humor, honesty, fairness, and love for children. They also include sharing, caring, village cooperation, responsibility to village, and respect for Elders and others and knowledge. Wisdom from life experiences, respect for the land, respect for nature, the practice of traditions, honoring ancestors and spirituality round out the outlook of Athabascans. In times of conflict or when mistakes are made the emphasis within the Indigenous world has been on reconciliation, healing, and fitting back in rather than on punishment and isolation.

Even when a person made mistakes in life, there were people that would counsel him or her. There was a process of reconciliation. It was done through the oral language. It was done through the Elders. This came about through discussions about how to get that person back into a balanced life and how to make that person aware of how to focus on what is important in life. And if that person had listened and taken the appropriate guidance from those kinds of people, he or she would get back into a balance and be able to be helped, to learn from these things, to become a part of the family, part of the nation.[3]

Songs and legends today strengthen community and predate recorded history. IK is not a singular body of knowledge but reflects many layers of being, knowing, and methods of expression. IK includes knowledge about economics, politics, music, leadership, transportation, building, astronomy, women's unique contributions, art, literature/stories, humor, and community conduct and values. Expressions of IK are interconnected; hence Indigenous science knowledge is not separate from our art knowledge. The lovely birch bark basket, which has been constructed and dyed, embodies knowledge of science, engineering for strength, and a botanical knowledge of plant dyes. Similarly, the ancient pot made from the clays of the Missinipe River in northern Saskatchewan is one that has the scientific properties to endure the extremes of heat and cold and is also lovely to behold.

Communities that have been exploited for their natural wealth (mining, deforestation, dams) and beauty (tourism) are now the least productive for hunting and gathering societies whose knowledge depends on these natural resources. That being said, IK is not something that is frozen in time; some knowledge adapts to reflect the dramatic changes occurring within Indigenous communities today. Some communities are in a state of disruption, with devastating impact, largely as the result of western encroachment and colonialism. These conditions and influences have been identified and addressed by activists and scholars alike who work to ensure that the future is secured for all humanity. I believe all of these factors must be figured into the IK equation.

This discussion was part of the author's master's thesis entitled "Honoring Indigenous Science Knowledge as a Means of Ensuring Western Scientific Responsibility" for the University of Manitoba, completed in 1999.

6

Clear Thinking:
A Positive Solitary View of Nature

John Mohawk

I come from a complex tradition that acknowledges a wide range of beliefs. The fundamental thing about being Iroquois is that people will not argue about beliefs or religions. Inside our traditional religion are all kinds of different beliefs, and not everyone shares all those beliefs.

But there is also in our culture a core requirement that ultimately, whatever our beliefs are, we are encouraged to maintain: the tradition of *clear thinking*. Clear thinking is the foundation of the Great Law and is an ever-recurring theme in what is known as the *Ganyodaiyo,* or Good Message of Handsome Lake. It's also discussed even in parts of our ancient tradition, the story of how the world came to be the way it is. We call this in English the Creation Story.

My version of Native American studies was that we would be the critics of Western culture. We would do what Western culture and anthropologists do to Indian culture: review it, point out what's wrong with it, explain where it went wrong, tell them it was wrong, and basically have a version and understanding of it. To do that meant that I had to take a close look at the origins and the philosophies around science, and the origins and philosophies about philosophy: the whole question of where the culture tells us it is coming from, where it says it is, and where it says it is going.

I am surprised a little, given that history, that we seem to be moving toward a different place. We have people now who are very clearly among the best scientists who are willing to agree that there are limits to the knowledge that science can have about nature. We're reaching a place in which there's ever-wider agreement that poetry gives us as much information about our relationship with the universe as telescopes do, and that those two strains can live together and complement one another harmoniously. Those two things can happen, and that's actually not dissimilar to my culture, which asserts that on the one hand there are dreams and visions and on the other hand there's a responsibility to maintain a clear version of reality. Those two streams of thoughts and reactions have to live cooperatively together.

The idea that the spiritual and the secular can live side by side is extremely important at this time. I also believe that, while we may not agree on everything that we believe in, there are a few things that are emerging that almost everyone can believe in.

The Iroquois culture has a tradition that every time we gather together to have a meeting, we open with what is called a *ga no ya* or opening speech. Some people call it a thanksgiving address. That talk is what everyone who is sane in the world should agree on. It's kind of like Iroquois diplomacy: we start with what we agree on and then we keep going to the things that we cannot agree on.

So what is it that we all agree on? The speech starts with an opening that we see one another; we need each other; we need people to be in the world and it's a good thing that there are people in the world; we're grateful and thankful that there are other people in the world and it's good to see them here, so we give a greeting.

We acknowledge others in our greetings and thanksgiving and we greet one another with this in mind. Since that's how we do things amongst ourselves, we should be able to do that with other beings, and so it goes on and we do greetings to the earth. Everybody should be able to give greetings to the Mother Earth. She's a person, and—call it poetic—it's a way of us having a relationship with that, so we acknowledge that relationship, it's fundamental.

Right after people, earth. Then it goes to grasses, waters, trees, plants, winds, the moon, the stars, the sun, the universe, the whole thing. Everybody in the world ought to be able to agree that we depend on those things. Those things are actually essential to us, and that's the rational mind, with a poetic way of expressing a rational mind. Some people look at that and say that's spiritual. Whatever you call it is fine. It's us expressing our positive relationship to all the others, every other that we can think of. We have not separated ourselves from them. They are others and we are part of the others.

We do this speech at the beginning and the end of every meeting because people need to be reminded of that. It's a constant reminder.

I think that now we need also to acknowledge science as a form of gathering information, a very important one. In a way, science has claimed to be more than that. There has been a tradition in the West claiming that science had a power greater than a system that gathers information for us. I think that leaves a lot of people feeling negative about science. But I want to be positive about science because we are now beginning to have a moment when it is possible for people across cultures to have a positive view of nature. Nature is what keeps us alive. It is not our enemy. It is what gave us life in the first place.

In my culture they call the *givers* of life *Jo Ha Cho*. They call the *creator* of life *Ho Cha Ne Tom*. The creator of life and the givers of life are different. The creator of life is that which existed in the universe, and the Jo Ha Cho is what existed here on this planet in this sphere: the physical beings with a spiritual face that create our lives and make us live.

Now we're faced with a reality that people have been playing with the Jo Ha Cho. They've been concluding that they can play God, a version of God. They would claim the right to splice genes, to fool with the building blocks of life. I propose to you that they've been doing that for a long time. This isn't new. It's been happening for a long time, ever since the evolution of chemistry, and it is coming into everyday life. Every one of us has things in our bodies that our ancestors never had in their bodies. Everything that is alive on the whole planet has chemicals in its being that didn't used to be in its being.

The second thing is that the things of nature are no longer available to us. From the air we breathe to the water we drink to the food we eat, every one of these has been altered from the way our ancestors experienced those things. The earth itself, when you pick it up and analyze it, is not the same. Everything has been changed. Yet if nature is sacred, it would be our mind to change it back to make it the way it was when it was supportive of life on the earth. This would mean to make the food the way it was, to make the water the way it was, to make the air the way it was, to make our bodies and everything on the planet the way they were, the way nature made them to be. I can see now that scientists can help us do that. I can see now that there are scientists who think that way too, and in that regard it seems to me that the natural-world people and the scientific people—all kinds of other people, even business people—can be on the same side of something.

We all have to have as a goal that we should see nature restored. The word "nature" is a little bit fuzzy here. When I say nature, I mean everything that supports life on the planet is nature. Nature is so complex and its interactions so dynamic that the idea that science could ever understand it all is utterly laughable. We can understand the more simple things that we do to interfere with it: to degrade it, to wreck it. But we can never understand it. It is beyond our comprehension.

The Indian cultures that I know have said that nature is a great mystery. It is so complex, so great, so above us, that we should never be so arrogant to think that we can understand even a little bit of it. But we can understand our nature. We can understand the profit motive. We can understand wrong thinking. We can understand the concept of science as a revitalization movement that makes outlandish claims for itself, and of course the real scientists say that's not real science but pseudoscience. I have really come to embrace that idea, that real science doesn't do that. Of course, many of the pseudoscientists are paid to say that. Large corporations that have profits in mind head right for the universities and buy the guys who are supposed to be the experts. Then they have people who claim to be scientists saying, "Tobacco smoke doesn't cause illness. No, there's no problem with changing genes around. There's no problem with atomic bombs. What are you worried about? Okay, so things are dying, but what are you worried about?"

So I want to propose that I can see that we are headed into a new space that puts the natural-world people and the Indigenous People, who still maintain their mind about nature, with very vast allies in the industrialized world. I never thought I would have that thought.

We can look at this as a global consciousness that is rising; it is coming from people to whom nature is like religion. The culture that I come from sees the universe as the fountain of everything, including consciousness. In our culture we're scolded for being so arrogant to think that we're smart. An individual is not smart, according to our culture. An individual is merely lucky to be a part of a system that has intelligence that happens to reside in them. In other words, be humble about this always. The real intelligence isn't the property of an individual corporation—the real intelligence is the property of the universe itself.

This presentation took place at the Bioneers Conference in 1999.

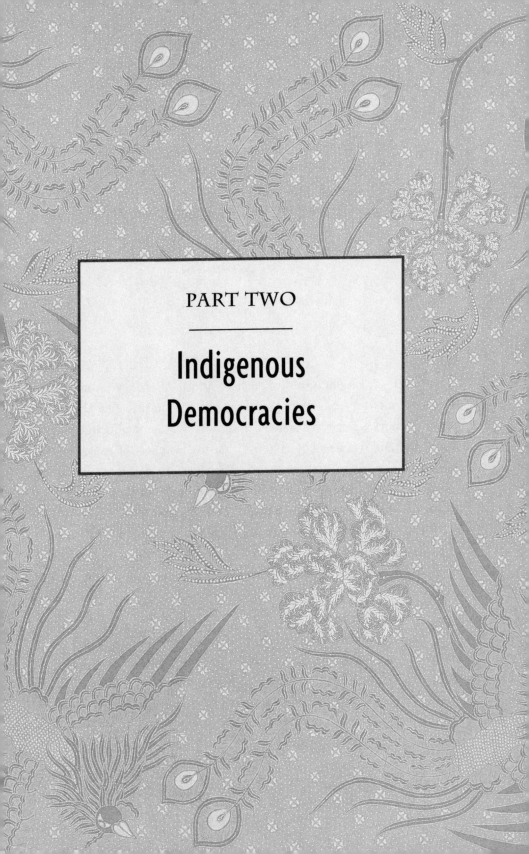

PART TWO

Indigenous Democracies

7

The Iroquois Confederacy

John Mohawk

Historically, the Indians of the Eastern woodlands had no coercive apparatus of state control. Those who knew them remarked that the reason their societies weren't in a state of chaos was because their culture was so powerful and so internally cohesive that the members of its society followed their cultural rules pretty well. They lived in relative peace and harmony amongst themselves for a long time. I think that's a very important message, just so we can understand that this is possible in the world.

The Iroquois Confederacy has many, many wonderful elements to it. We could talk about its spirituality. We could talk about its local structure and organization, about what its roles for women and children are, but I want to focus on one thing and one thing only: the origins of the Iroquois Confederacy.

The story has it that there was an individual born among the Hurons, on the north side of Lake Ontario, who grew up in a society that was each against all. Blood feuds left not only villages fighting villages but also individual households fighting individual households. Assassinations were common. Violence ruled the day. People committed atrocities of every kind against each other—from cannibalism to murder to mass murder. It was a time, not unlike the twentieth century, of absolute horror and the degradation of the human soul.

Coming out of this environment, one individual came up with an idea. He said that violence is a really bad idea. In all Western thought, by the way, this particular strain of thinking is never canonized anywhere. Anyway, this particular individual carries it further. According to the story, he is a young man, not yet twenty. He goes to the people he's living with, and he says to them, "You have to stop these cycles of violence." The cycles of violence were deeply embedded in the laws and customs of the Indian people, and they were about revenge, for real and imagined injuries.

Some of it was about thinking that someone had performed witchcraft on you, and therefore you had to get even for that. Or somebody had gotten killed and you had to get even for that. In the end, a single murder could cost thirty or forty lives in revenge killings and blood feuds. In those days, with the size of the populations being what they were, this was very significant. The way war was fought was also very significant because it was fought by sneaking up on villages with war parties and rushing through these villages, taking prisoners and killing people.

So this individual, whom we'll call the Peacemaker, began to say, to put it in modern English, that essentially war makes people crazy. When people are at war, they're not thinking clearly, and this is a problem. Then he goes on to try to define what it means to think clearly. Here's a fellow who actually belongs on the list of great philosophers of the world because he addresses two questions: How do we know when we're thinking clearly? And what does it mean to pursue peace?

He begins to talk to people, and his argument is, "We don't need to live this way. We have the power of our collective minds so that we can create a world in which people do not use violence, but rather use thinking. We could replace violence with thinking, and then go from there." He goes from village to village and persuades people that first we have to have a pact that says that we're not going to commit violence anymore. It's hard to tell exactly what's going on, because these are orally transmitted traditions. But you have to know that when you walk into a village and you say, "We have to put down our weapons of war and have peace," that they're going to say, "Not 'til the other guys do." To which the initial party will say, "Okay, let's go talk to the other guys." "Can't talk to them. They're all crazy."

So Peacemaker Dekanawidah starts out by saying, "When you tell yourself that your enemy can't think, you destroy your own power to make peace with him." It falls into a whole philosophy of peace, one that's designed to help diplomats walk into incredibly tough situations knowing that, unless they use their minds to solve their problems, the problems will get worse. To use their minds to solve their problems, they have to first acknowledge that the guy on the other side of the negotiation—whatever he's been doing—probably wants his people to live and probably wants a lot of the same things you do. So this process starts by looking for common ground with the enemy.

In the course of these conversations, what came up was that we're at war with these people because they've harmed us. They've done wrong to us, and we made a list of what these wrongs were. One of the wrongs was that the other group claimed an exclusive right of property that we needed to use. In the discussion, the Peacemaker says that the pursuit of peace is not merely the pursuit of the absence of violence, because peace is never achieved until justice is achieved. And justice is not achieved until everyone's interests are addressed. But, he says, you will never actually finish addressing everyone's issues. There will always be unfinished business. You can't achieve peace unless it's accompanied by a constant striving to address the issues of justice. This means that your job will never end. It will never end.

Then he says that we have to build an institution to represent this. Of course, he puts together the chiefs of the Five Nations. They come together, and they form the Confederacy. But who are the chiefs of the Confederacy? What's their job? They're not actually civil chiefs, certainly not in the sense Thomas Hobbes was talking about. The chiefs of the Confederacy convene a meeting, the purpose of which is to demonstrate clear thinking. There is a tradition in the Confederacy to question fuzzy thinking. They were constantly called upon to answer the question, "What is it that you meant by such and such when you said that?"

This meeting was conducted in a couple of different languages. The

Confederacy has a wonderful tradition that, when someone has a proposition, they get up and they articulate their proposition to the other side, and the other side has to tell them back what it was. Interestingly, sometimes the original proposition is in one language and it comes back in a different language. When it's in two languages and there is agreement on what it was, then we're on track. We're getting there.

The Peacemaker said that the problem that humanity faces—and all humanity faces this problem—is that the absence of peace will lead to the end of human life on this planet. He said also that injustice is the big disturber of peace. It's not even combat or warfare; it's injustice. So long as there is injustice, the people of the planet face the possibility of extinction. He believed, and the words here are clear, that unless we solve the problem of injustice, we will take steps that will lead to the extermination of our species on the planet. He didn't say that we'd kill each other off with war clubs. He said that in the end, unless we achieve peace among ourselves, the people of the planet will be eliminated.

I propose to you that he was exactly right. We're living in a period of warfare between the rich and poor. The rich people do things that have no virtue at all, by buying into the ideologies of things like globalization and the World Bank. How people are treating one another in the world has no relationship at all to thinking about how we sustain human life on the planet—not in terms of pollution, not in terms of food supply, not in terms of the oceans, not in terms of the air, not in terms of anything.

There's no virtue in any sense that Socrates would have understood; no virtue at all in any sense that the Peacemaker would have understood. Neither of them would have thought that clear thinking is prevailing in the world system that is, at this very moment, deciding who gets to eat and who does not get to eat, who has a place to lay down and who does not have a place to lay down, whose children will survive even their infancies, and whose will not.

If this system continues on and on in the way we're going now, the Peacemaker will be proved right. In the absence of a clear-minded idea that virtue means social justice in an economic as well as a military sense in the world, our species faces serious and almost overwhelming odds for the long-term future. I propose to you that Dekanawidah's thinking was as clear and as correct and as right as any, and that his version of virtue needs to be adopted by us all.

Having adopted that version, we can apply it to our ideas about what we need to do about the food supply, technology, the world economic situation, hungry children in the world, world hunger in general, militarism, and other issues troubling our global community today.

If our thinking changes from the question of how to enrich the rich to the question of how to obtain the sustainability of our species on the planet, as we make that our shift we would be engaging ourselves in an enormous revolution. It would be one to which the West has contributed very little thus far, even though I know many do want to contribute to it. It's an idea of the people, not an idea yet found in the philosophy textbooks. And hopefully it's an idea whose time has come.

In any event, I brought this discussion to you because I've been thinking for a long time now about how interesting it is that we've had all these wonderful and brilliant thinkers over all these centuries, and so few of them are engaged in looking at the most important things that we need to be looking at, the most fundamental things: What is in the best interests of future generations of the peoples of the world and of other species of the world? Certainly these issues need a lot more focus than we've been giving them.

This presentation took place at the Bioneers Conference in 1998.

8

A Democracy Based on Peace

Chief Oren Lyons

The history of democracy in this country, Western democracy, is very old. But what is democracy? Our people have been involved in this discussion from the beginning, from the first meeting that we made with the Dutch in 1613. This meeting established our style of interaction and relationship and was symbolized by the Two Row Wampum Belt, which represented our two different cultures.

At that time, we said, "We have a canoe and you have a boat, and in your boat you have many religions and many colors of people and ways of life." We said, "In our canoe we have simple life. We have what you might call a hard life, but a life that we like."

"In our canoe is our people, our government, our way of life. We'll connect our two boats, our ships, and our two vessels with what we'll call the covenant chain of peace. They'll be made of three links, the first link is peace, the second link is friendship, and the third link is how long it will last." And we said, "When we make this agreement it should last as long as the sun rises in the East, and sets in the West, as long as the rivers run downhill, and as long as the grass grows green" (of which there are some contradictions already).

But still, the sun is still rising and setting and so we made this agreement, this covenant chain, and we hooked our two vessels together and we said, "We're going to float down *Guswenta,* the great river of life, side by side. In peace and friendship for as long as we exist." That was the essence of our agreement in the beginning. At that time, the people who were talking said, "Well, what will happen if some of our people want to get into your canoe? Or some of your people want to get into our boat?" Our leaders said, "That's going to happen, but mostly it will be our people getting into your boat, because our life is hard and because it's not something that your people are used to. There will probably be a few of your people in our boat, but many of our people in your boat." But they replied, "That won't be the issue, the issue will be for those that have one foot in the canoe and one foot in the boat. That's not a good place to be." And they said, "Some time in the future a great wind will come and it will blow the vessels apart and those that are there will fall into this river of life and no one will be able to help them on this side of the creation."

Indian Nations believe in the creation. We believe in a higher power. We believe in a great authority. We believe that we're hooked together, the way that we are intertwined, the way that we live with one another, all of this one being. So that's what we've been gauging all of our agreements with down through the centuries, first with the Two Row Belt and with many nations that have held that belt. Then the English landed on Cape Cod. The Englishmen landed there in about 1620 although there had been many people voyaging back and forth across the sea before that. They were coming for real on this one. And we watched them settle.

Several hundred years later, in 1776, they declared themselves Americans and they said they no longer had allegiance to their father the king of England, that they were separate, that they were sovereign, that they were independent from England. A question arises, How did they make this transition? How did they change from Englishmen to Americans, because in 1776 or 1750 or 1700 Indians were known as Americans. The colonies were loyal to their countries. Now these Englishmen said that they were Americans. They made this transition through hundreds and hundreds of meetings that we held with them up and down the coast. They learned from us. The meetings were always over land, always over problems, and we came to know them very well and they came to know our leaders very well.

Our leaders spent a lot of time in Philadelphia and in New York and in Albany. The new Americans saw and came to understand our idea of being free. The idea of being independent was everywhere they looked and they liked it and they wanted to become like us. All of those people who were out there on the frontiers loved to be free. As soon as more people came, they moved, just like the Indians did—it was getting crowded. They, like us, didn't like being crowded. They didn't like towns. They wanted to be in the woods. So at one point, in a meeting in Lancaster, Pennsylvania, in 1744 when several of the governors were arguing among themselves, one of the Onandaga leaders stood up and said to them, "You know, you're never going to amount to anything until you quit arguing with one another."

He said, "Why don't you make a union like ours, why don't you make a league like our great league of peace?" And so began the instruction on unity, peace, and democracy. Those notes at that meeting were taken to Philadelphia and printed, and the printer was none other than Benjamin Franklin. He read these notes and said, "That's a good idea. It makes some common sense here." So in 1754 he called the Albany Plan of Union to create this league of peace, like the Indians, like the Haudenosaunee whom the French called Iroquois. At this meeting there was a spy for the English king. He sent word back to England and said, "Your Royal Highness, you must be aware, the colonies are talking about government by the people here." Over the next nineteen years the relationship between the king of England and the colonists deteriorated over issues of money and taxes.

When the Continental Congress joined together, they called themselves the Thirteen Fires. They had a Grand Council. They used all of our terms. They also used wampum the way we did because that's what they learned over these hundreds of years of meeting with us. In 1775 they met again with us and they asked us to join them in the battle coming and our chief said, "We know your father, and we have a lot of agreements and treaties with your father. And we know you; we also have agreements and treaties with you. We think this is a battle between father and son, best we stay out."

The Six Nations at that time were trying to stay neutral because they knew that a fierce fight was coming and it was going to rage over our lands, so we were caught in the middle of a great battle. After hearing our first response, the Continental Congressional Delegation said, "Good, that was going to be our second request. If you were not going to fight with us, then do not fight against us." A treaty of neutrality was struck that day. When they returned to Philadelphia and reported the agreement, President John Hancock began preparations to formalize this treaty and ordered a wampum belt to be made with thirteen diamonds (symbols) and the formal treaty was made at Fort Pitt the following year prior to their announcement of independence in 1776. Thus, this treaty, a treaty of peace and neutrality with the Haudenosaunee (the Six Nations Iroquois Confederacy), was their first treaty made as a new nation.

But actually in the event itself, Mohawks fought heavily on the side of the English. Oneidas fought heavily on the side of the colonies. In fact, it was the Oneidas who carried three hundred bushels of corn to Valley Forge when the troops were starving. They kept them alive. It takes a lot to cook corn. You can't cook corn in one hour. It takes about six hours to make corn soup and the Indians had to fight the troops while they cooked for them, because you can't eat raw corn. This is a part of history that you don't hear about and a primary reason why you're sitting here as Americans.

The history of us being together is important, but where did it come from? In 1774 Connasetaga talked about this to your people. He talked to them about democracy. How did he know about this? There was a time—a thousand years ago or more, give or take a hundred years, we don't know, we don't keep those kinds of records, but it was a long, long time ago, long before the white man—when we were fighting among ourselves. At that time, a great Peacemaker came among our nations and brought peace. This is an epic story. Some say it took him a hundred years to do that. Again, we don't know. We know it was a long and difficult job.

The Peacemaker finally brought together the leaders of the original Five Nations: the Mohawks, the Oneidas, the Onondagas, the Cayugas, and the Senecas. He had changed their minds. They were sitting in a group in a peaceful manner and then he laid down the Great Law of Peace. He laid down our confederacy constitution and said, "I'm going to base this constitution on the first principle which is peace, the second principle which is equity for the people, and the third principle which is power, the power of the good minds." Those are the principles and they're dual principles. When I greeted you I said *skannoh*, our greeting, in our native tongue. This word is the same word for peace, so health and peace are the same thing. You can't have peace without health.

Our Peacemaker said, "*Skannoh*, peace, equity for the people." Be fair. Be fair to the people. You can't have justice without equity. Justice comes with equity. Dual principle. Then he said, "The power of the good minds, the council of chiefs and the people themselves, the good minds." He was talking about unity, which is what we are talking about now—to be united, to be of one mind. And when you do that you have great power, great strength.

This is what Connasetaga was talking about in 1774. He instructed the Virginia, Pennsylvania, and New York governors to work together in unity. That's what we're going to do now. We're thinking now, how are we going to do this together, to be united, to be of one mind? Great power comes from that. So their discussion resonates today. When he talked to the leaders, first he said, "How shall you know your nation?" He said, "You shall know your nation through the women. They will be carrying the line." He said, "Because the earth is female the women will be working with the earth. The earth will belong to them."

So when a girl was born you had a landholder and when a boy was born you had a lacrosse player, a good singer, a good dancer—maybe he'd even be a chief one day. But he gave responsibility to the women; he made clan mothers and gave them the duty to choose all the leaders.

He gave us a process of raising leaders that did not involve politics. So at the end of the day you got a leader, not a politician.

It's a very extensive process to hold a title in the Haudenosaunee. First, the clan mother will choose, from her clan, the leader that she wants, and that has to be agreed upon by a consensus of the clan she represents. If they don't agree, she has to find somebody else. So it's the clan that's agreeable, but it's her choice. If they agree, she takes her choice to the chief's council and they also have the right of veto. If they don't agree, she has to start again, but if they do agree now you have a real candidate for this title that she holds, which was the name of the original leader at that time of the Peacemaker. So the titles we hold are the names of those original fifty leaders.

Each title denotes an office and each leader has a deputy. There is a clan mother, a chief, a subchief (a partner), and a faith keeper (a male faith keeper and a female faith keeper); all together they look after the welfare of the clan itself. And so, the process begins by choosing the leader. Now the nation will send a messenger to the other house, which is comprised of the younger brothers, the Cayugas, the Oneidas, and the Tuscaroras, and they will accept the message and they will say, "Good news. We will prepare because your house, the Elder brothers, are in mourning. You have a chief down, we the younger brothers will do all the work."

When this work is complete, they will send to our nation a runner and upon receiving this news, say, "This is the time, these are the speakers, this is the place where we the Haudenosaunee will raise the new leader." We send runners to all the Six Nations announcing that news and we gather at that appointed time and place and begin this great Condolence. At that appointed time the two houses will now judge this man and determine, by consensus, if he will hold the title.

The day begins when the host nation and his house (his brother nations) greet the arriving leaders and people (their side, their house) at the edge of the woods where ritual ceremony and greetings are exchanged for about an hour. Then the host nation leads the way to the Long House, led by a man singing the *Hi-Hi*—the role call of the fifty original chiefs. When they enter and are seated on their respective sides, the role call and duties of the fifty original chiefs' names are recited again to completion, and then another speaker rises and recites the story of the Peacemaker. Then the "twenty words" are recited.

When that is completed, the grieving house is condoled with a set of wampum strings by the opposite house, each string taking a certain amount of time. The strings move into the duties of the clan mother, the chiefs, the faith keepers, and the people—the people have more duties. Each string is passed to the opposite house. This takes a long time. Then the great hymn is sung by the condoling chiefs, then each string is returned by the condoled house, repeating in full each message. So the people hear the laws twice.

On this day the men without titles prepare the food. The women must be inside to hear and observe everything. They keep the records and teach their children. Finally, the candidate is brought forward by the clan mother and her leaders and he is judged again. It is the grand council of chiefs who determine if he will sit with them, all by consensus.

So we hear all of the laws, we hear all of that. At the end of the day, if he passes all of these examinations on his own merits as a human being, we will bring him forth as the titleholder of that clan. He must simply be a man of good health and courage, a family man, responsible and honest. If he's accepted then they'll all agree. But then they turn to the people and they say, "Does anyone here know a reason why this man should not be here?" And the final word is the people. That is democracy in its full form.

I know nations across this great Turtle Island that raise their leaders a similar way. They're chosen by the people. They're there by the will of the people and when they don't perform, the will of the people will remove them, and that's what you've got to do now. You must raise good leaders dedicated to peace, and to the welfare of the coming generations.

This presentation took place at the Bioneers Conference in 2003.

9

An Okanagan Worldview of Society

Jeannette Armstrong

I grew up in a remote part of the Okanagan on the Penticton Indian reservation in British Columbia, Canada. I was born on the reservation, at home, and I was fortunate to be born into a family that was considered by many people in our area to be a traditional Okanagan family. Our first language was Okanagan and we practiced hunting/gathering traditions on the land. I'm still immersed in that family today.

And while I've lived that life and I continue that practice with my family, my community was one that had been fractionalized by colonization, fractionalized in many ways in terms of the community itself. This gave me some valuable insights and observations. Thus, I have these two perspectives in terms of looking at society: the perspective of the small, extended, traditional family support system that I grew up in, and that of the larger community fractionalized by colonization.

One of the observations I have in regard to human relationships has to do with the relationships we have with each other and how these relationships impact what we do to the land. In other words, what we do to each other and how we look at each other—how we interact with each other—is one of the reasons that some things then happen to the land. In the extended-family community that I grew up in, our people organized themselves in a very different way than what I see happening outside of that. I want to describe some of my perspective, from that point of view, to you now.

The land that I come from is very dry and semiarid. It's considered the northern tip of the Great Basin Desert and the ecosystem there is very, very fragile. At this time, the Okanagan is one of the most damaged areas and ecosystems in Canada because of its fragility. In our area many conservationists and environmentalists are very concerned about the species that are endangered and disappearing there. We live in an area where extirpations have been happening over the last one hundred years; I've seen some of those extirpations myself.

This has been difficult because we grew up loving the land. We grew up loving each other on the land and loving each plant and each species the way we love our brothers and sisters and that's the point I want to get across. That doesn't just happen as an intellectual process. That doesn't just happen as a process of needing to gather food and needing to sustain our bodies for health. It happens as a result of how we interact with each other in our families, in our family units, in our extended family units, and in our communities; the networks that we make outward to other people who surround us on the land. Those networks are extremely important insofar as what happens to the land and how we interact with the land.

Part of the educational work that I do is to find a way to interpret some of that and to bring reconciliation to members of my community on my land to bring health back to the land. I cannot do that responsibly if I cannot create that kind of understanding. In the Okanagan, our understanding of the land is that it's not just that we're part of the land, it's not just that we're *part* of the vast system that operates on the land, but that the *land is us*. In our language, the word for our bodies contains the word for land, so when I say that word, it means that not only is my ability to think and to dream present in that word but the last part of that word also means "the land."

Thus, in my mind, every time I say that word and I refer to myself, I realize that I am from the land. I'm saying that I'm from the land and that my body is the land. We love to go out to the land to gather food.

I have done this every year of my life and continue to do so; I look forward to it every year. I go out to the land to gather the foods that have given me life, and given my grandmothers life, and given my great-great-grandmothers life for many, many generations. When we go out to the land, our people have perfected a way of interacting with each other that is respectful to the land and respectful to each other but also fulfills some needs that we have that are human in terms of interaction and relationship to one another.

What our grandparents have said is that the land feeds us but we feed the land as well. What they meant by that was that we give our bodies back to the land in a very physical way but we also do other things to the land. We live on the land and we use the land and, in so doing, we impact the land: we can destroy it, or we can love the land and it can love us back.

So one of the things that I was looking at in the development of our educational program was to find a way to teach about how we, as a society, interact. I wanted to explore how members of our community interact with each other and to find a way to distill that, describe that, and to teach and reconstruct that in our communities.

In the most basic sense, our use of the land relates to our need for food, for shelter, for clothing, and beyond. When we look at society, we need to look at how society is constructed. There are things that we need to live and breathe every day. But beside that we need pleasure. We need to be loved and we need to have the support of our community and the love that people surrounding us can give us. If we think about how those two things are combined together and work together, if those two ideas and ideals can work together, then we can see how we can either impact the land in a negative way or in a positive way.

If I look around at how the land has been impacted by what I call the Western culture, one of the things I see is an overuse of resources by some people and a lack of access to those same resources for others. In other words, there are some people with a right to have more and some people with no right. There are some people who cannot access even the most basic things that they need. When you look at the idea of democracy from that perspective, you can see there's something profoundly wrong with a hierarchical system in which people sitting next to you or next door to you don't have access to the same things you do. That seems to me to be a profoundly basic communal principle: Everyone in a community needs to have the same access to the basics and the same access to the joys and pleasures of life.

One of the things I was looking at with regard to this was the idea of the construct of how we make decisions. I looked at the Okanagan decision-making process in its traditional sense. I'm not saying that it's there today, that it works today, but elements of it are still present and have been carried forward because we are only two generations since colonization began.

One of the things that I came to understand is that in our decision-making we have a word, *en'owkinwiwx,* that demands a number of things from us. Specifically, there are four things that it demands from us; we use that process continuously in an informal way in our community. We can also engage it in a formal way and it's something like a framework or construct. Robert's Rules of Order,* for instance, is thought of as a democratic construct or an understanding of democracy wherein the decision-making power rests with the majority, as opposed to the minority.

From my perspective, embedded in that construct is an adversarial approach. It sets up the oppression of the minority, it sets up a dissention. It sets up a construct in which there is always going to be conflict. There are always going to be people who are in the minority and people who are in the majority. I do understand that this is probably the easiest way for decisions to be made, however, in terms of looking at what the outcome is, in terms of a decision-making process in this country and on the land and globally—systemically we might have to rethink how this works.

From our point of view the minority voice is the most important

---

*Robert's Rules of Order is a set of meeting rules and refers to the proper way to conduct a meeting.

voice to consider. The minority voice expresses the things that are going wrong, the things that we're not looking after, the things that we're not doing, the things that we're not being responsible toward, the things that we're being aggressive about or trying to overlook and sweep under the carpet or shove out the door. One of the things our leaders said is that if you ignore this minority voice it will create conflict in your community and this conflict is going to create a breakdown that's going to endanger *everyone*. This conflict will endanger how we cooperate, how we use community as a process, how we think of ourselves as a cooperative unit, a harmonious unit, a unit that knows how to work together and enjoys working together and enjoys being together and loves one another.

If that happens then the things that we need to do on an everyday basis for meeting all of our needs starts to break apart. I can see how that's working today. I understand that if we think about looking at the minority, if we use the process to think about why there *is* a minority, why there is poverty, then we should be able to find creative ways to meet the needs of the minorities. Is it about economics? Is it about societal access? What are those minorities about?

If we think of ourselves as human beings with minds, with the creativity that we have, we should be able to take into consideration how we can meet the needs of those minorities. We should be able to find every possible mechanism that we can to bring that minority group into balance with the majority. The process that we call en'owkinwiwx asks us to do that and tells us that if we can't do that in our community then our humanity is at stake, and our intelligence is at stake. We can't call ourselves Okanagan if we can't provide for the weak and the sick and the hungry and the old and the people who do not have skills.

In the same way, when we approach the decision-making process, one component is reserved for *the land*. We have one component in which we have people who are called "land speakers." We have a word for it in our language. I was fortunate in that I was trained and brought up as a land speaker in my community. We are different than other communities in that we have different people, trained as part of the family system, to be speakers for the children, for the mothers, for the Elders, for the medicine people, for the land, for the water—for all of these different components that make up our existence.

My part has been to be trained by my Elders to think about the land and to speak about the land. What that means is that I don't represent the people's view and I don't think of myself as an expert; I think of myself as one person who must continuously be responsible to my community. Each time a decision is made, even the smallest decision, my responsibility is to stand up and ask, How will it impact the land? How is it going to impact our food? How is it going to impact our water? How is it going to impact my children, my grandchildren, my great-grandchildren, what's the land going to look like in their time? So in that process of en'owkinwiwx, there's a built-in principle in terms of how we interact.

Another part of the process requires people to look at relationships. There are people who represent how a decision is going to impact people. How is it going to impact the children, what are the children's needs? What are the Elders' needs? What are the mothers' needs? What are the working peoples' needs? Someone has to ask those questions. That's their responsibility. When they stand up to ask those questions they also give their views in the same way part of our community is asked to think about the actions that need to be taken. Part of our community stands up and says, What are the things that need to be built? What are the things that need to be implemented and how much is it going to cost? All of those important details need to be examined and discussed.

Those people who are doers are given the responsibility of continuously reminding our people that there are actions that are going to have an impact. There are actions that are going to cause a number of *different effects* later on down the road. If we overuse something or if we take too much of a resource there are those people who are continuously asked to stand up to let us know that.

There is another group of people in our community who we call the visionaries, the creative people. They are the artists, the writers, and the performers, whose responsibility is to bring their perspective into the community; a perspective that tells everyone that there are innovations, there are *creative solutions,* and there are new ways we can look at things. We should always make room for newness because we need to be creative when we come up against something that we can't resolve and that we haven't come up against before. So those people are always brought forward to look for new ways to bring creative ideas forth and discuss them.

All four of these components within a community can participate in a decision-making process. The process then becomes, in terms of a democratic process, a different one than that of Robert's Rules. The process becomes something that is participatory, that is inclusive, and that gives people a deeper understanding of the variety of components that are required to create harmony within community. When we include the perspective of land and we include the perspective of human relationship, one of the things that happens is that community changes. People in the community change. Something happens inside where the material things don't have a lot of meaning, where material wealth and the securing of it or being fearful and being frightened about not having "things" to sustain you, disappears. They start to lose their power. They start to lose their impact.

The realization that people and community are there to sustain you creates the most secure feeling in the world. When you feel that and you're immersed in that, then the fear starts to leave. When that happens, you're imbued with the hope that others surrounding you in your community can provide.

This is the kind of work that I'm involved in at the En'owkin Centre. I'm talking about all of the community. I'm talking about all of the people who live in the Okanagan and people who we reach outside of that. Not just the Indigenous People, because at this time in our lives, our Elders have said that unless we can "Okanaganize" those people in their thinking, we're all in danger in the Okanagan. It sounds very simple and yet it seems to be an overwhelming task—a huge task—and some days it feels like that.

Some days it seems to be something that one person has no power over. But I think about my aunt who was talking to me the other day. She said, "Where are you headed off to now?" And I said, "Oh, I'm going to this conference, the Bioneers conference." And she said, "Oh, what is that about?" So I did my best to explain it to her. And she said, "That's a really good thing. How did you manage to do that?" And I said, "I'm not really sure, but I think I managed to do that by talking about some of the things that seem so simple and everyday to us. Things that seem to make sense to us, that seem to make complete strangers into loved ones of ours, ones that we've brought into our community who are now part of my family and part of my extended community. People like Fritjof Capra and people like Zenobia Barlow and other people who are friends, who are part of this movement."

For me, inside of me, they feel the same as my aunt to me, and I think that's how we all need to relate to each other. I think that's how we need to be with each other for us to be the way we need to be on the land, so that those things that are material lose their power over us. The voice that says, "You need a new car, you need lots of money, you need to do this and you need to do that." All of that starts to dissipate when we understand that the power is us, that we are our security on the land; *that's* what's going to sustain us.

The last thing that I want to share with you is something that makes a lot of sense to me and that is my father's words for insanity. For us it means that too many people are talking about different things rather than people talking about the same thing. There does seem to be insanity in the world because of what's missing inside in terms of our humanity with each other. When we start to take care of that, everything else will naturally follow.

In the work that we do, one of the things I've learned is the power of taking our young people out to the land to gather seeds or to gather our Indigenous foods. We started a program to replant Indigenous plants to renew the imperiled habitat that we share with some endangered animal species; we've got about ten thousand plants going now.

What we have found is that when we take the young people out to restore the land, all kinds of community members from the nonnative community come out to participate, from multicultural societies or from the senior people's communities, for instance. They just love going out there, to gather seeds and pot them and replant the habitat.

One offshoot of this is that for the young people who are having such a difficult time (all young people are having a difficult time) it heals them. The process of being with people, out there on the land, has a healing impact. It's not just the work of collecting the seeds. People who are in farming know this: It's not just the work of collecting but it's being with people, the community, and communing with each other. It is how the land communes its spirit to you: it heals people and it does this in an incredibly profound way.

We need to think about how we can do more of that.

This presentation took place at the Bioneers Conference in 2002.

10

Peace Technologies from the San Bushmen of Africa

*Megan Biesele, Kxao =Oma.,
and /'Angn!ao /'Un*

There are amazing intellectual achievements of Indigenous societies who have honed, over long periods of time, specific ways to keep peace and harmony in their societies. They are a type of peace technology. I have been privileged in my life to observe firsthand some of the wonderful and ancient processes of the Ju/'hoan San people. These are the obvious ways that human beings should behave. Some of the things I saw in this society were different from my own society, very basic things like keeping everybody in the loop of communication, making sure that everybody is at the same level, important leveling mechanisms reinforced in every way through folklore, through songs, through many kinds of social rituals. And, last, making sure that everybody in the whole society has a voice, mutuality.

These ancient methods of keeping the peace, of keeping the communication flowing in their society, are being used to run their Conservancy, which is a brand new experiment for their people, a brand new kind of social organism requiring its own brand new kind of social technology, and they have honed this very carefully and organically from their ancient traditions.

I think that the response of these people and the new little government that they are forming is the exact opposite of what we saw in this country. Ever since 9/11 it seems that secrets are coming out, and it is the opposite of the kind of sharing, mutual consultation, and negotiation that has gone on for a very long time with these people. So I think that that's the kind of lesson that we can learn from some of these longest tenured societies, which is what these people have been.

They've found that confrontation and polarization do not work, and wide consultation, wide discussion, and consensus decision-making do work. This can be seen as a form of turning the other cheek—when somebody's hard you need to be soft. The whole point of it is to preserve the social fiber because I think they realize that's where their wealth lies, that's where their strength and their safety is. They don't have the kinds of more artificial safety nets that we do, with money, with health insurance, and with social security and so forth. They've got to rely on the goodwill of living people, because what else is there?

I think that is a lesson the Western world can very well take from this Ju/'hoan San society: we have to realize we all do live together on this planet, and we're going to have to depend on each other because those illusory safety nets we thought we had are disappearing one by one.

The San Bushmen ancestors have obviously honed, to a fine point of artistry, that method of getting along with each other. There are some very important components to this. One, of course, is not dealing in secrecy; opening up your heart to each other, understanding where another person's coming from when they're feeling badly, and realizing that it depends on you to take that person's pain seriously and try to do something about it.

Perhaps last, they have a healing tradition that embodies all of these family values and makes them possible. I have seen this many, many times: If there are two people who are not getting along with each other, in the healing dance, they try to put these two people next to each other so that they can come into harmony by dancing together. Would you say that that is true, Kxao?

Kxao: I think that is true. Because when they're dancing with the spirits, it takes a strong person to send the arrows of power, the healing power that the spirits send. These arrows are sent between healers by "shooting" them. The shooting happens by snapping the fingers in a certain direction. If a healer is shooting you, if you fall down, you will feel that: okay, this one is very strong. If he shoots you and you're still on your feet, he is too weak for you. It will take a stronger healer to transfer the power to you. So it's how they're testing each other while they are dancing.

Megan: These are arrows of *n/om*. N/om is a spiritual substance, kind of like electricity that passes between the spirits and the dancers. If you are a person who is in good control of n/om, then you know how to deal with these arrows that are flying around. (Older people who have danced for many, many, many years, for instance, know very well how to deal with these arrows.) For instance, this man, /'Angn!ao (this older man sitting here), is a *n/omkxao,* meaning an "owner of n/om, or spiritual power." He easily goes into altered states of consciousness to heal people by the laying on of hands and he can deal with these chaotic things that happen between people. The dance is to cure what we think of as physical illness, but most of all it's to cure problems between people because those are the worst kinds of illnesses that there are.

What people have told me about what's going on in these beautiful dances is that it's a technology of opening the heart so that healing energy can enter and so that people's hearts will be revealed to each other and any problems or enmity will go out from between them. I started studying folklore and oral traditions of these people and I kept finding that everything comes back to the healing dance. Everything points to the healing dance. It's like the central metaphor. All the stories refer to it. Many of the metaphors have that at its heart—the metaphor of healing and of opening your heart. It's like a touchstone of the Bushmen culture, and I think for that reason this must be something that goes way back to the way that they established a workable social fabric.

I saw that people were very, very careful never to make themselves bigger than anybody else in that culture, and that has huge ramifications. It's a culture that is fiercely egalitarian, and this egalitarian ethos is reinforced in hundreds and hundreds of ways all the time through songs, through stories, through the way children are brought up and so forth.

My story concerns a young man named Kxami whom I met in Botswana years ago, and he went on his very first hunt. He was able to put an arrow, a poisoned arrow, into a large kudu, but he came back to his camp after doing this and people said, Well, did you get something? He said, I didn't see anything. That was a very modest way of saying, Yes, I've got a poisoned arrow into something. Everybody in the camp knew the code. His mother was there and she kind of nodded her head, Yes, it's going to take some tracking while the poison kills the animal, but my son has gotten an arrow into his first large animal. So, early the next morning Kxami left the camp. He went out and tracked the animal, all by himself for several days, and a few days later he came back with some of the meat and the news to the group that there was a big piece of meat that he needed help in carrying home.

I thought he would then become a lauded hero. I thought that he would be the hottest thing around. Instead, what did I find? I found that his mother, his grandmother, and all of his relatives in the camp said, "Oh, Kxami, this is a scrawny piece of meat you've brought home. This is just terrible. You know? Can't you do any better than this?" He also didn't have the right to pass the meat out or distribute it because it turned out that his grandmother, who was blind, was the owner of that arrow and she had loaned it to him and had asked him to hunt for her, so she was the owner of the meat and she was the one who was able to pass it around.

So I was watching Kxami out of the corner of my eye during this whole interchange, which went on over the course of a couple of days, and I thought, now surely his feelings are going to be hurt, surely he's going to feel belittled. But on the contrary, this young man seemed to have grown at least a foot while this was happening. His eyes were sparkling and I had no idea what was going on. What I realized later is that this was their way of acknowledging that he was just one person among the group, all of whom needed the protein from that killed animal and that if he puffed himself up in any way, then he would not be able to hunt as well in the future.

So, they insulted the meat, they insulted him, they brought him down a peg or two, off a potential boastfulness that he might have been into, and he was able to bring the social fabric of his group forward. He had that wonderful effect. His killing that animal had that wonderful effect, and it also was part of his growing up. It was recognized by everyone. This was Kxami's first large animal.

But all of that happened behind the scenes, quietly, with no overt recognition to this young man. He obviously grew up, his family was obviously glad of the meat, but they leveled him, unmercifully. You see that happening over and over and over again with these people.

/'Angn!ao ("Kiewiet") is from Namibia, and he is the chairman of the Nyae Nyae Conservancy, which was the very first conservancy established in Namibia after independence. Kxao =Oma is the program manager of the Conservancy.

Kxao will explain the social technology by which the Nyae Nyae Conservancy keeps control not only of its natural resources but also of the admittedly negative spectrum, from bad to good, that exists in all people. These are people who are very realistic. Nobody is perfect. No society is perfect. There have to be ways of managing people for them to live together in societies.

Kxao: This Conservancy was started in the 1950s with the help of the Marshall family from the United States. It has almost two thousand Ju/'hoan San people, and it covers 903 hectares. The organization began formally in the 1980s with John Marshall's help, when it formed the Nyae Nyae Farmers Cooperative, and then became the first communal conservancy in Namibia in 1998.

The traditional hunting/gathering society works with some subsidies in farming now. This community has a lower development and the highest poverty of any group in Namibia. Conservancy status enables the community to use the natural resources found in the area. The Conservancy has increased income through safari hunting for the community. This increases their security, increases employment, and empowers the community. The Conservancy is supported by a number of NGOs, which have helped the Conservancy to develop management skills for resources and to create self-sufficiency and a sustainable future for the community. It also works closely with local governmental organizations that support environmental, wildlife, water, and education projects.

A component of these projects is to make provisions to ensure the protection of the water supply from wildlife and, in particular, from elephants who often break down water points used by the villagers and even also the game water points that animals rely on. When this happens, the availability of local water, for the villagers and for the animals, is compromised in that humans and animals are not able to access the water.

The wildlife management segment intends to increase the game for the trophy hunting business, so that we can get more income from the wildlife.

Then there is the agricultural segment. Two initial local gardens and educated schools train in traditional foods. We are trying to bring small gardening projects to the schools so that the small children for the new generation can learn about different foods of the world.

The crafts are mostly produced by the women, which are then marketed. There is also woodcraft, which is done by the men. We can sell these crafted objects to tourists so that the Conservancy gains income for the community. In the transportation arena, we bought some donkey carts to enable children to be brought to the schools. The introduction of the donkey carts initially improved transportation but ultimately failed because the donkeys were killed by lions. Also, when the donkey carts broke down, there was no repair possible.

Now, to the peacekeeping. The Elders or the parents of any people fighting will intervene in any disputes. The people fighting will be encouraged to go off gathering instead and the dangers of fighting with dangerous weapons will be explained to them. This is effective because Elders or parents are still respected in the Ju/'hoan culture. This means that the peacekeeping happens as a result of people coming to a solution whereby they understand one another. This is also a way to ensure life for the generations to come. Today, life is difficult with some of the individuals, and a part of our world—we're still in this situation.

Maybe your culture is different from our culture, but sometimes when our people are fighting, they fight with weapons, which can be a knife or a bow and arrow. These are very dangerous weapons. That is why if somebody tries to fight with somebody, we have to try to stop him in a good manner, otherwise, he will continue fighting. We have to come and cool him down, speak nicely to him, so that he can understand that maybe he is wrong and the other person is right. That's how you build up your peace.

With regard to decision-making, let me give you an example of how we operate. A family requests a move to another village. This request is taken to the owner of the present village so that they can understand each other before this person moves to the other village. This takes place through the Elder from the village and an agreement will be reached. Then, as the agreement is being reached, it is accepted by all the members of the village.

That was the old way of peacekeeping. Now let's look at the current method of peacekeeping. Today, Ju/'hoan communities use their formerly given rights to stay in *n!oresi*. N!oresi means traditional hunting territories, and this meaning is now being extended to include the concept of settled villages. The people's rights were recognized by the new Nyae Nyae Farmer's Cooperative when it was established. For each n!ore there are Elders who have the right to make a decision regarding the resources and the people who can stay on the n!ore. These Elders are the same traditional Elders as before, but there is now more formality to the process.

Lately, we have also changed considerably in that our young people are receiving more education than before, which increases their chances of leaving the villages and finding employment with the government or the tourism industries. Currently, we are now on our way to building up some village preschools. We have large schools in the area but we have small children to start educating, from the youngest ages upward. The Nyae Nyae land is secured for the Ju/'hoan people. Education in the mother tongue is valuable for children, however, even given that, few children are progressing beyond four school grades. This means that some of our people have not completed their grade tens or twelves because they are not able to pay school fees and so on.

There is a lodge about to be built that will be providing more jobs and income to the Conservancy. We are still waiting for Country Lodges to build a tourist lodge so that we can increase employment opportunities for our people.

We have problems with the wide scale introduction of crops. Earlier we used to provide some people seed so that they could grow crops, but the crops were damaged by elephants. With the introduction of cattle to the community, some individuals had success. Some people applied themselves to the cattle. Some people still do have cattle, but some were losing their cattle to wild animals such as lions, leopards, and others.

What can provide accessibility and security for the villages and the wildlife? As stated above, we work to increase the wildlife population to benefit community through trophy hunting income and harvesting meat. Our Conservancy has one of the largest incomes in the country, with livelihood opportunities generated through craft sales and campsites. The Conservancy is being run by its own people; one of them is me. I'm the program manager. There's not just one person leading the Conservancy, there's also a chairperson. Our current chairperson is here with me today, Mr. /'Angn!ao /'Un. None of us make decisions alone: we do everything in consultation with each other.

Management of the Conservancy funds still need close monitoring and support. The funds of the Conservancy are not well managed. Limited learning and poor recordkeeping meant reports were taking place without mentoring support. The reports were not given correction when it was needed.

With regard to staff management in the Conservancy, our staff is respectful maybe but not according to what the policies of the organization say. Continuously we need to define the rights. We still have to build up our land rights so that everybody can be organized and be happy with the rights given to them.

Megan Biesele: I love the way Kxao has ended what he said about the Conservancy. It's all about what we said at the start of this piece, that the Ju/'hoansi realize that their most important natural resource is themselves, the mutual understanding and cooperation they can maintain among themselves. They know that what I've clumsily called "social technology" is one of the oldest and most important human technologies for survival.

They have made efforts in the last few decades to define and polish the workings of their original small-group democracy, their governance by consensus, and to use it for the higher level of regional governance required by their changed circumstances in the new Namibia. I think we in Western countries have a great deal to learn from the Ju/'hoansi—and from other hunting/gathering societies around the world—while we still can.

This discussion took place at the Bioneers Conference in 2006.

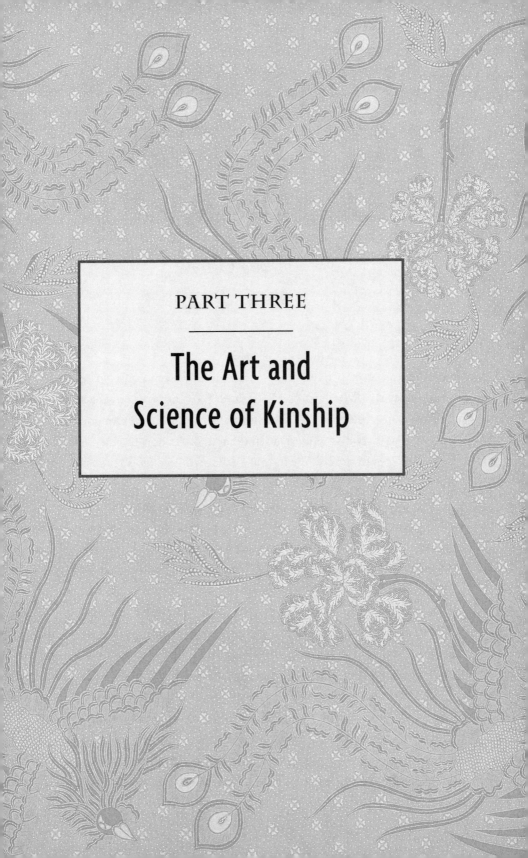

PART THREE

The Art and Science of Kinship

11
Where Is the Holy Land?

Leslie Gray

A basic question I invite students in my ecopsychology classes to ask themselves is, "Where is the Holy Land?" I invite you now to ask yourself the same question. It is illustrative to note that it can sound a bit peculiar to a Native American Indian to hear non-Indians refer to a specified area of the Middle East as the Holy Land. *This* land is the Holy Land. Right here on this North American continent.

This is where Onondaga is. The sacred council fire burns at Onondaga still. This is where the Black Hills—the traditional vision-questing place of Black Elk, Lame Deer, and other great teachers—are. This is where the spiritual city of Chaco Canyon was constructed with every point in alignment with the heavens. This is where pilgrims crawl on their knees to be healed at Chimayo. This is where Blue Lake is. This is where Big Mountain is. This is the Holy Land. In fact, aboriginal peoples of the Americas have always wisely acknowledged that the earth itself is everywhere and in all parts sacred.

Indeed, all over the planet you will find sacred sites that were honored and preserved by the Indigenous People of that bioregion. Everywhere you step you step on the sacred bones of ancestors. So this is the Holy Land—right here—the very soil upon which I am standing. And, of course, it lies beneath your feet as well, wherever *you* may be standing.

Why is it important to acknowledge the sacredness of the land you are on? Because at the dawn of the twenty-first century, people are still going to war over the idea that one spot in the Middle East is the Sacred Place. Or another way to say it is that it is still easy for a few people motivated by power and greed to bamboozle those populations who see only one place (and one religion based upon the spiritual story of that place) as sacred.

Here in the United States for example, where the prevailing culture still clings to a narrow conception of a distant holy land, the public is easily duped into righteous wars that are, in fact, ultimately aimed at control of distant natural resources. Correspondingly, we see heinous crimes against humanity enthusiastically committed by individuals and groups who have been persuaded that their particular spiritual story, from their particular part of the Middle East, must prevail throughout the world.

Seeing only one place as holy, and by inference others as not holy, is a great source of problems. There is a very high cost indeed for failing to acknowledge the whole earth as sacred.

This presentation took place at the Bioneers Conference in 2002.

12

Restoring Indigenous History and Culture to Nature

Dennis Martinez, Enrique Salmón, and Melissa K. Nelson

"Restoring Indigenous History and Culture to Nature" is a unique educational approach different from what is generally done in either academia (history, anthropology, ecology) or the environmental movement (with the exception of the environmental justice and Indigenous rights movements). In Indian country, ecological and cultural restoration are intimately entwined and vital to the health and well-being of Native American communities. This approach requires careful observations of natural cycles and time-tested practical cultural responses and accommodations.

Dennis Martinez: I've been doing Indigenous restoration work long enough to know that there was a time we couldn't have filled one small tent with people interested in hearing about this type of work. That wasn't that many years ago. I noticed a change for the better in the mid-1990s at international scientific conferences when I tried to get Indigenous presenters to talk about their issues and about traditional ecological knowledge and Western science. At these conferences, we'd usually be relegated to the smallest possible room, but typically so many people would come that we'd have to interrupt the session to get a larger room to accommodate everyone. You can always read the science in the literature, but you're not going to get much of what Indigenous Peoples have to offer about their unique perspectives unless you hear it from them directly.

But now in the literature, in the last ten years internationally, traditional ecological knowledge and Indigenous landcare systems have caught the attention of many scientists globally. This is a good trend. We don't know how long this postmodern deconstructionist window of cultural relativity is going to be open. We're damn glad it's open. We hope it stays open long enough to kind of sneak through and get some of our ideas across.

In this chapter I will discuss the fundamental difference between the Western scientific-oriented environmental movement and Indigenous worldviews and practices. Western science has many good aspects as a useful quantitative tool, but it does not fit with Indigenous cosmologies and worldviews. In these modern times of unprecedented environmental degradation, we need both; our goal here is to find out how and where they can work together.

In wilderness preservation, in land management, forestry, and resource management of all kinds, Native Peoples offer a kind of model. But it's not the biocentric model that you're familiar with from deep ecology or Aldo Leopold's land ethic. It's fundamentally different because it is primarily kincentric. That's the word that I have coined to describe a unique Indigenous cosmology and relationship to nature. It's not in the dictionary. I had to think of something that would work to explain that what this relationship is about in the universe is one of equality. Humans don't even have the moral authority to extend ethics to the land community, as the Leopold land ethic and deep ecology do.

Traditionally, we work with animals and plants. We are comanagers with animals and plants. We don't have the right to extend anything. What we have the right to do is to make our case, as human beings, to the natural world. That compact, that kind of contract between animals and human beings, is what has guided Indians' subsistent livelihoods—hunting and gathering—and Indian agroecology and agriculture in the world for a very, very long time.

There was a time when Indigenous Peoples in one part of this continent during the fur trading years lost faith in that compact, lost faith in that treaty between the animals and the people. Due to European diseases and the Jesuit conversion, or the attempt to convert mainly the Algonquin peoples of Eastern Canada and the Northeastern United States to Christianity, they broke this contract. There was a time, the Elders say, the oral tradition says, when animals and human beings could talk to one another—that was when these compacts were made. This is metaphorical, this is symbolic, but it guides, nonetheless, how traditional Indigenous Peoples have related to the animal and plant world. Eventually, after the near total decimation of most fur-bearing animals, Indians came back to their traditional respect for all relatives in the natural world.

This was a relationship model, a kincentric model, one in which we are all equal, but we have different jobs to do here on earth. If an Indian woman, for example, were digging in the old days here in California, probably in this very place in San Rafael, she would be digging up what we call Indian potatoes. By digging up that soil, mixing nutrients, aerating it, taking off little corms* that stick to the mother corm and replanting them, she would improve the health of those corms. They would propagate those little ones and then extend the size of that tract and increase the health and fertility of that tract. Where federal land agencies have come in and fenced off those places to preserve them, those tracts of Indian potatoes have disappeared. They've contracted to the point where they're nothing like they were formerly.

These valleys around here, 150 years ago, were amazing seas of blue camas in May and June, as far as the eye could see. We barely find any camas anymore. The Elders say that if you don't care for the plants and animals, they don't take care of you. That's reciprocity.

---

*A corm is an underground part of a plant that helps the plant to reproduce as a tuber or a bulb.

It's not so much a moral universe in the Western sense. It's more about practical reciprocity. It's more of a compact. We agree to do certain things and the animals and plants agree to do other things, and we honor that commitment; we honor that contract. It's like a league of sovereign nations working together.

In the 1920s in Tomales Bay in Marin County, California, there were eleven major clam beds basically semidomesticated and harvested by Indian people, the Coast Miwok, the very people whose land we are on in Marin County. The Department of Fish and Game in California stopped the harvesting to protect the resource, and the clam population crashed. Only one clam bed was left that had any clams. Why? Because by moving those clams around as they harvested them, Indians spread out the population, and by mitigating against any densities, they mitigated in the same move against any diseases that would afflict very tightly growing clam populations. And so the clams, by being moved, thrived.

At the openings of river mouths on this north coast of California up into Oregon, tribal members used to clear away the sand spits that closed off the lagoons and closed off the mouths of the rivers. In late summer there was a Chinook salmon run that was totally dependent on that clearing of the sand spits so that the salmon could get up before the rains came. They had to move fast so they wouldn't get eaten by the pelicans and the cormorants and the seals that were hanging out there, milling around waiting for the rains to come to lift the salmon over that blockage, which made them easy prey for the birds and seals. Today, that late summer Chinook run is extinct.

Indian people in British Columbia used to take fish eggs, salmon eggs, and they would transplant them in moss from one stream to another. When the ice ages came, they were there to move those salmon around. When those rivers were blocked (such as what happened on the Frazier River in 1911 due to logjams), the Indians made a wooden flume and allowed the salmon around. Where they couldn't build a flume to the upper regions they would carry the eggs so that those salmon could spawn. They had weirs across the rivers near the mouth of those rivers, and they would let the salmon through once they'd done the harvesting in the morning.

There are many stories like this. They would clean spawning beds for the salmon, they would break up logjams on steep gradient creeks to allow the salmon up, but most importantly, they didn't fish the open ocean for salmon or anadromous fish, they fished at the mouths of the rivers. By fishing at the mouths of the rivers, the mouths of the streams, they could control the harvest, they could control how they built their fish traps and selected their fishing hooks, and the size and the species of fish they needed. The others would be let go. If they were circling a herd of elk with fire, as they did in the Willamette Valley in Oregon and in the San Joaquin Valley and the Sacramento Valley in California, they'd concentrate those deer into a small place, then they'd go in and take the fair to middling ones out, not the best ones. They'd let the best go because the Indian people had a sense of genetics, of selective breeding and selective harvesting.

A tobacco, *Nicotiana quadrivalvis,* used to be a very important medicine plant that was sowed out in the ashes of slash at midslope in the Klamath Mountains where I live. It is virtually extinct because no one is doing that anymore. When they burned in the Willamette Valley in Oregon, they backburned around Douglas fir and western hemlock groves at the edges of the valley in the foothills, so the elk would have thermal cover in the summer time. All this was conscious. There's a lot of academic nonsense in the literature these days that asks whether or not Indians were conservationists, or whether they were the first ecologists or not.

The words conservation and ecology, as we use them in the Western sense, don't exactly fit what Indian people did or do with the land. It was their livelihood, which depended on reciprocity. Thus, the trees were not seen just as trees, they were also seen as relatives. The trees are relatives and other species are relatives and they watched you all the time. It was a forest of eyes that looked at you to see how you were handling the remains of plants and animals.

An animal's shadow soul is alive for a long time after an animal is killed, and it watches how you treat the remains. Among the Koyukon in Central Alaska, if you came across a moose that had already died, and it was somewhat decomposed, you would still stop and cut it into edible pieces like you would if it were ready to be eaten. You would do this to show the shadow soul that you cared for and respected that animal, no matter how it died. You still had to show respect. That was the agreement, the compact, between the animals and the people. That's how it worked.

So what does that have to do with where we are today? We could go on and on about the codependency and the coevolution through selective harvesting and gathering between Indigenous Peoples and plants and animals (of course, everyone's ancestors were once Indigenous). Ninety-nine percent of our human existence has been nonindustrial, nonmajor agricultural, it has been hunting, gathering, and agroecology, all mixed up together depending on the season and the resource that needed to be exploited.

One recent author claimed that Indians only occupied 0.02 percent of North America land area, so therefore they didn't really manage very much land. That's just where the villages were. But they forget that they did seasonal roundups to the highest elevations, they burned at virtually every elevation from sea level and foothill and valley all the way across the high peaks of the Sierra Nevada and the Cascades. They traded with their neighbors beyond, harvesting and burning along the way where and when it was needed.

Due to this intensive and extensive management by Indigenous Peoples nearly everywhere in North America—as forest ecologists, as native scientists, and environmental activists—we need to recognize that there is a model here. This model is a baseline that we can derive from the oral tradition and the literature and from various scientific techniques such as pyrodendrochronology (the reading of fire-scar history, which indicates how many fires occurred).

Given that most Indian fires set by the women in this area did not show up as fire scars, we can get only a little bit of an idea about lightning frequency data and even mean return intervals (the average times a fire comes through in any given place) from the scientific community. We need to look at what it would have taken for Indigenous People to survive at very high, precontact, predisease populations, and the amount of burning that would have been required. It would probably be ten times what is currently estimated by formal anthropology for population numbers.

An enormous number of plants would have to have been burned to be able to create approximately twelve major categories of cultural use. Eighty-five percent of the plants that were used by Indian people in California were plants that had been burned the year before to make them useful for basketry, cordage, for ceremonies, for games, for musical instruments, for fishing and hunting gear, for structures, for clothing, medicine and food, and deer and elk habitat improvement. There are two to three hunts of deer where I am living every year. To make the deer forage correctly, the habitat is burned to make it suitable for wildlife.

By combining Indigenous Knowledge and our knowledge of Indigenous land practices with Western ecological science, we can create better land care. We can then work from a reference ecosystem model that guides us to the present time. The landscape has changed; we have fragmentation, exotic plant invasions, toxic pollutants, and all that. So it's not that we're imitating the past, we can't really do that. Once an ecosystem is gone, it's gone; that's why conservation is always the first choice.

So while we can't really re-create the past, we can emulate it to the extent that we can attempt to restore the basic structure, composition, and function or integrity of ecosystems during precontact times. Western science can assist our restoration efforts with its powerful quantitative toolkit, its technology. Indigenous Peoples can make use of this, according to their own traditions and restoration objectives, and guided by Traditional Knowledge. By working the two systems of knowledge together, even though we can't translate cosmologies across the board, I think we can create better ecological science.

QUESTIONS AND ANSWERS WITH
DENNIS MARTINEZ

Question: How do we make an alliance with nature, how do we establish a relationship with nature in sites that are severely degraded like ones that have been mined?

Dennis Martinez: I live in Trinity County in northwest California and most of the soil around streams and rivers, for example, has been turned upside down due to mining, so I can relate to that. What you do is you find out what you can about plants from your local area that can begin to restore fertility to that site.

I was recently at Chemawa Indian School near Salem, Oregon, working on Opal Creek. Some environmental activists will remember the Opal Creek forest struggle in the 1980s. We had the same situation at this site, a mining site, and we had thirty students and the soil was so hard it took a bar and a shovel and a pick to loosen it up. In five hours 150 red alders were planted. Red alders were chosen because they fix nitrogen in the soil.

In the process of doing that, you start to come together, you start to develop a relationship with the land, the plants, and each other. Your sense of ownership comes in; those are your plants and those students will come back and they'll look at those plants and say, this is my plant, look how it's doing.

Question: Do you pick up roadkill, dead animals, along the roads? If so, what do you do with them?

Dennis Martinez: Yes, I do, although not as frequently as I would like because some curves on roads where I live in the woods are pretty dangerous and scary, however, to the extent I can, yes; I carry a short-handled shovel in my rig. One of the reasons I do that is because birds like ravens and crows and magpies will come to feed on the carcasses and then *they'll* get hit by cars coming around curves. I wish I could take more dead animals from the curves; sometimes I'll walk back a block or two to do that.

Second, it's a respectful way to honor the remains of that bird or animal. As I mentioned earlier, it's how you treat an animal's remains that counts. In the past, people didn't just throw things away willy-nilly. They didn't put them in the garbage can, they put those bones carefully up in the knot-crotches of trees. They had a way of dealing with remains. In a sense, this was not unlike the Christian idea of the blood of Christ and the body of Christ being transformed by eating it in the form of a wafer—a symbolic eating of the flesh of God. We consider wildlife to be people just like us, with the same kind of psychology as us. Wildlife becomes, eventually, a sacred substance, and in some cases, tribal rules dictate that you have to eat all of something right away, and sometimes you can wait. But there are strict protocols and rules on how to dispose of the remains of animals. That's a very important part of traditional culture.

Question: Did the Indian people of the Plains actually manage the buffalo or did they just take from the bounty of the land when they could?

Dennis Martinez: I think we have to get rid of this notion that nature was so bountiful in every place, the Indians didn't have to do much, and if they'd had higher population numbers or if they had sophisticated technology like we have now, they would have also destroyed wildlife. I gave you the reasons why they didn't do that: they had respect for the remains of the animals and the reciprocity of their pact. With respect to buffalo and many, many other forms of wildlife, they definitely were thinking ahead to the future, and they deliberately burned the landscape to direct and manage the herds, much like they did here in California on the ridgetops.

Ridges used to be kept open for elk and deer in late winter, and that was an important deer hunt because stored food supplies were getting low and fish runs hadn't yet occurred. Indian greens, Indian potatoes were not available, but they began to get fresh meat because their burns in the fall stimulated new browse. It was the same thing with the buffalo. Besides enriching the prairie grasses and flowers the bison fed on, fire directed the buffalo to where Indians were waiting. Both Indian and lightning ignited fire, which kept trees from invading the tall-grass prairie and extended the bison prairie habitat all the way through the eastern woodlands to western Massachusetts. But when the cattle came on the Oregon Trail and other trails, and began to bisect the hunting grounds of the Indian peoples there and changed bison migrations, Indian peoples began to burn vast areas to deprive European stock of any forage.

QUESTIONS AND ANSWERS WITH ENRIQUE SALMÓN

Enrique Salmón: *Cuira-ba*! (Greetings in Rarámuri). That's my Rarámuri language (also known as Tarahumara). I start that way because when I think about ecological and Indigenous issues I can't help but think about how we talk about these issues, how we talk about the environment, how we talk about traditional culture, how we talk about our own connection to place. Using the right words, finding the right words, is often difficult, because half the time it's an intuitive process that we're all struggling with, trying to find a way to describe and express this very deep and emotional connection.

For me, it takes me down into the core of my being, of being a Rarámuri—how I identify myself when I wake up every morning and think about who I am and what I am. When I think of being a Rarámuri, it implies a very deep responsibility. Let me tell you a story about that.

I like to tell stories. This is a key way to get encoded knowledge across, and in this case, ecological knowledge. I remember a number of years ago when I was back down in Chihuahua where my people are from. It's the center of the universe, by the way, not Marin County like some people like to believe. Although Marin's an incredible place. To me it's become home.

But I was down in Chihuahua at the edge of the Barranca del Cobre or what we call in our language *Urique*. This is a canyon that is deeper than the Grand Canyon, and you can fit three Grand Canyons into it. And this is the homeland. I was there with some of my friends in a place called Norogachi and we were talking about going to a community called Creel, which is the nearest community where there's actually electricity and running water, and we were going to go do some things there with some of my relatives and friends.

That morning, when we got up and went to leave, I noticed that my friends had all changed from the traditional clothing into what we call Western clothing. There's a reason for this, because when the Rarámuri go into places like Creel, where there's a lot of Méstizos and nonnative people, we often get picked on and get beat up and sometimes even murdered. So it's to people's advantage to put on Western clothing. But I was teasing my buddies and saying, "Oh, you're not Rarámuri anymore; you don't have the clothing on." So we were teasing each other about that.

Then we got into one car and it took us five hours to go fifteen miles on the super highway across the Sierra Madres. We got to Creel and we did our thing, and being that there was electricity, there was an ice cream shop. So we went and had ice cream, and we came out and we were just sitting on the curb eating our ice cream. Then from across the street this traditionally dressed Rarámuri comes out of a shop, and again, I started teasing my buddies and I said, "Now there's a real Rarámuri!" My buddies said, "No he's not." I said, "Yeah, look, he has the traditional clothing on—the aca'ca, the sandals that we wear and so on." And he says, "No. He's a Mormon."

Now, what's the reason that sounds funny? When Mormon missionaries come down into Northern Mexico and to other places around the world and do their mission of missionizing, they bring their beliefs. A part of their belief is that when you become a Mormon, you can't dance and you can't drink.

Part of being a Rarámuri is dancing and drinking, and not just for the hell of it. When we dance, we play a certain kind of music, and Onoruame our creator, likes to hear this, he likes to watch us dance; he likes to hear the music. When we drink our corn beer, it's a sacrament. Our origins are from the corn, we are the children of corn. We literally emerged from ears of corn. So when we drink corn beer, we're becoming one with our origins, one with ourselves, because we are the corn, the corn is us, and as a result, we are the land. When we drink this corn beer and we get drunk on it, Onoruame likes to hear our laughter, and likes to hear us being Rarámuri, he gets strong, and he brings the rain. And when the rain comes, of course, we can grow things. The land is strong, the animals are strong. Part of being a Rarámuri implies dancing and drinking and making sure that cycle continues on this landscape.

This is key to what Dennis was talking about when it comes to Indigenous communities and individuals of any landscape connecting to their place, being that this implies action; it implies a practice; it implies centuries of observing what works. What we often think of today as being sacred knowledge is just as my friend Dennis has said—it's practical knowledge. This so-called sacred kind of secret stuff is just what works. *Que dice.*

Part of what I used to do as a program officer for a private foundation that works with Indigenous communities and what I still do as an Indigenous ethnoecologist and educator is I go around and talk with people about their places. In this talking I hear all sorts of history—cultural history—or what you might think of as stories: origin stories. I get to see ceremonies and dances and rituals. This is not just about doing the dances and singing the songs for tourists. They're for ourselves. They are metaphors, they're moving metaphors of our relationship to place. When we hear the songs, we're also hearing these metaphors that are motivated by experiences with our cultural spaces. Let me see if I can give you an example.

A long time ago in another world there was this woman that we often called Sita; her full name was Sitakame. She was a lousy gambler. She was always losing, and as a result of all this losing, she was always angry and people didn't like to be around her. So she didn't have many friends at all. One day, Onoruame approaches her and just kind of tells her, "Hey, I'm tired of this. We're going to have to change you." Can you imagine God coming along and telling you you're not going to be a human being anymore, I'm going to change you into something else?

This is what happened to Sitakame. Creator comes along and says I'm going to change you into something that you can be that's going to contribute to this community, and he changes her into a tree, which, today, is referred to as Brazil wood. As a result of her being changed into Brazil wood, she's now very useful to this community because from Brazil wood we get all sorts of incredible medicines, and a wood that we use for making many cultural objects.

Now the whole story, the rest of the story is: What happens when the Rarámuri now come across Brazil wood? All these cultural metaphors of proper behavior are activated in our minds. The way we think about and talk about this place is activated, it's changed. The landscape becomes a moral landscape. As we move across the landscape, it's not like we go across thinking of these stories all the time, we are remembering this story and that story and so on, but it's just a sort of automatic, subconscious connection to all these things in our environment, to the plants, to the animals, to geographic or geologic formations, and so on. As a result, our morality is directive, or comes directly from a landscape. Consequently, we find a way to interact in a kind way with our landscape (as Dennis discussed earlier). All these sustainable ways to manage the landscape come directly from this way of thinking and talking about the landscape.

Because this is a living knowledge, it can't be put into a memory bank. We shouldn't be thinking about preserving this stuff. We often read about how it's important to preserve traditional knowledge. Well, what's another word for preserve? We can pickle it, can't we? It's not good enough to just pickle this traditional knowledge and pickle how to interact with the landscape, we need to keep the actions and the practices alive. When we preserve and pickle, or do what some ethnoecologists or anthropologists do (take this knowledge), they have to translate it. They have to transform the knowledge and they take it out of its context. They write about it in one of these journal articles that maybe ten other people are going to read, or undergrads at a college are forced to read. Then it gets archived, it gets stored. The knowledge is out of its place.

It's the same thing if we go along and we take a picture of a bunch of Navajos from say, the 1870s, and then we say this is how Navajos always have been and how they always will be, not allowing the community, the people, to be dynamic, to live, to become a living community. The knowledge is also a living thing, and we have to allow this to continue as it is, and to be creatively changed, because, of course, the people and the land also change.

Memory banks are not going to do a whole lot for us. There's not much context. We have to think then, if we're not going to store or pickle or preserve this knowledge, what's the alternative? We always talk about maintaining our biosphere, our biodiversity. But we've got to keep it going, and we've got to make sure it's alive. What about what Wade Davis calls the ethnosphere? The sphere of human creativity and cultural diversity? Indigenous Peoples are trying to find a way to continue this human legacy of living sustainably with this land, with our different landscapes. Because when we start to lose the ethnosphere, we're losing all of these cultural translations of specific ecosystems.

The Lakota way of dealing with their landscape is not going to work for the Hopi in Northern Arizona, and vice versa. We have to pay attention to the context of their specific models and their moral metaphors and their moral landscapes, or what Leslie Marmon Silko referred to as their cognitive journeys across a landscape. We all have to find our unique ways of taking our own cognitive journeys on our landscapes, as the woman here asked about with this land that she has adopted. She has to find her cognitive journey on that landscape. Dennis suggested a great way to do this: find the plants. Connect with them and then your cognitive journey begins, and then next your metaphors will begin, and that place becomes your moral landscape.

So, let's find a way to maintain these cultures, in situ, on their places. If the people own land, then the land will stay healthy. It's not an accident that in the most biodiverse regions around the world, we also find traditional cultures, people who are speaking their languages, who are maintaining these sustainable land-management practices. So, despite what so many environmental NGOs have been telling us for a long time—that humans are bad for the land—humans are actually good for the landscape if they find this proper behavior with their landscapes, this moral behavior. I know that many NGOs are changing, I'll give them that credit.

So, what does this mean for us today when I talk about talking about place, talking about environment? Why is it that most Americans, when polled, agree that we have major environmental concerns that need to be addressed? In fact, a lot of Americans say they are environmentalists, yet "environmentalist" and "environment" have become bad words. We have to change our language about this issue. We have to stop talking about the environment. We have to stop setting up this barrier, this wall, between what we feel is good and proper behavior, and apply it to our language, and take it into a deeper sense, a deeper truth, which is what? That we *are* the environment, and if we are harming the environment, we're harming ourselves.

So, in other words, we have to talk about things like global warming and climate change, not as an environmental issue, but as a human health issue. This is what it's really about. When we can start to do that, we can stop separating humans from the environment and place humans smack in the middle of the environment, which is not just native peoples, all of us have to *be the environment*. We need to stop separating ourselves from what's in our own front and backyards, because we're all of that as human beings.

QUESTION & ANSWER WITH
ENRIQUE SALMÓN, DENNIS MARTINEZ, AND
WORKSHOP MODERATOR MELISSA K. NELSON

Question: What happens when you approach an Indigenous community that has decided that they want to allow roads, modern conveniences, logging, and do economic development?

Enrique Salmón: Normally the Christensen Fund doesn't work with those communities, because when they've reached that point then they're not really living a sustainable lifestyle anymore. These sustainable communities are actually few and far between. The key for those kinds of communities is to find a way to adapt the modern conveniences so that it works for them, so that they still can maintain what is the core of their philosophy and their values within modern development.

I'll never forget when I taught a semester at Hampshire College in western Massachusetts and I had some native students I had taken with me from Fort Lewis College. One of them was Tlingit and she was telling me about midway through the semester that she had gotten into this huge debate with some of the Hampshire students because she was talking about how her family used snowmobiles to hunt. They were getting all over her case about it, saying that it is not traditional to hunt with snowmobiles and if you do so, then you're not being a true Tlingit anymore.

She responded by saying, "You go out and hunt in the middle of winter on snowshoes, and if there's a snowmobile there and there's snowshoes here, I'm going to take the snowmobile." It doesn't mean that they're not Tlingit anymore. They're still hunting the old way, they're still following the traditional spaces that clans are assigned to for hunting and so on, they're still managing the landscape, but they're taking advantage of this modern convenience for something that is still a good thing.

Question: You have a pretty strong critique of Western anthropology and what's called ethnographic fieldwork. What's the better way to go about doing it?

Enrique Salmón: I think the first thing that anthropologists today need to do is to make a long-term commitment with a community, because traditionally, anthropologists would go into the field and plan to spend some time there, maybe eighteen months, and, if they're lucky, possibly two or three years. But it takes at minimum that long just to learn the language, which is the next key point: learn the language. Once you start to learn the language, then it begins, and you start to really understand these metaphors I was talking about. These are the true ways that people talk about who they are and how they reveal their connection to place. Anthropologists need to recognize that it's a long-term commitment with one community—ten years, even more. Another important thing is to not treat the people as just data, as informants. I hate that term informant. We're all human, we're all friends and relatives. Many times people became relatives within a community, and they need to pay attention to those things.

Melissa K. Nelson: I'd like to comment that one area I've seen that really helps is when anthropologists understand there are human rights issues and cultural development issues involved with the community. Thus, it's not just a matter of going in and extracting their ceremonial knowledge or their other traditional knowledge without understanding that maybe the majority of their tribal members do not have running water in their house, or that their sacred sites are being endangered by adjacent land uses. It's important for contemporary anthropologists to understand that tribal peoples are much more than repositories of knowledge and, as human beings, have larger human rights, political, and social justice issues that need to be addressed.

When anthropologists partner up with Native Peoples in those struggles to protect their land rights and sacred places, they can be very powerful and important allies. Today there is finally a more community-based approach to research emerging within anthropology and, more importantly, tribes are creating their own research protocols and review processes to determine what type of research they would like to see within their nations and communities.

Dennis Martinez: A lot of people in the environmental wilderness preservation movement draw inspiration from the noble savage stereotyped Indian who walks on the earth very lightly, leaving nothing but footprints. There is great ignorance about the true role of Indigenous Peoples as caregivers of the land! There is great ignorance about how much impact Indian peoples have had on vegetation patterns and species' composition.

What we need is support for cultural survival, which involves guaranteeing access, equity, and sustainability of cultural resource management on public lands, what we call the commons and customary use rights. That is barely underway in the United States. So, support reserved treaty rights, support comanagement, support and protest against relocation of Indigenous Peoples globally from their homelands in the name of science.

Enrique Salmón: Dennis, you bring up something else that's important here when you mention the idea of the noble savage. What does that imply when we use that concept, when we think about this? A lot of times I run into people who just assume that because I'm a native I'm also inherently an ecologist, that I walk around barefoot all the time, walking lightly in the woods, and so on. It's not like ten thousand years ago after the Ice Age, Native Peoples all woke up around the world and said, "Hey, let's be ecologists now." This is just the way of living on a place. It's just like I said; it's a result of centuries of observation of what works and of recognizing that we have to be in this place so we better not make a mess of things.

Question: Isn't it true that the world's biodiversity started to go down when modern humans started to emerge and develop?

Enrique Salmón: We have to be careful about that sort of thinking because biodiversity maintains a stochastic continuum. It's always going up or down, it's never in this one simple, harmonic state where something reaches a certain number and then stays there. It's always moving—that's the history of this planet, and human beings have experienced the same thing. I think I know what you're getting at, though, partly with Paul Martin and that research about extinction rates after the Ice Age, and Indigenous Peoples having a role in that. But that's up for debate whether or not that was true, or whether or not it was actually a combination of human hunting, climate change, and all sorts of other factors that affected mammoths and other large megafauna.

You can't deny, however, that in the last hundred years diversity has plummeted, and that's, of course, a direct result of modern industrialized society, not traditional human communities that still manage their landscape. That's why I said that, of the remaining high biodiversity areas in the world, the Indigenous communities are there maintaining those traditions and enhancing their biodiversity, as opposed to decreasing diversity. Unfortunately, there aren't enough of these traditional communities still around in the world.

Dennis Martinez: I just wanted to add one thing to that: This idea of a reference restoration model for science based on Indigenous management techniques and practices and knowledge is a relative thing. Before there were humans there was a different vegetation configuration structurally and compositionally in nature when there were different climactic weather regimes. There were differences even when humans were here. Over the last six thousand years there has generally been a cooling trend in climatic regimes.

Fire has been used by Indigenous People to maintain oaks that were retreating south as the climate cooled. Their burning removed advancing conifers like fir, cedar, hemlock, and Douglas fir, which were displacing oaks. We still have to work hard to keep Douglas fir out of oak groves. Fire was the main architect, in North America, of the structure and composition of forest and prairie and wetland ecosystems, so to the degree that fire has been made illegal or suppressed, biodiversity has suffered tremendously. Indian people were the ones primarily using fire, which supplemented lightning fire in some areas. There were other areas where lightning fires supplemented Indian fires.

Question: What are some models of ecological restoration that are being successful right now in the American Southwest? What are people doing now? How can we get involved?

Enrique Salmón: One of my favorite models is right here at the California-Arizona border down into the Colorado Delta. There's a community of native folks that not a whole lot of people know are down there.

They've kind of kept themselves quiet; they're the Cocopahs. They live on both sides of the Mexican-American border, traditionally they were there, and the border just kind of came along and split them up. They are currently working on a restoration of the Delta. They are doing a combination of dredging—because the Delta has silted up and affected their traditional fishing grounds—and building weirs and dykes to hold the water in certain places or, in other words, to lift the level of the water there in the Delta.

This is something that they did before. For centuries they've done this work to maintain the Delta. So they're returning to this way of managing the Delta there and, as a result, the fish species are coming back and certain shoreline plant species are returning. When that happens, of course, the small mammals and the birds, insects, and other life, all start to come and fall back into place. Once you start to restore an important part of an ecosystem, what we call the keystone species have to return. This raises a very interesting question, then, in light of that concept: Are humans a keystone species? Dennis, what do you think about that?

Dennis Martinez: Humans are keystone species where they have been involved in ecosystem dynamics for millennia, and even for shorter periods of time when their actions and practices have been ecologically appropriate. Humans are not innately destructive, innately exploitive; it has to do with culture, it has to do with a way of relating to the land that implies both spiritual and ecological wisdom, and this is embodied in Traditional Ecological Knowledge. It's how we fit in with that, which the forest, for example, is familiar with over coevolutionary time. Humans in most ecosystems in North American, and many globally, have been intimately involved as top carnivores and as keystone species, and when they've been removed from those practices that were ecologically appropriate, systems have tended to unravel and unintended negative cascading ecological consequences have occurred. We're also keystone if we're doing destructive practices, but by changing our practices, we can have a positive effect on the ecosystems.

That is the role of culture and the Indigenous model I've been talking about.

Question: The greatest healing that needs to be done is the healing of this European idea of the separation of people from nature, and its modern counterpart, which is that humans are bad, and our children now are depressed about being a human because they see what we're doing out there destructively.

Dennis Martinez: But cultures that practice ecologically appropriate practices are in a different bag altogether. There is no Indian word for wilderness. There are words that correspond to "wild"—that which we don't control. Wilderness implies a lack of a relationship, even though it means in its earliest meaning, "self-willed." We don't manage nature, we work with nature. But we don't control nature. In restoration, we nudge nature just a little bit to assist in recovering natural processes, just like a doctor would by using medicine in the human body. It's a matter of our relationship in a spiritual sense. We come as suppliants, we pray in ceremonies to set the world right because we use it up; we re-create the world with plants and animals. We are cocreators with the plants and animals; and unlike Islam, Judaism, and Christianity, God did not create the earth and then rest on the seventh day. Every day is Creation. Every day is Earth Day and ceremonies of world renewal are carried on every year by Indigenous Peoples worldwide.

Melissa K. Nelson: I want to comment as well that a linguist, Dan Moonhawk Alford, wrote a wonderful paper called "God Is Not a Noun in Native America." That gets to the point that Dennis just made, that God is not simply a transcendent, divine force or power outside of our human experience, or outside of nature and after the seventh day he stopped all his creative activities. The divine or the sacred is something that's a verb; it is active, it is a cocreative process that Indigenous Peoples and all peoples have a right and obligation to participate in on a moment-to-moment basis through our actions, thoughts, and behavior. That seems to be a very different worldview from the Eurocentric perspective of a monotheistic Divinity, of a single God that is a noun, an authority, a thing that is a transcendent entity separate from our world. That message has great power but as Dennis pointed out, it doesn't necessarily help with giving a practical responsibility to all of creation, all of our relatives on the earth.

Dennis Martinez: It's no accident that tricksters like coyote and raven were often a tribe's original Creator because they're very sneaky and they combine both the worst and the best in human character. Unfortunately, the Babylonians also had a God that combined those two things, but who was basically ignored when the Jews, the Israelites, were in Babylon. They chose to separate that one God that had two faces—into one black God and one white God, one good and one evil—and to this day, just look at the current political situation. We have the same kind of dichotomy facing the world due to religious ideology.

Question: Are there any efforts today to get back to traditional eating, to eating traditional foods, foods that come naturally from the landscape without the need for pesticides? Simply, what's being done to bring back Indigenous traditional foods?

Enrique Salmón: You're speaking my language. This is actually key to any kind of ecological restoration because what is the bottom line for why we want to sustainably live on any landscape wherever we are in the world? We have to eat! We don't do it just because it looks good. We make these parks in the forests and we restore these rivers, the Colorado River Delta, and we work to harmonize with the land because it's all about eating. We have to get food to sustain ourselves and our communities.

A key to any kind of restoration is to think about the traditional diets of communities. Once these diets are returned to the community it means that these people are living sustainably with their environment. The diet also does something else then, it's returning a form of nutrition that is unique to the specific place. Indigenous Peoples around the world have coevolved with the plants and the animals that are in their regions.

I think about, for example, the first time I had potatoes directly from the Andes. I don't know if you guys have ever eaten traditional potatoes from the Andes. You eat a plate of these things and you want to take a long nap for about twenty hours. That's because they're so full of these glycosides and other nutrients that we're not used to eating. They have that effect on us, they literally shut down a certain degree of oxygen in our blood system, but for people who have coevolved with these potatoes, it doesn't affect them. This is key, again, to restoring Indigenous health, restoring the food ways.

A lot of us know already that here in the United States and in parts of Mexico and Canada, as well, diabetes—adult onset, Type II, diabetes— is out of control. In some communities like the Gila River Pima in Arizona, 50 percent of the adults over the age of thirty-five can assume that they're going to die from diabetes. This impact, of course, is horrendous on families and the community at large, the traditional knowledge we've been talking about.

Diabetes can be easily prevented by returning to a traditional diet. Very simple. But then, of course, we ask, Why don't people just do that? Well, it's not that easy, because there are all these other economic, social, and political factors that just don't allow this to happen. But, fortunately, in our case here today, there are some organizations working very hard to return at least some of the communities on the reservation to traditional food through traditional farming methods and by getting the youth involved in farming, and getting the food into the educational system on the reservation. For example, on the Tohono O'Odham reservation in Southern Arizona there is a group called Tohono O'Odham Community Action (TOCA) that is doing this sort of thing.

It takes these smaller efforts to eventually reach a tipping point and then it just can't be stopped; they take on a life of their own. And we have to keep supporting it. We can support it by trying to not just eat organically—eating organically isn't enough—we have to eat locally. I was talking to Melissa's class yesterday at San Francisco State and I challenged the students. I said to them, I'd like for you to center yourself in San Francisco, draw a circle that goes seventy miles in all directions, and for three months, eat food that only comes from within that circle and see what happens. If we all could do that, imagine the impact it would have on our health and on the planet.

Dennis Martinez: Frybread is great, it tastes really good but frybread is pure poison if eaten all the time. Frybread is an example of people adapting to what is available; making lemonade out of lemons because the USDA commodities have been one of the worst and most destructive things that have happened to reservations since the 1950s. At that time and in some parts even today, all that the government gave Indians to eat on reservations was white flour, white sugar, dairy products, and canned foods.

Question: When you talk about restoration and you recognize that landscapes and cultures are constantly adapting and changing over time to new things that come around, then there's no set point, or specific time, for restoration to go back to. Trying to go back to a certain time of cultural practices or a certain time of ecological functions assumes stability in the system, and is that sustainable?

Dennis Martinez: The answer is no, in my view it does not assume stability. We have relative stability. We don't want, for example, forests to grow up and get burned down every thirty years—they used to get burned down every 150 to 300 years—because we're not creating the fire that we need to relieve the fuel buildup. We only have, in a sense, a moving photograph or video, as opposed to a still photograph of the past, so we're looking at the flow or ecological trajectory and we're trying to capture it as best we can in its most salient and characteristic aspects. For example, how many trees were there per acre? What kinds of species were dominant? What was the forest structure? What were the keystone species? We're trying to get those back.

The system functions on its own once we nudge it a little bit in that direction, but we don't restore back to a set time and expect it to stay there. I don't know any restoration ecologist who believes that. It's a common environmental philosopher's critique of practitioners in restoration, but they're generally not practitioners, and that makes a huge difference.

So, it's all relative, it continues to evolve. We want the rate of change, the kind of change, and the intensity of change to be within the historical range of variability of how ecosystems have evolved and coevolved with people. When it exceeds that rate, then there's an ecological and a cultural problem. Cultures can't adapt fast enough to the changes. Forests cannot adapt fast enough to the changes either. So with people and trees, it's the same idea. We need to adapt the same slow pace of change through restoration. That's why we use a historical model as a guide, but we don't entirely stay there, because so much has changed.

To put it another way, we don't set back the ecological clock. We reset the coevolutionary clock so that it may run again at its optimum rate. That's the broad evolutionary trajectory we hope to nudge back into place. Indigenous cultures have always had to adapt to changed conditions—remember the ice ages, great floods, warming or cooling climates? As my friend Enrique noted, using a snowmobile doesn't make you less of a hunter. What we want to see happen is the restoration of the coevolutionary and coadaptive role between culture and nature at the appropriate temporal and spatial scales of the earth's own schedule.

Question: Enrique emphasized language and how we talk about landscape. Do academics or linguists who study different languages begin to talk differently about the land or nature based on their study of all the various languages?

Enrique Salmón: First, if linguists are going to pay attention to language, they need to not remove it from its context. That's usually the first thing that happens: They take the language and they treat it like it's just a store of data, of words, and some grammatical structure. Then it gets placed into some sort of interpretive model, and it's not allowed to grow or change. I think linguists need to stop doing that. It has to become an action or practice to stop taking these languages out of context. And what does that mean, then? That means finding a way to keep the language alive in the speakers themselves.

Melissa K. Nelson: There are actually many important native efforts underway to work with Indigenous languages in North America. One exciting model of Indigenous language work is coming from an organization called Advocates for Indigenous California Language Survival (AICLS). Rather than the usual anthropological model where Indian language keepers are consulted and recorded by linguists, it is the reverse situation. Grassroots Indigenous language advocates are employing and consulting with academic linguists to assist them in recovering their language under *their* terms.

There is a biannual conference, "Breath of Life: Silent No More," at UC Berkeley, organized by AICLS and hosted in part by their linguistics department, where traditional Elders and primarily California Indian language learners come together to revitalize their languages. In many cases, the Elders that come are the last speakers of their language, or their language has been "extinct" for decades. Sometimes there may be only four or five Elders in their sixties and seventies who have a fluent understanding of their language.

AICLS also sponsors what's called a Master Apprenticeship Program, which many tribes and organizations use, to partner a fluent Elder with a tribal language learner. Also at the Berkeley conference these Elders and learners work with a linguist. The linguist works for the native master and apprentice, and they go through ethnographic notes, they go through linguistic notes, and they create dictionaries and vocabularies. It's a great example of grassroots Indigenous language keepers and advocates working with linguists in a new, more balanced way. If scholars want their work to be relevant or useful to communities, then academics need checks and balances by affected communities and especially by Indigenous Knowledge keepers.

Dennis Martinez: One thing to add to Melissa's comments, and this is not usually thought about in respect to the preservation of language: We need economies in our wildlands that will keep tribal people in their local communities long enough for the kids to keep the language and keep the knowledge, and maintain the connection between the Elders and the youth. So when I work in forestry in the Pacific Northwest in Canada and the United States, I emphasize small-diameter thinning, niche markets, nontimber products—things that the tribe agrees can be commercialized, knowing there are things that can't and shouldn't be commercialized.

We explore all those areas. Thus, we need jobs in the woods, not only for Indian people to keep that connection, but also for the non-Indian, rural lifestyle, which is now disappearing as Wal-Marts come in and the tourist service industry tries to have its way. In the process of this, we're also losing the good stuff, which is the relationship that local people have with the land. We're not going to have any caregivers or caretakers of our land if we remove all the people from our wildlands. We need both Indian and non-Indian people to be responsible for areas they derive their livelihoods from. That's how the system worked in the old days, it was a secure land tenure. You took care of your turf, as an individual, as a family, as a clan, as a band, as a tribe. You took care of that. You were responsible for that. When that doesn't happen, we have what Garrett Hardin called the "tragedy of the commons," and we're heading in that direction right now. Language loss is one of its consequences.

Enrique Salmón: Dennis, you remind me of a little story. A number of years ago I had some of my students at San Juan Pueblo and we were visiting with one of my friends there. He used to be the governor of San Juan Pueblo. We were talking about the ceremonies, and one of the students had asked if the young people were dancing anymore, and he said, "Well, yeah, they're all coming back! They're all dancing! We have more dancers than we ever had at these corn dances and these butterfly dances." He seemed kind of upset or distraught by the question and so

I asked him what was wrong. He said, "They don't know why they're dancing. They're all coming back from Albuquerque and Santa Fe and Española and so on from their jobs, they leave their community and they go take up these jobs. They're not growing the food anymore out in the fields. The fields are just empty. They're not growing corn anymore and the beans and the chili and squashes and so on, and as a result, they're not speaking the language."

What he was saying was that they may know the words, but they don't know the context, the metaphors, that reveal these very deep and significant relationships with place. They don't know the stories that are associated and encoded with the metaphors in these ecological understandings. So that's what he meant, and this is what I'm saying when I bring up the concept of context, we've got to keep the living context of the language alive, not just the dictionaries and the words.

This discussion took place at the Bioneers Conference in 2005.

13

Protecting Water Quality and Religious Freedom at the Isleta Pueblo

Verna Williamson-Teller

I'm from Isleta Pueblo, which is located about thirteen miles south of Albuquerque, New Mexico. Our reservation abuts the City of Albuquerque on the south. We've been there for a very long time. I imagine there are some anthropologists that can give us dates we don't agree with, but we've been there for a very long time. Back in the 1500s we started seeing changes coming our way and those have continued in a bad way for us. The population of my community is about four thousand tribal members. We have about six to eight thousand people that live on the reservation. We have a reservation that is about 350,000 square acres and that land has a valley through which the Rio Grande runs.

The Rio Grande runs right through our reservation, right down the middle of it. The topography of our land is such that the village itself, the pueblo is right in the valley and everything else goes up. Albuquerque is upstream from us so we get everything that comes out of the city of Albuquerque, including bad air and bad water and many times, bad people. So this is what we are dealing with in our community at Isleta.

Isleta Pueblo and the Pueblo people in general are a very traditional people. I guess we consider ourselves to be some of the more traditional of the tribes in the nation. There are over five hundred tribes in the United States and there are nineteen pueblos in New Mexico, starting with Taos Pueblo at the north and ending at the southern portion of Pueblo Country land that is Isleta Pueblo. So we're the southernmost pueblo and we get it all.

Starting in the 1500s and afterward, outsiders were amazed to see there were hundreds of villages in New Mexico at that time. Today, there are only nineteen. The traditional structure of the community was very strong. Our religion had to go underground when the Europeans came because of the Catholicism that they brought. They were trying to get rid of all the "pagans and the heathens" and trying to Christianize everyone. So our religious practice went underground basically. That is probably the reason why our religion is so strong today and it is very strong. It's amazing the kinds of things that go on in our pueblo communities that our neighbors are just not aware of, very sacred and religious ceremonies that occur throughout the year.

In September we perform a month-long ceremony in Isleta Pueblo, which is a combination of the equinox ceremony that is leading us into fall and winter, and also a harvest ceremony. This particular month-long ceremony culminates with dancing that is open to the public. Most of our ceremonies are not open to the public. This ceremony also culminates with cleansing and bathing in the river and also ingesting river water at the closing ceremony. This is a little bit of background that will help you understand what's going on in Isleta with our water issues. You'll be able to see where Isleta is coming from with this issue of challenging the state of New Mexico, the city of Albuquerque, and the United States for clean water.

In 1986 I was elected governor of the Pueblo of Isleta. At that time we had two major agendas, one of them was to begin to address the governmental infrastructure of the tribe and the other one was to address health and environmental issues. Mostly because of where we're located geographically in reference to the city of Albuquerque, we began to collect data with the assistance, very limited assistance, of the Bureau of

Indian Affairs (BIA), and also from the Indian Health Service (IHS), again, very limited assistance from them. We ended up having to go out and seek experts to assist us. We had to get people to volunteer for us and do pro bono work for us to collect the kind of data that we needed to begin to build a database to use for comparison purposes as this agenda progressed.

Also adjacent to the reservation, right on our north boundary, is Sandia National Laboratories and Kirtland Air Force Base. Sandia National Laboratories has been involved over the years with different kinds of nuclear experimentation and the development of weapons using radioactive materials. Around 1989–1990, the Sandia National Laboratories approached the Albuquerque Council, requesting them to amend their wastewater quality standards to allow for more low-level radioactive waste to enter the Rio Grande. Being that we're two inches from the Albuquerque line, that water is immediately going to enter our reservation. Besides that, which we felt was a very serious situation, we're already dealing with all the wastewater that comes out of Albuquerque. The waste treatment facility plant that services all of Albuquerque is located six miles north of our reservation and dumps right into the river, which comes immediately onto the reservation. Our community is a farming community and our people have made their living for many centuries from farming, so we were looking at the effects of that water coming into the river, into our irrigation canals, into our ditches, watering our food, and eventually getting into the food chain.

We started with a major effort of community education. Though many native people are sensitive to "environmental issues" like everyone else, we tend to take our environment for granted. Our older people especially have a hard time understanding that when you turn on the tap water and it's coming out clear that it's not necessarily clean, that there might be something bad in there. So we started having a number of water fairs and trying to bring awareness up in our community because we needed that support, because we were going to be confronting the city of Albuquerque, which is a city that's not used to being confronted by a little tribe.

I think our efforts made them awaken to the fact that there was a tribe that existed right down the road from them. We have many people coming into the Albuquerque area from outside the state, a lot of easterners. I think they take the state of New Mexico for granted. That's one of the problems we're facing and we're getting the backlash from it, those of us who have been here forever. We made contact with the Albuquerque Council and invited them down to Isleta Pueblo to meet with us on a government-to-government basis. I think it was really a learning experience for them. They never had to deal with a tribe and I don't think they really recognized or understood the whole issue of tribal sovereignty and tribal jurisdiction. Therefore, I believe it was a real learning experience for all of us.

We had done a lot of work in terms of understanding and learning about environmental quality, water quality, and we got into some technical, scientific areas. We learned a lot, but we wanted to make sure we had our homework done when we sat at the table with the council members. Our plan and our goal was to establish water quality standards for the Pueblo of Isleta that would exceed, certainly not only the city's water quality standards but also the state's—and everyone else's for that matter. We were able to get that opportunity when there were some amendments made to the Clean Water Act, which gave the tribes an opportunity to address and establish water quality standards on their lands.

We pursued that process, working very closely with the Environmental Protection Agency (EPA), Region 6. They gave us some money to do some model projects and we eventually worked our way to establishing water quality standards for our community. Our water quality standards were drinking-water safe. Because of the high standard, Albuquerque's hair stood up because they thought we were out of our minds to establish a water quality standard that was so strict. It was certainly strategic on our part. Why start any lower than that? They were going to try to pound us down anyway so we figured we might as well start at the highest level that we could.

The state of New Mexico, interestingly enough, did not support the city of Albuquerque. Albuquerque ran crying to Santa Fe asking for some support from the state legislators to fight the Indians because they were getting crazy down there asking for clean water. The state refused to get involved and said, "Hey, you guys better learn how to deal with those Indians down there because they are asserting their sovereignty and they have that right. They've been granted that authority by EPA and that's your problem. You deal with them."

It was helpful to us that the state wasn't willing to deal with us at that point either so it gave us a bit more strength in dealing with the city of Albuquerque. We have a number of issues that we're dealing with besides the radioactive "low-level" issue—I'm not sure what that means. It's all the same level, as far as we're concerned. What's the difference if it has a half-life of a million years or ten thousand?

We had to get politically savvy and public-relations-wise. We were able to get support from all the local governments south of us and, as a matter of fact, many of the local governments north of us also gave us support through resolutions and letters that we used as we sat and talked with the city of Albuquerque and also with EPA. It took us eighteen months to get William Riley to come to Isleta Pueblo and visit us. We asked him to take a swim with us! He finally realized that we were right. We do need to clean up the Rio Grande. He sent a team of people in their white suits to Isleta a few weeks later and they did a bunch of soil testing and water testing. We were very happy about that, but it was interesting in that we had to go through so much trouble, and it took us so long to be able to get them down here to listen to our needs. It was really kind of disheartening that we had to go through all that trouble just to be heard.

Many tribes out there are sitting in the same situation we are in terms of their location near a city or a facility that discharges toxins into their area. They do not always have the wherewithal or the political know-how to be able to get the powers-that-be to come to their lands to look at the problem directly. So they kind of get bypassed. One of the things that we are doing in Isleta is trying to share that information with other tribes, with the hope of helping them work with EPA and the state governments to get them to pay attention to these environmental concerns that tribes have.

Probably within the last ten years or so, tribes are finally beginning to assert their sovereignty and assert that we are dealing with the states on a government-to-government basis. We do consider ourselves independent nations. If the feds owe us something, if the United States owes us something, that's their problem. We are going to hold them to their trust responsibility to tribes and to treaties they signed and it is time that tribes hold the feet of the federal government to the fire.

We were here first so we have been victimized by a lot of bad stuff that has come down politically, environmentally, socially, and in a number of different ways. The city of Albuquerque filed a lawsuit against the EPA for approving our water quality standards. There was also a mayor's race going on at that time in Albuquerque so that put everything on hold for a while. They were waiting to find out who their new mayor was and see what direction he would take in either working with or fighting with the Pueblo of Isleta on this water issue.

The mayor of Albuquerque, at that time, was never seen at Isleta Pueblo. We had invited him a number of times to our meetings and our sit-down sessions to talk about these issues and he refused to meet with us. When he filed the lawsuit against EPA on behalf of Albuquerque, he took it to the City Council because he needed their approval for funds to file those lawsuits. The City Council refused to give him any money to pursue that litigation. So we were real pleased about that and thankfully that put everything on hold for a while.

We hope that new mayors and political leaders, whoever they are, will be willing to work with the pueblo on our water quality concerns. Right now, we have radioactive isotopes going into the river. We have storm runoff, or nonpoint source pollution, which the city of Albuquerque is saying they are not responsible for. The city of Albuquerque claimed that they were only responsible for 2 percent of the pollution that goes into the river. We contend that that's a very low percentage and we assert that it's actually much higher than that. The city was basically trying to get out of the liability of having to clean it up for everybody upstream.

In February of 1993 the Pueblo of Isleta received what's called "Treatment as State Status" from the Environmental Protection Agency. That gives the Pueblo of Isleta permitting authority for anyone upstream who wishes to discharge into the Rio Grande. That puts the Pueblo of Isleta in a very powerful position. It also puts us in a position of great responsibility because we have to set up an infrastructure that can enforce the standard that we have established. One day in the Albuquerque papers they had headlines that said, "Isleta Pueblo's water quality standards are going to cost the City of Albuquerque $150 million to comply with." The next day, the same headline was used except it went up another $100 million dollars, so it was $250 million that the city was claiming it was going to cost them to clean up the water. Our reaction to that was, "Jeez, if it's going to cost that much, then it must really, really be filthy, so yeah, we need to have it done!"

The Rio Grande is the life source in New Mexico. It is the biggest waterway that runs through the state. Water is a scarce commodity in the southwest. Many people in the southwest—in the state of New Mexico—make their living from farming. Somebody's got to stand up and fight for that. Somebody's got to do it and if it means a little bitty tribe that many people have never heard of, if that's who's got to do it, then that's who's got to do it. So we've been out there fighting for support. All the tribes in New Mexico are supporting our effort. Many of the little towns and communities are supporting our effort and we're looking for a long, drawn-out battle.

The interesting part of our fight with the city of Albuquerque was that not only did we assert that it's detrimental to the health and environment of our people and our community, we also brought forth the issue of religious freedom. We have annual ceremonies at Isleta Pueblo that require immersion and ingestion of the river water. We have a number of other very sacred ceremonies that also require ingestion of that water or to immerse in it. Probably for the last ten or fifteen years our religious Elders have been very concerned that the water is too dangerous to drink.

This became even more of a reality for us when we learned what's going into that water from the labs and the hospitals and also from Sandia Labs, which is a lot of low-level radioactive waste. This makes it very unsafe to even go *into* the water, much less drink it, or eat any of the fish that are in there. It's a perspective that hasn't been brought forth before. I think that the EPA officials that were at the table with us the day that we brought this issue out were just flabbergasted. They couldn't believe it and asked, "What are you talking about, religious freedom? This is a new idea. We've never heard of it. What are you talking about?"

What we were saying is if we can't drink the water we cannot complete our ceremonies because the water is not clean. If we can't drink it because of all the toxins in it, then our religious freedom is being impinged upon. It's being infringed upon. We cannot complete our ceremonies the way we should. And that is a very serious situation for Indian people. Having been brought up as a Catholic, it is like going to church and not being able to have Holy Communion because somebody dropped the host in the toilet bowl and you can't eat it. It's something like that. I am not trying to be sacrilegious, although the Pueblo of Isleta did throw out their Catholic priest in 1965 in handcuffs. Isleta Pueblo has always been known to be a little bit on the radical side, if you will.

What happened in Isleta during that time is not unusual in terms of what other tribes think of Isleta and how far they'll go to get things done. So we're real pleased about that. We're still out looking for as much expertise and technical assistance as we can get. We do have a number of educated people in Isleta Pueblo. We are very proud to say that we have five or six tribal members who are attorneys, who have been doing a lot of pro bono work for us and we have many national organizations that have volunteered to help us out with our effort.

Many tribes throughout the country were looking at Isleta Pueblo because of this cutting-edge, precedent-setting situation. What happened at Isleta—asserting our religious freedom and water rights—has positively affected many tribes throughout the country. We have a lot of other tribes in New Mexico that are also being threatened in various ways. We have several tribes that sit right below Los Alamos Laboratories. We all know what happened at Los Alamos and what's still happening there.

They're finding more and more toxins that have leached into the water, both surface and subsurface waters, and it's really scary. All that is coming down.

We're hearing about all kinds of things going on in southern Colorado with the old mines. All that stuff is leaching and everything goes down, so Isleta Pueblo is eventually going to be getting a lot of that. We've worked with people all the way down to Mexico and we've gotten a lot of support from them and we're hoping to continue that relationship until we turn New Mexico around and work with people who are concerned about the environment. I hope that we will be able to turn it around.

The Pueblo of Isleta pushed for this significant effort that we called Native American 2000. It was a long-term approach to addressing the issue of environmental quality. We integrated an environmental program into our elementary school. We have one school on the reservation that's kindergarten through sixth grade. Thereafter our children go to public school in Albuquerque or in another little town south of us. We're hoping to build a high school on the reservation and keep our children on the reservation and begin to start teaching about the environment, planning, and teamwork. All those kinds of things that our young people need to be skilled in to continue this work for us for the next twenty-five or thirty years, which is probably how long it's going to take us to clean up the waterways in our area. We're looking at that hopefully as a viable target time frame.

We'll be working closely with tribes throughout the country. We're getting together with an organization called Windriver Associates. They're out of Wyoming. They're also doing a number of training sessions for tribes and we're working with tribes right now trying to provide them with a kind of how-to manual for how to work with EPA and the state and federal governments to address some of these environmental quality issues. It's a big task. It's been interesting for tribes to have to integrate that whole technological perspective and the jargon and everything else that goes along with being real scientific about it. Indian people have always been more spiritual about it, so we're trying to establish that balance for ourselves also, and then sharing the spiritual part with everybody else that's technical about it, if you will. We're hoping to create a balance.

The environmental issue is a very spiritual one. It takes an understanding and a recognition that water, and all natural resources, are really spirits. Indian people recognize that and so when those spirits are wounded or soiled, then it is very much a degradation of that spirit. Moreover, we are all going to pay and we are all paying for it now. Therefore, it is very important that we recognize the power of these spirits. We have no control over them. They are very powerful and if we're not really careful how we treat them, we may be seeing some very serious end to us, because the spirits can only put up with so much, and we have to be very careful to work with them. They are very real.

Native Peoples recognize this and I think after a long time of being underground, especially in the pueblos with our religion and our sacred beliefs, we are finally beginning to become a little bit more open about it and beginning to share it a little more, because we are finding that it's very important that the world recognizes the spirituality of it all.

This presentation took place at the Bioneers Conference in 1993.

14

The Art of Thriving in Place

John Mohawk

First I want to state that it is my opinion that Native American studies as a discipline anticipates that there is an intelligence in the cultures of the Indigenous Peoples of the Americas, and that it's an intelligence that can be discovered. This is completely contrary to the expectations of the nineteenth century, when it was thought that there was no real intelligence in these cultures.

I want to begin this discussion by talking about how to see this world, because people *can* get a view of it. I would recommend that when you go on your Internet and do a little browsing, you take a minute or two and type in the key words "snowball earth." Because when you do this, websites come up that have a discussion about our planet six hundred million years ago. Many scientists believe that there was a time when the whole of the planet was covered with ice, quite deep ice.

For those in the government who don't believe in global warming, the big question is, how did the earth escape this ice? The answer, they think, was that volcanoes erupted over millions of years and the volcanoes spewed forth what we now call greenhouse gases, and the greenhouse gases eventually heated up the earth, and the earth melted the ice, and we began to have the whole process kick into gear. There was a great flourishing of evolution that took place in the millions of years following the meltdown, and it took us to the place where we can almost imagine what the world might have looked like so long ago.

Then there came another moment when it is believed that a species, our species, radiated out of somewhere. Now, I'm going to leave open where it radiated from. Some people want to say it radiated from Africa. Wherever it radiated from though, it reached a point where there were so many people concentrated in some areas that it was no longer possible for hunter-gatherers to keep radiating. Something must have happened to cause this to occur, and our best bet is it was climate change; probably a more arid climate forced people to consider trying to control their own food supply.

So there was something that happened in approximately 5000 BCE that caused people to consider the possibility of domesticating plants and animals. These people were settled in a place and they could no longer migrate to another place because that other place was already occupied. Here starts the kind of story we need to think about. There is a predilection in our species, you could call it our primate instincts, that has groups of us forever aggressively looking at the possibility of expanding and taking over and plundering others. From the beginning until now the whole of civilization hasn't very successfully addressed this shortcoming.

Many people believe that civilization has been a movement from our lowest potential to our highest potential, yet it seems to me that the history of our domestication of plants and animals for food proves that that's not entirely accurate. What happened was that we chose— somebody chose—to domesticate plants, but this has problems associated with it. For one thing, you can only domesticate the plants that allow themselves to be domesticated; you can't domesticate *all* plants. When you begin this process of domestication, it means that of the one hundred or so plants that you were used to eating, only three or four subject themselves very well to domestication. So you've actually reduced your choices of what to eat, as it were.

You did it because there wasn't enough food to eat so it was kind of a desperate measure. Yet it will turn out that the plants that you have planted in your garden have their own agenda, as all plants do. Not only do Indigenous cultures have intelligence, believe me the DNA factor has intelligence too. And plants act in the plant's own best interest. They don't act in another species' best interest.

So plants around the world, generally speaking, will produce chemicals in their bodies that are intended to keep them from being eaten. Even the domesticated plants did that. So not only did we not get the best plants, we got the plants that we *could* get, but by domesticating them we were domesticating plants that sometimes had defensive mechanisms in them that made them not the perfect food for humans.

In fact, this is the specific problem with the domestication of plants: Domestic plants are not the perfect food for humans. The perfect food for humans is made up of the plants that humans evolved from. The ones that humans went out and gathered, usually the fruits and nuts and whatever it was that they found, these were the survival plants. So when we think of agriculture, we might start thinking about survival plants.

One of the legacies that we get from domesticated plants is the fact that there is some portion of our society, some number of us in almost every instance who are unable to eat whatever the domestic plant is. There are some of us who can't eat wheat. Some of us can't eat barley. Whatever it is, some of us can't eat it. Then there's the other problem that quite often we look at: The reality that almost all of the domesticated grains are poison until they're cooked. They have to be cooked before you can eat them on some level.

From the beginning we had these problems with agriculture. Yet in spite of calling them problems, ever since we radiated out from wherever it was that we started out from, we've had to adapt to new environments. The adaptation to new environments has always meant that humans had to find new plants to have a new relationships with. For the most part, humans found plants that already grew in the wild, in nature. So, for most of the existence of our species, our ancestors have been eating the plants that nature provided for them and supplementing their diet with some things that they grew. In some cases humans relied on domesticated animals and in some cases they were basically hunting some part of their diet.

For the most part, however, with the exception of the high arctic, meat played a fairly minimal role in the ultimate survival of the human species. Our species survived because we inhabited new environments and when we did, we learned about the edible plants that lived in those environments. We learned how to live with those plants and, in fact, those plants made it possible for our species to survive in almost every environment that is presently inhabited across the planet. Our cumulative knowledge of plants made this a reality. It was our cumulative knowledge and shared, passed-down knowledge that made long-term survival possible. It's what I like to call our collective human heritage, which is the knowledge of our relationship to plants.

Some of that relationship had to do with what *we* did. We call it domesticated. I don't like that word because it doesn't sound reciprocal enough to me. The healthy relationship between a human society and a plant has to be reciprocal. The plant has to benefit from it and the human has to benefit from it. Alas, I'm not clear whether some of these plants have been colonized by humans, or whether the humans have been colonized by the plants! The clearest one of all of these is corn. Corn, it turns out, is really quite a mystical plant. In some places, in some cultures, it assumes the stature of goddess, but it is one of those plants that can't survive in the wild. It has to have humans.

It has a reciprocal relationship with humans but that reciprocal relationship can be abused. We can look at the modern condition of corn plants. Corn is so powerful in our culture that if we were to take all of the corn in the whole of the United States and put it into one cornfield, that single cornfield would be the size of New York State. It would be unbelievably large, five hundred miles across and four hundred miles the other way across. From that cornfield, which we have scattered across the continent, will come all of the modern maladies. All of the things that humans have done to a plant have been done to corn—all of the poisons, all the biological modifications, all the hybridization, all of that.

What is resulting from this abuse is visible in other parts of the country. If we look into the Gulf of Mexico, where most of the watershed goes for most of the cornfields in the country, coming out of the Mississippi River into the Gulf of Mexico is a plume of dead water. That dead water comes from all of the chemicals that are put into growing corn. Yes, we're raising corn, but if you really think about it, it's not a reciprocal process. On the one side the corn benefits but on the other side the species of humans for generations to come will not benefit because what's happening is that we're eating up the biological savings bank of the planet, planting a plant for the wrong purpose. The corn doesn't actually produce food. The corn produces money. We have transformed our basic relationship from one species of corn to a corporate species.

When I was first in graduate school I had the very good timing to arrive on the scene at about the same moment that some Hopi Elders were going across the country meeting with other Indigenous Peoples, traditional societies, and talking about their prophecy.

I was very fascinated by that for a reason. When I was growing up as a Seneca—and I grew up in the traditional Seneca community—I was always struck by something about the Seneca and the Iroquois: they're what you might think of as practical. You talk to them about something and if they can't actually see it, and put their finger on it, and touch it, if you ask them to have faith in it and believe in it, they won't. The old ones didn't.

They had this idea that if it's not practical and we can't actually experience it, see it, understand it, then they kind of put it into another category. In any case, the Hopi came—and listening to the Hopi we discovered that contrary to some ways of thinking, the Hopi were also very practical. Just recently, some people have rediscovered the Native American origins of pragmatism. The book that talks about this is called *Native American Pragmatism*. Native American pragmatism is a way of thinking about the world that demands that the thinker look at the outcomes.

When you think about the great quotes from Native American people you get quotes like, "Let us look forward to what we do today and how it benefits the coming generations, seven generations in the future."

"Let's put our minds together to see what kind of life we'll give to our children," etc. This is the concept of outcome. And it's different than Kissingerian realism in that it requires that all elements of an outcome be desirable. For instance, keeping a president like Nixon in power might not have been desirable to many of us, so it's not Machiavellianist, it has a kind of requirement that you look far into the future and ask, "What are going to be the results of what it is that you are doing today?" That way of thinking used to astonish the British who came to meeting after meeting with the Iroquois and were pounded with oratory. The Iroquois kept asking the British to think, you know, think, what is this going to do in the future?

The British. Think? The future?

So I came along about the right time because I was doing a lot of public speaking then, traveling around the country, and again and again I'd end up at a place where the other speaker in the program was none other than Thomas Banyacya. (The late Thomas Banyacya, as discussed earlier in this book, was a Hopi tribal Elder active in promoting the Indigenous worldview to outside agencies.) I was also meeting with Thomas Banyacya when the Hopi came into Iroquois country. I was at those meetings and I had a pretty good idea what his message was. There were a couple of times we went somewhere to give a talk, and Thomas would come over to me and he'd say, "I'm going to have to tell this story, but I need someone to hold up the other end." He had a thing on fabric, a fabric depiction of the pictograph that he wanted to talk about to illustrate his story, so he'd come over and say, "Will you hold the other end of this?"

I have to say, he was over seventy years old and he could hold that fabric for a long time and talk for quite a while. He told a story and the Hopi Elders who came with him told a story. I've seen this story rehashed and rehashed since then, but they leave out a couple things. In Thomas's version of the story, he said that, in the past, there were previous worlds, and he says that we emerged from one of those worlds into this one, the fourth world. But in the past worlds human beings misbehaved in such a way that they offended the spirits of nature, and the spirits of nature retaliated by causing disasters. He said the offensive things that the humans did are the same things that modern American society is doing, and we need to go to the United Nations and explain to all of the world that what they're doing is the wrong thing, that society is letting greed and animosity and unclear thinking take over. In so doing they're destroying the earth, and what's going to happen is that the earth is going to strike back.

At one point, the Hopi Elders came to Onandaga country and asked the Six Nations of the Iroquois Confederacy to help them on a mission. The Six Nations had a treaty with the Hopi, still commemorated by a small feather in the old long house over there on the ceiling. The treaty was a commitment by the Iroquois, to the Hopi, which said, "Okay, we'll do our best to help you fulfill your mission." The mission of the Hopi was that they had to go to a house of mica on the edge of the waters in the East, and they had to tell the world—warn the world—that what the world was doing was going to lead to disaster.

Now, I was always kind of puzzled about this in a little way because my question, even to them then, was, okay, then what? We go there. We tell them this. They're not going to listen. What's the point? They said, "Well, we were told that's what we were supposed to do. We go tell them." Then they said something else I thought was kind of interesting: "The evidence, the proof that what we're saying is true, they have that already. It's in their libraries, it's in their science—they already know that this is true, they just haven't absorbed it yet so our job is to go there and tell them that this is the case. This is what's going to happen."

The relationship between the Hopi and Iroquois goes back at least to the 1940s. As the story goes, some of their boys worked for the carnivals and so did some of our Iroquois boys and they met that way, going place to place setting up carnivals. The word got back to the Hopi that there were Indians in the East. (The Hopi had been told that all the Indians in the East had been killed and there weren't any Indians left there.) So the Hopi slowly started this trek, initially to the Allegheny reservation in 1948 and then in 1970 a big delegation came to upstate New

York. They stopped at Allegheny again on the way. I was there for that and then we went to Onondaga. All of this, what was going on with the Indians, unfolded well out of sight of the mainstream American public. So the conversation was happening and I went around with Thomas. I thought, "Hmm, there's a lot to this, but what is their primary, fundamental message really?" Because there was a piece of it that I couldn't quite understand.

In the end, Thomas did get to address the United Nations. I wasn't there for that but others were. The day he addressed the United Nations was the day that the worst storm in New York City's history took place. As Thomas was in the United Nations building telling people that the world was going to experience a horrible backlash by nature, outside in the street the water was three feet deep: it was from the rainstorm that was blowing in off the Atlantic. The whole place was shut down. All the delegates from the UN went running home and they've never invited any Indians back to tell their story since. It turns out, though, that the Hopi prophecy is not the only Indian prophecy that talked about these things. There are others. The Iroquois have them, the Cree Indians have them, different Indians have them.

So here's what's changed in thirty years about thinking—in the last thirty years there's been a ton of revolution in thought. It's happening in a very, very small group of people but it certainly is very powerful.

Among those things that are happening is a linguistic anthropologist named Robert Bringhurst, who is also a poet, translated or retranslated a Haida myth. The book that came out of it is called *Raven Steals the Light*. Today, *Raven Steals the Light* is being touted as a kind of world literature. What it is about is how human beings come into a relationship with nature that works with people. It shares an understanding that nature can be hard on people, and they understand how it works a bit, and they don't see nature as the enemy. The ancient stories of the Indians, what some call mythologies, are a little bit like Greek mythologies in that they're really deep psychological sorts of conversations about fears, about dreams, and about how people relate to gods that are not predictable and are at some times even avaricious.

Basically you could summarize to some degree what the Greeks think by their mythologies. A lot of the stories are saying, "Well, shit happens," and sometimes it's just really bad shit. But the Greeks anthropomorphized their gods. The Greek gods sound and look like humans. Sometimes they come to earth and have sex with humans and they do all sorts of things. They have names like humans, whereas in the Native American stories, quite often the spirits that are creating the earth sometimes are not human. And they're not really even animals either; raven really isn't a raven, you understand, but he acts funny if you read the stories.

Here's an interesting thing about pre-Christian Native American thought—it did not require you to have faith. In fact, it discouraged it. You don't need to be a believer but you can be an appreciator. You can appreciate the gifts of nature, but it doesn't ask you to believe in anything, but you have to be there for it. I think that when all those people arrived in all those ecosystems we talk about now, when they came to a specific place, their problem was: How do I adapt to this place? What is this place? They came to deserts, to plains, and they looked at this place where maybe nothing was; it may have been a very barren place.

Some of them went to places that were dark half the year. Some of them went to places that were water, covered with snow and ice. Others went to places that were so dense with foliage they couldn't see five feet ahead of them. In these places, they had to come up with a culture that not only enabled them to survive in the place, they had to come up with a culture that made them *thrive* in it. They had to come up with a culture that made them *it*. They blended into that culture. They became part of that culture. That is the marvelous capacity of our species to survive. Our adaptation isn't built on our ability to build a new machine. It's not built on our ability to alter a plant.

It's built on our ability to live where people have not lived before, under conditions they have not lived under before. Look at where they live. They live on deserts on which there's practically nothing. They live in islands that sometimes offer very little in the way of sustenance. They live where nature put them and they adapt to that place. To those who think that the concept of global warming is a new concept let me turn you to the Hopi. Listen to the Hopi's story of the four worlds and think about climate change.

The Hopi come out of a cultured complex and if you go down there today—it's a nice drive down there, take a run down there and have a look. Start with the complexes in northern New Mexico and in Colorado, and then go to see all the so-called ruins. Don't stop when you get to the Mexican border. Keep going. The Indians of the Americas built civilization after civilization. They built irrigation complexes. They put together more food species, more cultivars, than all the rest of the world put together.

In so doing, for centuries and centuries they fought against climate change in place after place and in culture after culture. Dozens of them left behind a record of that. Some of them left behind some of the most sophisticated alternatives in their quest to successfully live in a new place. It is hard for us to imagine the accomplishments of a classic Maya who was living on a shelf of rock, and had no water under that, and to look at everything he did. Then time after time and place after place they lost the battle. They lost the war over climate change.

When our turn comes, when the climate change comes back, when the day after tomorrow turns into the day after the day after tomorrow, here's my question—where's our relationship to those plants? *What* are those plants? *Where* are those plants? Where is everything that we learned in the one interglacial period where things got warm and we got a chance to fix things up all over the world? All of the survival techniques we learned, about our relations to cultivars and everything, at this hour stands in peril. And our relationship to wild plants stands in peril. The big human relationship to our cultural heritage is on the verge of extinction and we need to change that. There are still enough plants left, but we don't have enough humans exploring enough relationships with enough plants to ensure that when climate change happens—not *if* it happens—but *when* it happens, that we'll have some plant foods to go on with, from there.

Humans will survive the next climate change. Trust me. Humans will survive anything. Corporations won't necessarily survive it though; Monsanto won't survive it. But right now Monsanto produces almost all of our food seed products and that's the problem. We need to move away from that.

This presentation took place at the Bioneers Conference in 2004.

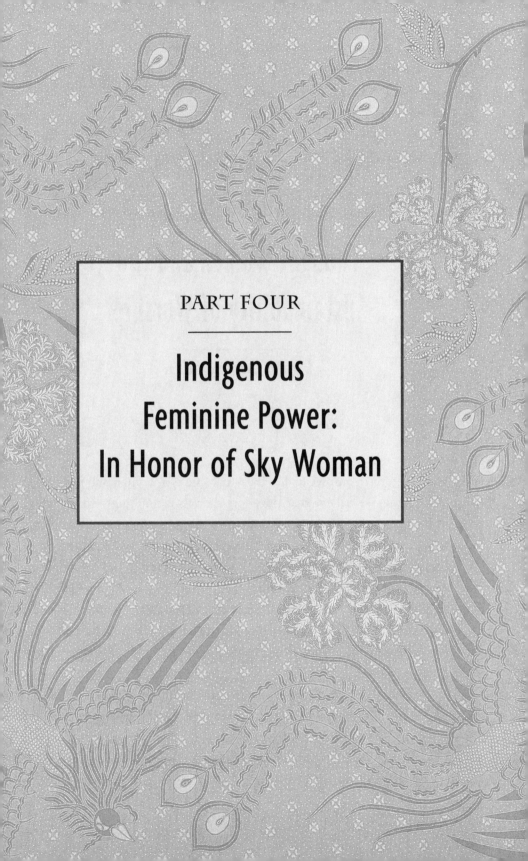

PART FOUR

Indigenous Feminine Power: In Honor of Sky Woman

15

She Is Us:
Thought Woman and the
Sustainability of Worship

Paula Gunn Allen

Where I come from, we like to think our god is a woman and her name is Thought. We believe that the entire cosmos is thinking—not the sort of blathering that we all do, subvocalization in our brains, all the blah, blah, blah—but something else, more like sorcery, like fragility, like transformation. It was Elisabet Sahtouris who said it's energy becoming energy becoming energy becoming energy. And it takes all these forms. I hope you've seen photos and films of the Mandelbrot set and the Julius set because to see that, you see her. There she is. If you look at the Mandelbrot set and you turn it right side up, it's the Great Mother. There she is.

So what do we do when we restore the planet? This is urgently important. We are not restoring the planet; she is restoring us. We've got to get over this sense of power, ego, and hierarchy so prevalent in this culture. The thing about hierarchies and heroes is that we accept it as THE main narrative to live by. But the truth is, there aren't any main narratives. We don't need to invent the story. For one thing, there's already a perfectly good story and it's very old. But I want to go beyond that and say there isn't a story. There are *jillions* of stories. There are as many stories as there are blades of grass in the lawns of the Marin Civic Center. And more. The problem is, because of patriarchy, because of monarchy, and because of monotony, we keep thinking there's only supposed to be one—the Great Mother.

What do you mean, the Great Mother? Or God the Father? We're told there's only one. No there's not. There's not only one. Look at the world. Did you ever see one blade of grass? You think you did because you've been raised to think of it that way. But you can't see one blade of grass; it isn't a possibility. You can't see one raindrop, one snowflake. You think you can. But it's a scam. You've been drugged, hypnotized into thinking there's such a thing as one.

The thing about tribal systems, about the old, old stories is that they recognize multiplicity at every single level. It's always interaction. There isn't any other way to talk about it. Which makes trying to talk about our tribal systems—not only in English, but in the Western paradigms and the contexts, like essays, or even poems—so difficult. You always have to have a subject, you have to have a verb, and you have to have an object. That's the way the language works. And you have to have a main theme. You have to have a single thread of thought. The minute I start doing that with native systems I start telling it wrong. Then I start creating misunderstanding.

When I was little my mother used to say that all life is a circle, and everything has its place within it. She used to say that in English. It already sounds weird. All life's plural, and there are lots and lots of circles, they dither about in circles, all these lives. Within all of those circular, circular, circulars, everything has an interactive capacity with everything else. As the Lakota medicine man and teacher said, "If it weren't for that beetle"—and he pointed to a beetle on the ground right at that moment—he said, "I wouldn't exist."

What did he mean? He meant that we're all here. That's how it is. When She thinks, then we be. But now I just made it sound like cause and effect, and of course if we didn't be, She wouldn't be thinking. You can't separate the subject from the object. It doesn't separate. Or as they told me in multiplication and division, it doesn't go. You can't put three into one. That's the problem with monarchy. That's the problem with monotheism. That's the problem with hierarchy. Twenty-nine billion into one doesn't go.

Of course, we need models. We need feminine models. We need these systems that I call gynocratic. And why do I call them that? Because they're based on the feminine principle. Oops, I just said "The . . . feminine . . . principle." There's only one and it's the right one and we don't want any of the wrong ones. No lesbians and no Communists in our women's group. Feminine principles mean organizing ourselves around the idea of interactive communities. Now, those communities are plant communities and critter communities and spirit communities and supernatural communities and human communities. We have to take all of them into account.

One of the problems with the Western world, in all of its aspects today, right now in white folk's time, is that we don't understand the spirits. We don't understand the supernaturals. We don't understand that right here standing with us are multiple worlds coexisting, cohabiting, and occupying the same space with us.

What the tribal people all recognize is that those communities are absolutely real and have everything to do with us. What we've done in the West is walk away from them and say, "Oh, superstition. Oh, devil. Oh, evil. We've done more interesting things." We've put military bases on sacred spots, as a friend of mine was pointing out yesterday. Another interesting thing we've done is we've found the sacred places and we've bombed them. Not in war, we call it target practice.

I'm not entirely sure what we're trying to bomb because you can't bomb the spirit. There's just no way you can do that. There's a great, great fear of that Other. Women, of course, have been identified for five hundred or five thousand years, depending on where you're counting from, with that Other. With that evil. With that which is supernatural. With the void. With what you can't control. With irrationality and hysteria, the energy of the womb. With deconstructing everything and then reconstructing it in new forms over and over again.

Women have been associated with that and then we've been demonized. Women were demonized then Native Peoples were, all over the world. Then anybody else that comes along that you might possibly be able to add to that pile of that which recognizes the imminent real existence of what some systems have referred to in English as "the Great Mystery." You can't really walk out that door, because it isn't there. You can't really sit in this room because it isn't here.

As Leslie Silko puts it in her novel *Ceremony,* she has Ohkoshta, the Laguna medicine man saying, "But grandson, you know, this earth is fragile." He doesn't mean we better take care of it because, you know, we're going to run out of resources and then what will we eat. Shame on us for thinking that way. Excuse me, but here we go again. I've got to get new things that are sustainable because otherwise I'm going to die. Well, you're going to die. As far as I know, there's no way out.

I've got to make sustainable systems because I worship Her. Now that's another thing. That's something else. Because I honor and respect Her. That's something else entirely and that's a good step; a step to go. I give back more than I take, because it's my nature to transform energy through this conglomerate of critters that I like to call my body. Energy comes through me so I can energize any place I am. That's my magic.

The reason She gives rise to this formulation is because she's reenergizing herself. She's so good at it. She knows. She's so old. Fragile. She is in that. She's continually transforming. Because She's an old medicine woman. Because She's an old sorceress. And from time to time She thinks up things. She thinks up dinosaurs and She thinks up human beings and She thinks up cockroaches. Actually, I'm not sure that She isn't a cockroach. They seem to be quite intelligent. They dreamed up all these cities because they thrive in them. They love them. Electric light is great fun for them because they can play more games because they never quite know when one's going to go on and they're going to have to go run away! They have a good time. I'm not sure that the cockroaches are not the smartest beings on the planet.

I do know that we take too much power. We in the West believe that we can do anything. We actually think that we can destroy the planet. Try it. We actually believe that we can create a planet. Try it. We can't do any of those things. We aren't that big. We're not that important. We just are here because we're here. And when my mother said all life is a circle and everything has its place within it, she meant many, many things.

I was born in 1939 and they nuked New Mexico in 1945 and so by the time she's telling me these things it's 1947. So she's saying, nuclear weapons are part of the hoop. Droughts, great, great droughts that devastated my country in New Mexico are part of the hoop. Greedy, fearful, frightened megalomaniacs are part of the hoop. How do I know that? Because we're all here, aren't we? Here we are.

What we've learned to do since the burning times, as Westerners, is choose sides and then go to war. Here we are, we're all the cool people and there they are out there eating at Denny's and they're the not-cool people. I don't know that I'm so cool. I do know that I'm here and I'm getting old and that's how it goes, that's the natural transformation. And it's a good trip quite a bit of the time.

The Great Mother is beautiful, no matter what. And she's perfectly willing to fall on my head. She's perfectly willing to erupt right now into a volcano like the movies they make in L.A. She doesn't care. She does what she does. She's not nice. She's not pretty; she's beautiful. And I'm telling you something about the feminine, what the feminine means. She is one scary bitch. She gives real meaning to the word. We run around as humans because we're weak, and that's okay. We're human. That's all right. That's how we are. We try to control her. You can't control a madwoman who's a sorceress. I can see why we try. Lord knows I try all the time. But I try to keep it in perspective. I'm trying because I feel vulnerable, not because I'm going to save the world. The world can save itself quite well. It's doing it. There are so many good people who are involved in a new form of saving the world. It's a wonderful thing. You're doing it because She told you to. She comes through your bodies and hands and minds and mouths.

Gynocracy is more about grandmothers' femininity than about mothers' femininity. Because where I come from, all over native country, there isn't the goddess, we talk about grandmother. There's not the grandmother, there's grandmother tree, and grandmother this and grandmother that. There are lots of grandmas.

The thing about grandmothers is that they've stopped menstruating. And what's happened is that the fire is inside now. But it doesn't stay inside, of course. What it does is radiate out and empower the community. All of the communities—the cockroaches, the beetles, the humans, the trees, the horses—everybody gets empowered by that.

Grandmothers are funny because they think in very connected ways. If you've reached grandmotherly age you have discovered you can't find a central thought no matter how hard you try. And you say, oh my God, I'm losing my mind. And you are, and isn't that wonderful because you're plugging into mindfulness, the great big ones, the huge systems that are always interacting and interconnecting.

So the grandmother system is the one that says okay, you've got to feed the kids, all the kids—the cockroach kids and the beetle kids and the forest kids and the Echinacea kids, and all the kids. You've got to keep everything in balance because that's your job because you're a grandma and that's what you do. I hope it makes you a wonderful life, because you're supposed to be here to have a good time. You're supposed to be here to honor the earth, to honor the feminine, to honor chaos, to honor terror, to honor fear, to honor the supernatural, which is what you are. Which is what we all are.

We go off in search of the miraculous and yet we *are* it. The very fact that this amazing conglomerate of critters is our body is a miracle. There's this whole world that lives in your eyelashes and when you wash your face you kill everybody. Did you know that? Think about it next time you wash your face. All of us are this walking planetary ecosystem. And somehow you say, I'm going to go have lunch and they all come along. That's sorcery at its finest.

We work to restore the planet, and the reason we're doing that is because the grandmothers are coming back and they're not pissed.

They're tacky old ladies and a bawdy story, let's face it. As they come back, as we come back, keep in mind that the earth herself is blooming again. The earth herself has gone into her postmenopausal self and I know this is true. She's saying, here I am. Or as my grandma used to say, "Here's me."

So what we need to do is exactly what we're all doing without the judgment part, without the critical part. Without the "Oh, I've got to be good." You don't have to be good. You just have to be. Because there's no way to stop being. You can drop dead, but it doesn't matter, you're still going to be. You can't change, fix, or solve anything. But you can live and learn and have gratitude and love. Then you're here because you're here because you're Her, because we're us. Now let's get on with being and with nurturing each other and all the children and everything around us.

This presentation took place at the Bioneers Conference in 1997.

16

Ethiopian Women: From Passive Resources to Active Citizens

Bogaletch Gebre

Although literacy allowed me to escape many of the harsher realities of my childhood and those of my sisters and my mother, one thing I did not escape is female genital excision (FGE). My parents weren't educated but they were wise and intelligent. They would never intentionally hurt their daughters. For you to understand what I'm trying to say, I would like to take you back to my home in rural Ethiopia. I need to transport you back there so you can imagine what it was like to be a twelve-year-old girl being taken out of your home like a sheep to a slaughter by your own aunts and cousins.

This was supposed to be a momentous, proud occasion in my life, but I kept crying. My mom was also crying. I heard her repeating over and over, "I wish they would do away with this. I wish they would do away with this." But we both accepted the practice because that's what we thought we should undergo to make us "whole women"—taking away the very thing that makes us feel like a woman.

Girls are often forced into marriage at an early age, sometimes by abduction. Many women, including two of my sisters, died in childbirth. Other women are destined to live in backbreaking, tedious, abusive circumstances like my mother did. I do not usually like to speak about myself, but I decided to do so today. I have never spoken frankly about my own life in public before. I was never meant to be here, never to be educated or to think for myself. Not because I'm unique, but because I am a woman: a woman from the village of Zato in remote Ethiopia.

One day when I was in graduate school here in the United States, I met a wonderful person who became my best friend. We started talking about female genital excision. She was horrified; I was outraged. How dare she question the most sacred, the most precious part of my life? The part that made me a "whole woman." Even as I defended my culture I experienced an incredible awakening, then a tidal wave of anger, as I began to comprehend all that had been taken from me in ignorance. I began to understand that the real purpose of female genital excision was to excise my mind; my ability to live my life with all my senses intact.

Tears of understanding flooded from me as I allowed the scientist in me to see, to examine in a new light, all that I remembered: the infections, the deaths of my sisters, the chronic pain, and the physical and psychological numbing left with the scars. You can't imagine how hard it is for me to speak about this in public and share it with you. I choose to speak, to do so now, because in the past five years I have been asking families and communities to speak against FGE. Just now, for the first time in our history, young girls, young men, mothers, even circumcisers—the very people who make a living out of this practice—are speaking out by the hundreds, even thousands. I must speak in front of you because today when little girls compose songs and sing against female genital mutilation, when circumcisers stand up and strike a match and burn a plastic bag (which demonstrates the scarring of the female genitalia), they are saying "See, this is what you ask us to do to your children," then I, too, must stand up in front of you and speak out so that you can understand.

All of these people in my home region who are standing up against FGE allow me to dare to think that our strategies have the potential to spread through my homeland and beyond. After my awakening, I began to dream of returning to my birthplace to start an NGO that would help women address their concerns, including the traditional practices that negatively impact us.

I dreamed of developing three comprehensive interconnected programs: health, livelihood, and environment protection—like the three-legged stool I used to sit on in the traditional, thatched-roof roundhouse I grew up in. If one of the legs breaks, you cannot sit on the stool; it cannot support you. For once I was determined that we would treat women as if they are entitled to a whole life as whole human beings, with whole families, within communities capable of producing values that nurture and support them. We would not see women as only basket weavers while men are trained in new technologies. We would not come as outsiders, like foreigners, and impose programs. We would facilitate and discuss things with them, not dictate to them.

With many small contributions and a major start-up fund by one of the funders of Bioneers and a member of our board, I went home, finally, in October of 1997 to begin working toward our vision for the future. We were able to establish our NGO on seven precious acres granted to our Kembatta Women's Self-Help Center (KMG) by the municipality of Durame township. As the first woman from my village to be educated abroad, many people expected me to establish clinics, schools, factories, but they did not expect me to do so in the name of "Woman." No. It was mind-boggling for women in my home region to see the center named for them. For the men, too, it was hard to accept. For some, it seemed like a waste of time. But we continued. And today the center is a place of hope for everybody, not just for women.

We built the first public library in the whole region (but it is still empty). We built a Women's Dialogue House, which is the heart of the Women's Center. Traditionally, Elders (always men) would convene under a large tree to dialogue, to resolve conflict, to determine how the village should live. Their sons were allowed to sit with the Elders to learn their wisdom. Women never sat with them under that big tree.

Today, we have a place for women to discuss issues that concern them, and believe me, it's not just chitchat. We started small, in just two districts so we could expand as we gained experience, and learn from it and from our mistakes. But as we looked for support, potential funders told us our vision was too big. I wanted to shout: "But look! Everything is connected! You can't address health without providing water; you can't address the need for water without protecting the environment! You can't address health without thinking of livelihood! Everything is connected. What's wrong with that? I'm giving it to you all in one package!" So we continued. We didn't despair. And this "package" is beginning to work.

The package linking economy, ecology, and social and political systems is producing results. Just recently we supported the wedding of the first girl who publicly refused to be cut. A rebel. Her husband happened to be a member of our women's advocacy and support group and facilitates discussions in his community. This couple is wonderful. They are the future. What I see in the pictures of their wedding is men and women making decisions together, as equals. People came to the celebration from all over; over twenty thousand of them. They organized theatrical performances and gave speeches and recited poems—all against female genital excision. A television crew from Addis Ababa traveled 378 kilometers to videotape this wedding, which was broadcast in four languages, nationally. Leaders who usually don't show up (particularly for women's concerns) came to watch and participate. Men realized that day how profoundly they need a revolution from the heart of women and the heart of nature.

The governor who attended the wedding heard the words of a mother who refused to have her daughter circumcised. Along with all of us, he saw this same daughter become an advocate for the Women's Center and participate in the dramatic performance by young students against FGE. As the men watched the play unfold, you could see they were bashful. We all wondered how they were going to be able to deal with this break from tradition. The bride herself was wearing a hand-lettered placard on her chest that proclaimed, "I am not circumcised. Learn from me." And this occurred in a region where a girl who is not married does not pronounce the word "circumcision." The term for the practice is "removing the dirt."

It took such courage for a young girl to make this public statement and for young men to stand up and say, "We want to marry uncut girls." What we found over and over again was that, in fact, these young people are way ahead of us. In one of our seminars at the center, a young man raised his hand and told us, "Don't worry, the days of circumcision are over. It may be around five or seven years more, but that's it. What you should worry about is how you're going to counsel those girls who have been circumcised because they will not find husbands."

At KMG, our methods to achieve our ends are not always conventional but the most important thing we can give is respect—respect and dignity to the people, to their culture, their wisdom, and their way of life. Without judging anyone we engage in dialogue and converse with communities as equals, allowing everyone to make his or her own informed decision.

You should see another young woman. Her name is Abarash. She has been called our "Rosa Parks," like the woman in the American South who sparked the Civil Rights Movement. Abarash was abducted when she was sixteen years old, an eleventh grader in school. We fought to bring her back and have the community accept her. Usually girls who are abducted and raped are considered to be "damaged goods" and shunned by their families and communities; these girls are forced to stay with their victimizers, their abductors.

A year after her abduction, Abarash stood up in front of a multitude of people and spoke publicly about her ordeal. This was a first. No girl had ever done that before. Today Abarash is a college student. She continues to speak out in schools and communities, and because of her courage, we now have ten other young girls who were abducted, but have returned to their families and are going to school. I have to tell you this didn't come easily. We must train the policemen, the judiciary, the community at large in human rights, in gender rights, in constitutional rights, you name it. Like I said, everything is a package. You cannot erase female genital excision without taking the rest of the social fabric into consideration.

I would like to tell you about our vocational training, and the business we are creating for women so that they can be more than basket-makers; so they can also be decision-makers. We are creating a system to get potable water close to their communities so their backs won't break as they walk for hours daily to distant springs to bring huge jugs of water to their families. This will give them time to go to school to learn new things, and to hear new ideas to create and earn a living, so that their work is given value, and they are valued as human beings.

Maybe you have read that Ethiopia is one of the four countries in the world that the United Nations says is at risk of an explosive growth of HIV/AIDS. In Ethiopia, the ratio of infection is seventeen women to ten men. The fastest-growing demographic is young women. With girls between the ages of fifteen and twenty-four, the infection rate is five to seven times higher than that of the boys their age.

Female excision is a silent facilitator of AIDS because scars tear during intercourse, increasing the exchange of fluids. We are sensitizing communities about HIV/AIDS—an amazing phenomenon. We are working with a United Nations Program (UNDP) on the prevention and control of HIV/AIDS. The UNDP chose KMG to advance this program because of our rootedness in the community. We started by showing videotapes of an actual female genital excision and discussing how FGE could exacerbate the spread of the pandemic. We put a generator, a TV, and a VCR on the back of our old four-wheel-drive vehicle and headed to remote areas and regions. Thousands of people came to see the video because for most of them this was the very first time they had ever seen a motion picture.

We know these screenings alone will never eradicate excision. Likewise, we can't tell women that they have the right to health without creating access to health. We cannot teach about sanitation, about the need to boil water before giving it to their babies, without giving them access to water and the means to boil it. Most women in Kembatta see a doctor only on their deathbed (and this is if they are lucky enough to see one even then). Only when things go terribly wrong—usually during labor to give birth to a healthy baby unable to break through the scarring caused by excision—do they seek help. Then, in a procession that breaks your heart, you see a bleeding woman being carried on a makeshift stretcher to a town in search of help. Many die along the way.

That's why our KMG Mother-Child Health Clinic is the most important, the most urgent, of all our projects to date. It will provide obstetrics, maternity, and pediatric services and preventive health care that is not available anywhere else. Buildings for the Woman-Child Health Clinic are going up, thanks to the European Union, which has partially funded the project. We are just about three hundred thousand dollars away from opening our doors.

Attempts have been made to stop the practice of FGE by edict, by dictate, and by persuasion. Christian missionaries told communities in Sudan and Kenya that if they didn't stop the practice, their children would not be allowed to attend school. The communities then built their own schools. Then the British colonial rulers tried making FGE illegal. People started circumcising their daughters at night, in secret, and more girls died, so the ban was revoked. Today, we are fighting new phenomenon known as the "medicalization" of female genital excision. In places where traditional circumcisers, convinced of the danger, have stopped the practice, a new practitioner has arisen: the "plastic bag doctor," as the local people call them. As the traditional practitioners turn away from FGE and join us as agents of change, medical assistants in a few medical clinics are taking advantage of the situation, making money on girls' lives. They charge five dollars per girl. But this is something we are fighting. Today the girls who have been educated in KMG centers are vigilant. They work with the police and the judiciary, and they bring the practitioners to court. Today, ten of them have been incarcerated.

There are so many amazing stories I could tell you. One of them is about our Hambericho Mountain, a beloved landmark that has become a symbol of our environmental protection program. Because our ratio of land to population is so small and crowded it is difficult to speak to communities about the need to protect the environment. But we have found a way. We reached peoples' hearts, the Elders' hearts, by calling on traditions that might otherwise be lost as we work to eliminate harmful practices like FGE.

In our KMG Center in Durame we built a traditional roundhouse with a thatched roof. This is another dying tradition. Its design is an art in itself; its internal organization is very sophisticated. This dying symbol has been reborn with the help of our Elders. When we raised the central post of this house, there was a big celebration. On the day of the postraising (called *Utubo*), we invited three hundred Elders from around the mountain to come and help us raise the Utubo, as the tradition dictates. In front of the roundhouse, with Hambericho Mountain overlooking the ceremony in the distance, we spoke to the Elders about the importance of the mountain to the community's life and imagination.

We talked about how the mountain is being deforested, how the wildlife is dying out. The Elders were moved to tears. They understood immediately. Some said, "You are bringing back to us what we have lost. Hambericho used to be our stomach, our backbone, a place where we used to worship. We used to protect it by only permitting one time during the year to hunt. What will we have left if our Hambericho dies?" Since then, Hambericho Mountain has become the symbol of our environmental movement, with the Elders spearheading our efforts to restore it and save it.

As I have said before, until we restore the health of our women, we'll never restore the health of our communities. Until we stop the maiming of women, we cannot turn the tide against the historic maiming of our culture and the modern maiming of our countryside. Until we empower women, we'll never activate the paradigm needed to heal our environment. Until we educate women, we'll never end the cycle of famine and build a sustainable economy.

I want to close these remarks by sharing something with you from that day when we raised the center post of our traditional roundhouse. We ended the celebration in the tradition of Kembatta, with a song. Sadly, many of our people's songs and dances are long gone. So that day, I created a new chorus:

"DAN-DIN-AMI METO-MAN! DAN-DIN-AMI METO-MAN! DAN-DIN-AMI METO-MAN! DAN-DIN-AMI METO-MAN! NU-GUS-ETE BE-ISSI. DAN-DIN-AMI METO-MAN!"

This is what we sang in Kembattisa, our local language: "Together, we can do it! Together, we can do it! Together, we can do it! To stop FGE! Together, we can do it!"

Thank you.

This presentation took place at the Bioneers Conference in 2002.

17

Powerful Like a River: Reweaving the Web of Our Lives in Defense of Environmental and Reproductive Justice

Katsi Cook

As a Mohawk traditional midwife and grandmother I have two agendas spinning in my life: a commitment to that area of sovereignty particular to women—control of our reproduction through advancing reproductive and environmental justice agendas—and the interpretation of the Indigenous reality to the larger world. Much of my work as a midwife and an environmental health researcher evolved organically as a result of the compelling impetus handed down to me from my parents, grandparents, and ancestors. Mohawk people are on both sides of my lineage, their traditional homelands are along the St. Lawrence River Valley on the United States–Canadian border. Here we had always lived a subsistence lifestyle that only changed in the 1950s with the post–World War II boom in industrial development.

The second largest federal industrial development program after

World War II—the Columbia River Basin Project in Washington state being the most massive—was the St. Lawrence Seaway Development Project that opened the Great Lakes ecosystem to industrial development and international trade. Robert Moses, one of the fathers of industry, has monuments dedicated to him and buildings named after him throughout the communities of the St. Lawrence Seaway, from Buffalo to Cleveland to Massena. He changed the whole nature of our environment by making cheap, easily available hydroelectric power to corporations like General Motors, Alcoa Aluminum Corporation of America, and Reynolds Metals. His legacy continues in the Power Authority of the state of New York. Their on-line company profile states: "Question authority? Well, without question, authority for power lies in the Power Authority of the state of New York (commonly referred to as NYPA)." The state-owned public power provider generates and transmits more than 20 percent of New York State's electricity through its hydroelectric and fossil-fueled generating facilities.

Growing up in my community, I'd swim in the grassy channels of the snye (chenail) portion of the great St. Lawrence River on our Mohawk reservation. I remember that at the age of five I witnessed this huge environmental change being undertaken there. The St. Lawrence River is our sacred *Kaniataraowaneneh,* the place where many waters converge. I would see these big, huge ships starting to make their way down the big shipping channels. Even the massive dredging of sediments from the river bottom to accommodate the ever-increasing size and number of international ships illustrates one environmental justice thread of concern in a weave of many. Robert Moses' engineers literally scooped up tons of contaminated material from the bottom of the St. Lawrence River and dumped it on the shores of our reservation community—called *Akwesasne,* the land where the partridge drums—so that we had these huge hills of uncovered, contaminated sediments along the shoreline in some sections. These areas were never planted with grass or trees—to bioaccumulate the heavy metals contained in these sediments—as they had been in the communities of Ogdensburg and Massena and on down into Oswego.

In my vision as a Mohawk midwife, reproductive justice and

environmental justice intersect at the nexus of woman's blood and voice; at the very centrality of woman's role in the processes and patterns of continuous creation. Of the sacred things that there are to be said about this, woman is the first environment; she is an original instruction. In pregnancy, our bodies sustain life. Our unborn see through our eyes and hear through our ears. Everything the mother feels, the baby feels, too. At the breast of women, the generations are nourished. From the bodies of women flow the relationships of those generations, both to society and to the natural world. In this way, our ancestors said, the earth is our mother. In this way, we as women are the earth.

Many Mohawk traditional cultural practices are protective of the health of women, children, and the community. I can think of no more powerful example of this than breastfeeding, the health benefits of which for the mother-infant pair are well documented elsewhere. It was in seeking to protect this valuable, sustainable cultural resource that I approached the St. Regis Mohawk Tribal Council and the Mohawk Council of Akwesasne to engage with them the democratizing constructs of participatory action research in collaboration with agencies inside and outside our community.

Our story and unique context as a designated environmental justice community coevolved with a struggle for reproductive justice. The restoration of culture-sustaining practitioners such as midwives and doulas (who provide woman-centered, continuous childbearing and childbirthing support) were always included with strategies for the restoration of the holism of our environment in the protection of women's health over the life span. We understood that many other aspects of women's health were at risk from exposure to industrial chemicals in our environment. Environmental estrogens, reproductive cancers, reproductive failure, autoimmune diseases, thyroid disease, and a host of other concerns fill our clinic charts and community meetings. The integration of multiple bases of knowledge and their translation across collaborative bridges engaged our community in the learning curve that always ensues when community members, organizations, and agencies attempt to understand each other's language, culture, and issues. This requires a willingness to see through another's eyes to overcome limited perspectives of what is possible; to hear through another's ears to develop joint strategies for action.

In some of the ecological analysis conducted by my community, of everything from plants in people's gardens to farm animals to wild animals and all the way up the food chain to the nursing infant, we began to see how heavy metals in these piles of contaminated sediments moved through the food chain into, for example, corn that was raised by a Mohawk grandfather and fed to his grandchildren. Our scientific partners at the University of Albany School of Public Health fingerprinted congeners, or specific molecular structures, of PCBs found in tissues of fish caught in Wildlife Pathologist Ward Stone's infamous Contaminant Cove, adjacent to the GM landfill. These same congeners or contaminants were also found in Mohawk mother's milk; I was one of the actual study participants. Because our nursing infants are at the top of the food chain, they inherit a body burden of industrial contaminants from our blood by way of our milk; thus are we part of the landfill, colonized.

This stark sacrilege came to my attention when a mother in my care who lived not far from the General Motors Corporation landfill asked if it was safe to breastfeed. The toxic waste site situated on the banks of the St. Lawrence River and named on the National Priorities List* of 1983 featured two PCB-filled open lagoons, which leaked into our St. Lawrence River—the lifeblood of our community—and contaminated the local food chain. Each generation of our vulnerable young inherited a body burden of local industrial contaminants from their mothers who consumed locally caught fish.

So in all of these insidious ways, we're exposed to toxic contaminants in the environment as a result of the industrialization of our world. From that moment at the age of five when I first noticed the coming changes in our land, water, and air, a number of generations would be

---

*The National Priorities List (NPL) is a roster of hazardous waste sites deemed to be eligible for long-term remedial action financed by the federal Superfund program. The Environmental Protection Agency (EPA) outlines a process whereby these hazardous waste sites are assessed for eligibility on the list.

born in our community before we understood that we needed to push for the remediation of these exposures to toxic chemicals and heavy metals that have some known and many more unknown individual and synergistic health effects.

Along those shores we've developed a lot of strength in responding to those kinds of crises, they are nothing new to us. Everything we do, everything that we are, comes to us from our environment. Our whole *Kahniakehaka,* our Mohawk way of life, has everything to do with the celebration of the cycles of life, from the time in the spring when the maple syrup runs. The maple is the leader of the trees, the chief of the Tree People. We give gratitude to the creation, to the maple for that gift, the sign that life will continue to the harvest, to the green corn, to the harvest ceremonies, the thanking of the thunders.

All of that we still continue to do, and we see the environmental justice movement as something that arose out of a world that began to pay attention to the destruction of ecological systems. From this attention to the details of how systems are affected arose the 1991 First National People of Color Environmental Leadership Summit Report to the United States Environmental Protection Agency and the Office of the President. It states: "The Environmental Justice movement is the confluence of three of America's greatest challenges: the struggle against racism and poverty; the effort to preserve and improve the environment; and the compelling need to shift social institutions from class decision and environmental depletion to social unity and global sustainability."

The environmental justice movement was a real beacon to minority and poor communities to wake up and look around and see what was being done in the name of the ideology of progress. The promise that Robert Moses made to our chiefs back in the 1950s has never been fulfilled. The subsequent centralization of schools and health care that was part and parcel of the ideology of progress that drove industrial development involved the larger process of assimilation and cultural disruption that disempowered and disinherited our children.

For this reason, there are leaders in my generation who have been dedicated to building a bridge between the powerlessness of our grandparents to empowering our children in a process of recovering our sovereignty. We have our own Akwesasne Freedom School, where our children can grow and learn within the Mohawk language where our Indigenous Knowledge is contained.

Thus, we stand in a position of strength and we have garnered more tools from the environmental justice movement. We are using the tools of science to weave our way out of this web of confusion that took five hundred years to envelop us.

I also started hearing about the PCB-contamination of Inuit mothers' milk in northern Quebec. These Inuit women were chosen by scientists at Laval University in Quebec City to be the control group for women in the south, in Montreal, who lived along the St. Lawrence River. Because they weren't exposed to St. Lawrence River fish, the scientists expected that these Inuit women who live in pristine environments—which are so remote that they are only accessible by bush plane—would be the control for women in the industrialized south. But lo and behold, because of the deposition of PCBs into James Bay and into the waters where these women consume nine meals of fish and sea mammals a month, they have the highest documented levels of PCBs on the entire planet in their breast milk.

In fact, wherever you go on this earth, you're going to find toxic contaminants in mothers' milk. But it doesn't mean that it's not safe to breast- feed. Our policy in our community is that breastfeeding is the safest route in this environment. That alone was a process of empowerment for Mohawk mothers themselves in that they were coinvestigators with research scientists who are very well-known in their fields. These scientist are the ones who read the papers at the scientific meetings across the country and internationally. We engaged their attention and their help in developing our hypothesis and using the tool that research process can be, to try to decipher a reality around the highly emotional nature of the reality of environmental contamination—not just of your environment but of your body, of the very life that you give to your suckling young.

It's highly emotional, highly depressing work and we must struggle against despair. For this reason, my work as a life-giver is always the antidote for me to maintain a sense of balance. In our creation story, it was a pregnant woman who fell from a hole in the Sky World, from another reality where the sacred Tree of Life was dying, to create the reality we're living now. As she fell through the hole in the Sky World created by the uprooting of the sacred Tree, she grasped at the edge of the hole. In so doing, seeds and bits of the sacred became embedded underneath her fingernails, as she grasped at the hole and the roots of the Tree as she tried to keep from falling. Falling to the great ocean below, she landed on the back of a great sea turtle.

With the assistance of the water animals who brought up from the bottom of the ocean a clump of soil, she planted those seeds and bits of sacred things that she brought to this world, dancing around that first garden with her left shoulder facing the fire at the center of the circle. Those things began to grow. Those things are our sacred Indian tobacco, our medicines, our corn, our beans, our squash, and those foods that come to us from the other world.

When we respond to these issues it adds strength to the generational impulse to regain who we are as Kahniakehaka people, to regain that *Kahniakehaka neha,* the way of the people of the flint, to keep that precious way of thinking, of being, of doing, of seeing, alive—not only in our own personal realities, our community realities, but in our children.

We have taken control of those institutions that have an impact on our lives and our community. My generation has worked to accomplish that. We've impacted the school systems; we've impacted the arena of health care. These are now places that integrate our Indigenous Knowledge. We're used to that now, how to do that in our community, and so when environmental justice began to be talked about, we realized we already had a model for how to integrate that into communities. In fact, environmental justice includes sustainable communities.

The grant program that funded Citizens for a Better Environment in Chicago and First Environment Communications in my community is the Environmental Justice: Partnerships for Communication of the National Institute of Environmental Health Sciences. Young leaders need to pay attention to those government agencies that have taken to heart the 1994 Executive Order 12898: Federal Actions to Address Environmental Justice in Minority Populations and Low-Income Populations of Former President Clinton's Administration. There has been a subsequent process of integrating environmental justice principles into federal agencies, from the DOE, NIH, EPA, CDC; the whole alphabet of government. The forerunner NIEHS EJ program has, as its purpose, bringing community members together with their health care providers and research scientists.

By the time that request for proposals came across my desk I realized we had already built that model. Akwesasne was one of the first of three national demonstration projects; we're in the senior class of that program. The abstract for our grant renewal reads: "This project will attempt to expand the classic risk assessment models to incorporate and integrate concepts of sociocultural risk. This work will focus on remediation, restoration and healing. Ultimately, the goal of this project is to develop a community-defined model in which health is protected at the same time that traditional cultural practices, which have long been the key to individual and community health are maintained and restored."

So what is the health reality in our community? We're finding in our research that Mohawk women around perimenopausal age have a sevenfold increase in risk for hypothyroidism. Metabolic diseases like diabetes affect everyone. We're seeing those possible endocrine effects of toxic chemicals playing in our daily lives with thyroid disease and we're following up now on a Mohawk children's wellness study where we'll be looking at Mohawk kids around puberty to do some anthropometric testing of their growth and development.

A lot of neurobehavioral tests have been done at Akwesasne. Science will often tell you things you already knew. It's only a tool. It is useful but it has its limits. As a community you can engage the research process as a process of empowerment, but we need to be very cautious in laying down the groundwork in negotiating our relationship with the scientific institutions. I was lucky to find a scientist whose family history was one of being in southern Minnesota in the late 1800s. He was from white farmers who were raided by the Lakota people and he had a memory in his family of being massacred by the Lakota and vice versa. When we got together he explained his family's history. During the course of our scientific research together he went back to his community where they had invited some chiefs from the Lakota people and they did a wiping of the tears ceremony to rebalance their relationship, after having those memories of trauma and suffering. I get amazed in this country at the negative dreams and images that people carry still; the essential fear of the Native American image.

One time, at the Open Center in New York City, a midwife told me about recurring dreams she had had since she was a little girl. She said, "I'm a little girl under wagons and there's Indians going round and round shooting arrows at us." This has been a recurring dream since her childhood. This illustrates how deeply embedded the fear of the Native, the Indigenous, what anthropologists call "the Other" is in the American psyche. So when I go around in my work, I have to remember the reality of that history and how that impacts whatever you're working on in social justice movements. We all need to seek healing.

There's a lot being written for those of you who are winding your way through the academy about the place of science, the philosophy of science, the limitations of science, and how science itself, by virtue of how it's funded, how it's supported, cannot be objective. Already, depending on the source of its funding, most science occurs in this country to serve that ideology of progress, to serve the consumer mentality.

The crisis that we see around us, spinning even now, beginning to further manifest itself in global warming issues is something that's going to wake all of us up to not just environmental justice issues but concerns that belong to every community and every individual.

QUESTION AND DISCUSSION

Question: My question to you comes from hearing Dr. Sandra Steingreber, and reading her book, *Living Downstream: An Ecologist Looks at Cancer and the Environment*. When she spoke in Santa Cruz, she was saying how it's intolerable to be regulating, monitoring, and permitting known and suspected carcinogens into the environment, that it's a form of homicide and that we need to do something about it because we know a certain number of vulnerable people will die.

I'm paraphrasing her, of course. She said we need a movement along the lines of the civil rights, suffragettes, and the abolition movements. The abolitionists didn't say, just ban slavery over there in that little area. It has to go across the board; we see our struggles all over. I'm with Pesticide Watch, Farm Without Harm, Toxics Action Coalition in our area. How can we forge a huge movement to stop this? Not to study it anymore, not to be put through the mazes of the EPA, which I call the Environmental Pollution Agency by the way, or the DPR, Department of Pesticide Representation. They've abdicated their responsibility to protect public health.

I'd like us to be working on a massive, stop the toxins, stop the corporate poisoning of the earth campaign. I wondered if you had comments on this?

Katsi Cook: The question is, how do we change the world? Sometimes it's good to look at how the world got to be where it is right now. For the part of the world where I come from it began in World War II and it began with the Christ-bearing colonizer, which is the translation of the name Christopher Columbus. I'm not here to insult or hurt the feelings of any Christians, but the reality is that when Christopher Columbus came there were debates in Spain about whether we were human beings because we didn't have souls. The only way to have a soul was to be baptized. As a recovered Roman Catholic and born-again pagan I see the roots of the mental issues, the thought process of my own people coming out of oppression, based on the capacity to believe in who you are and who you came on to this earth to be. I can only handle those issues that you had asked about in your eloquent question on a one-to-one, individual, interpersonal basis with the mothers and families that I serve.

Every time that I'm able to support a Kahniakehaka woman in giving birth, to come to her own blood and voice in the creation of her reality, is the only way that I can, in that macrolevel, solve that problem, because of the feeling we have as individuals that we can only do so much. It's about transformation and restoration. We want to know in our community how we get back to where we were, where we are, where we need to be. It's not a matter of romanticism or living in the past. It's a matter of making an environment where we can recover from the history that we've endured and now need to be able to think clearly about how to solve. You have to engage the same process in your own lives, in your own families, and in your own communities. Essentially to me this is a culture based on fear, and until you can cope with getting people to a place where they can think clearly, nothing will change. Everybody's afraid. That's what it's about.

Question: I just wanted to briefly mention that I believe that the environmental and ecological crisis is, at its roots, a crisis of culture. And by that, I'm talking about the dominant society culture that goes back to Cristobal Colon and even much earlier than that, specific to documents issued by the Vatican in the mid-fifteenth century, which said to capture, vanquish, and subdue all Saracens, pagans, and other enemies of Christ, to put them into perpetual slavery and take away all their possessions and their property.

That was followed by another document called the Inter Caetera Bull of 1493, which called for the subjugation of all barbarous nations to propagate the Christian empire. And so they've been bringing their empires across the whole western hemisphere and building them throughout the world. And that word "science" appears in the Papal Bull of 1493, it's referred to as the *cienca* of the papacy, or of the pope, the infallible knowledge of the pope, of the same institution that issued these documents of conquest. Then those end up being the entire basis for the Western so-called civilization that they have erected.

So the end result is a whole system of domination embodied in the federal Indian law system, and embodied in the whole mechanistic conception of reality and all the practice that follows from that.

It occurred to me the other day that people talk a lot and justifiably so about the saving of the old growth forests. It just seemed to me like it would be an excellent idea to talk about saving the old growth cultures, which are the Indigenous Peoples' cultures that have embodied wisdom and understanding over thousands upon thousands of years, and which provide alternative models to empire and domination.

Katsi Cook: I think that's a very important statement that he made. But the bottom line is that from the perspective of Indigenous Peoples the purpose to save us is because we're the ones who know how to relate to the earth, to the ecosystems, because cultural and biological diversity go hand in hand. It's impossible to unwind a thousand years of that mono-culture, that monopolistic kind of thinking. At work here is the very mind-body-spirit continuum that has been oppressed in so many ways, in each and every one of us.

I think the bottom line is that we need to support Indigenous cultures all over the planet and I'm not just talking about Mohawk people. That's why, in a community like mine, even though we struggle every day like you do to put food on the table and to get our kids health care, at the same time, we contribute our energies to keeping alive that vision of our primeval mother, Sky Woman. That's our duty on this earth. So I'm grateful to come from a generation that picked that duty up and didn't let it go.

Chief Oren Lyons, who is one of the carriers of our prophetic tra-ditions around the world, is a great leader and I like what he said to Greenpeace. Greenpeace staff always tends to be college-age kids and they wanted to know what to do, because they have a "Chicken Little attitude" of the sky is falling! The reality is that there is only so much that we can do, but part of what we're supposed to do is to maintain that cultural integrity—generation to generation—of our Indigenous values and ways of life. In our pitifully short time here on this earth, we are to maintain those cycles of continuous creation. Life exists on a continuum; it is all about the continuity. I think the key message is respect for life.

Question: I want to tell you an environmental justice story with a twist. I live here in Marin County, which is very beautiful and one of the most affluent counties in the country. We have the highest rate of breast cancer in the world. We were told that we do because we are rich, white, and educated. So I started an organization called Marin Breast Cancer Watch. Our purpose was to find out why we have the highest rate. I've always believed that it was the environment. You can't see it here, but something is really, really wrong.

We are finally getting people to cooperate with us. In the beginning nobody would cooperate. They said, "It's impossible. Look at how beautiful this place is." So, it's important that we can all work together, because it's in the communities of color, it's in the communities of poor and rich and we're all color. We all have something of color, so we need to work together if we're going to survive. I just wanted to say that environmental justice issues hit all of us.

Katsi Cook: The issue of toxic contamination isn't about pretty or not pretty either. One of the first things I learned working in this was trying to get scientists to move. I started looking at the research of a wildlife pathologist who found dead owls along the St. Lawrence River and when he tested their tissues, he found horrendous amounts of PCBs in their livers and brains. To our people, the owl is a messenger of death.

This pathologist showed slides of the Hudson River Valley—beautiful orchards, lovely golf courses—and it turns out, he says, these are all toxic hot spots. So it's easy to be seduced by the cultural thing that everything is supposed to be manicured and pretty and green and nice-looking, red apples. It's a seductive thing, but you're right. It's everywhere. Contaminants move through the air, without a passport. Look at the Inuit women who have no benefits from the industrialization of the south, but reap all its risks.

I'm lucky enough right now to have the opportunity and the ability to just pick up and go wherever I want to. I've been thinking about going to a reservation and saying, "Hi, can I help?" Do you think that would be welcome? Do you think it would be helpful?

Katsi Cook: I am a field coordinator and board member of Running Strong for American Indian Youth, one of many trustworthy community- and culture-based American Indian organizations that exist. Respectful support of them is needed and can be very welcome. Get on the Internet and connect to us or one of the many other organizations that need your support on many levels.

This presentation took place at the Bioneers Conference in 2002.

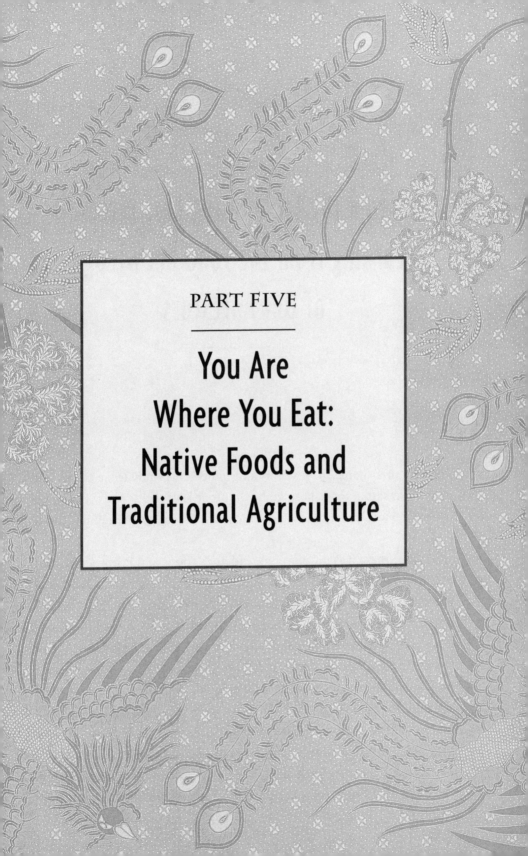

PART FIVE

You Are
Where You Eat:
Native Foods and
Traditional Agriculture

18

From the First to the Last Bite: Learning from the Food Knowledge of Our Ancestors

John Mohawk

The idea of Original Instructions and Indigenous Knowledge comes out of a conversation that's been going on for at least thirty years. I'm going to amalgamate history so you get a picture of what we're talking about now.

Before there was a Columbus, Indian Nations and Peoples occupied areas specific to themselves, something we might describe as a cultural eco region, and inside that, they had lots of things that they encountered: plants and animals and micro environments all over the continents, different landscapes, different seasons—a mind-boggling array of things. Even in a given small area, one group sharing the same language and having the same technologies would live in an area for a very long time. In that area they had to make choices about how they were going to expend their energies, how they were going to survive in the area they lived in. There were hundreds of cultures in hundreds of these little bioregions, cultural bioregions, and they all did things differently. But they all shared one thing in common: They stayed in the same place with the same animals and the same plants for sometimes hundreds of generations.

They lived in these conditions before anybody thought of having a money economy. That meant that their behaviors were predicated on concerns other than money. So what were these other concerns? First off, I'd like to propose that many Indian Nations lived in areas where they had to make many choices about various things. These were two essential areas that are also on people's minds today: they had to make a lot of choices about what plants and/or animals they were going to use for medicines and what plants and animals they were going to use and possibly cultivate for food.

To my knowledge, no one ever found a plant that had a medicinal use that the Indigenous Peoples who lived there (and lived with that plant) didn't know about. Anywhere. No one ever found one. When they found something, they usually had to ask the locals, What's this good for? The locals, if they felt like it, would tell them, Well, you know, that'll cure poison ivy or whatever, it is a medicine.

What did that mean in terms of their process of deduction, of discovering that some rare plant was good for a particular use in medicine? The only thing that we can be sure of is that they spent a lot of time experimenting on that. You could assume some of them spent thousands of years experimenting on it. If you have enough trials, once in a while you'll have a success, right? If you're good enough at memorizing the success, you have many choices to make. In medicine, the choices are daunting. What plant do you use? What *part* of a plant do you use? When do you *harvest* the plant? *How* do you use it; do you swallow it? Do you rub it on? What do you *do* with it? Maybe you just dance around it, who knows?

With any given illness, there would probably be thousands of plants, tens of thousands of *parts* of plants and numerous ways to treat with them—from a poultice to an elixir to consumption of that plant. Therefore, a lot of decisions had to be made. Somehow they whittled those down and by the time most of us heard about them, they said, here's how you use this plant for this purpose, which I say is a version of

Indigenous Knowledge. They did all that experimental work for us, and we inherited the end result of that experimentation, that native science. And that is Indigenous Knowledge.

What I find most interesting is Indigenous Knowledge about food. I'm going to look at a couple of specific examples, but please don't forget that there are thousands of Indians living in thousands of environments. These are the principles—the specifics are very diverse and very interesting.

Where I come from, people were very vigorous horticulturalists. They raised at least twenty different varieties of corn and probably more varieties of beans. They had squash, gourds, and melons of many different kinds. So at the time of the alleged contact, they raised a fair garden of plant foods.

They had more choices than we have now. Today you go to the grocery store and you're looking for corn. How many different kinds of corn can you have? One or two, right? You can have white sweet corn or yellow sweet corn, and the only other kind of corn you can get is chicken corn. Most of you probably wouldn't eat chicken corn. There's also popcorn. But that's pretty narrow compared to what an Iroquois gardener would have had to worry about because not only were there twenty varieties of corn, but there were different ways of eating corn.

Sometimes you picked the corn when it was green, sometimes you picked the corn when it was baby corn, sometimes you picked the corn late. Then you dried the corn and processed it. You had to hull some of it; you had to roast some of it. In my tribal tradition there are a lot more varieties of corn and many more ways to process and cook corn than you have today; certainly there are more varieties than the two you find in the grocery store and more ways to eat it than just boiling it. I'd make a bet that just with our white corn alone, there are probably twenty-five or more different ways to eat it. So my point again is that the tribes had a lot of choices to make.

Now with regard to beans, there was a whole array of beans. Today, how many kinds of beans can you get when you go to the store? In California you can get more beans than just about anywhere, and yet I don't think you can get ten in California. We're talking heritage beans here. But, generally speaking, if you're in the rest of the country, you'll get your choice, you can have pinto beans or you can have kidney beans, they'd have whites, but only about seven or eight beans.

Apart from beans, what about greens? A few years ago, you were limited to about three or four, but now I see someplace you can get seven or eight different greens. But just think about the Indians. The greens were just about anything growing in the woods that you could eat and keep down that wasn't too hard to chew. You threw them in a pot, boiled them, ate them, and many of these greens had not only nutritional value but medicinal properties.

So when you think about how many different foods the Indians ate, I want you to know that they ate a daunting variety of vegetables and grains. Compared to the modern diet it is amazing to think of the variety of foods that they consumed. But what I was told in school was that modern American agriculture brought us more choices than we had ever had in the history of mankind. That was a huge lie.

The reality is that the pre-1491 Indians were living in a world in which two things were the case. Number one is that nobody was whispering in their ear telling them what to do, and number two was they lived communally. In a society where the accumulation of knowledge is one of the reasons why Elders are revered, it was a good idea for a person who passed forty to start paying attention to things. If you're going to be revered as you're getting older, you should know something that's valuable to the survival of the people. So people, as they got older, actually became more and more responsible for being the repository of knowledge of the group.

One of the things about Indigenous languages is that they have a way of preserving knowledge in the language. The language would tell you things that you might want to know, or you might need to know to survive. The knowledge in the language was often responsible for life and death. Sometimes tribal communities were in groups of forty or fifty people, sometimes they were in groups of four hundred, sometimes in groups of two or three thousand, but the group was responsible for life and death. From the moment you were born, they were responsible for you. Not your mother, but the whole group. From the moment you're born, they're all paying attention; it's usually women who are paying attention to you when you're very small. As you get older, especially if you're a male, then the males take over at some point.

So everything that ever happens to you is watched. When you're small, if you don't thrive, they notice. If they feed you something and you don't thrive, they notice. If they feed you something else and you do thrive, they notice. Every single possibility that they have at their fingertips can be tried; they are motivated to watch and see which foods help people the most. Not which foods help people make money, which foods have the best biological impact, especially on young people, and old people.

Here's a society that would rightfully consider the idea that food is a medicine although to me this is obvious. I've been in a hospital and they'll kill you from the kitchen. They clearly don't believe that food is a medicine. Whatever medicine they're giving to you the food will counteract whatever good the medicine is doing. But this healthcare system is not about healing, it's about making money.

This 1491 society was motivated to find a diet that was the best diet. As a group they only had so many resources that they could expand on to produce their ideal diet. They could only produce so much of some thing, so they had to pick which corn they were going to produce, which beans they were going to grow. Essentially they had to be very strategic about how they were going to spend their time and energy getting food. It had to be proportionate to how they saw benefits coming from the food. And the only benefit they were interested in was the health of the people. The only one. Health of the little people, middle-size people, old people, but always they're thinking about the health.

So here's a diet that's based on the premise that food is medicine, that it starts on your first bite and ends with your last bite, literally, and that the society learns where it should spend its energy producing which foods. When the society was responsible for its own health, you had to say that they were very careful what it was they gave you.

I think this is why the food value in Indigenous, heritage foods is far greater than the food value in commercial food. The food value in commercial food is weighed in dollars, and the food value in heritage foods is weighed in something we might call life force. Somehow it was built around life. Subsequently, you could live on and thrive on heritage foods by actually eating quite a bit less vegetable matter than you would need to eat of commercial foods to get the same nutrition and life force.

I want to share one story that was striking to me years ago back during the 1960s, when people were trying to get back to the land. *Mother Earth News* ran an article about how Iroquois Indians lived pretty much on corn and beans and squash. So, at the time, I had written some articles and was corresponding with people. A couple of people wrote to me and they said the following thing. They said, We tried living on corn. We planted corn and all we ate was corn and beans and we almost got sick doing that.

So I wrote back to them, What kind of corn and beans? Well, they were planting essentially the kind of corn and beans you could order at that time out of the seed catalogs. But the corn that you can thrive on is the high-lysine corn and the beans have to be dense. It is the combination of dense beans and high-lysine corn hulled by lye that produces all the amino acids you need to make protein. This has a remarkable quality: it can be turned into something that a baby can swallow. It will keep a baby alive when the mother's milk goes dry. Try to find that with any other vegetable-based foods. With Iroquois Indians when a mother's milk went dry, they fed the baby a derivative of corn; it's the stuff the corn bread is boiled in.

It's not that different from what will happen with animals. One time a horse got loose at this farm and he wandered off and passed by a quarter mile of yellow corn to come over and eat white corn. The horse was a gourmet. He didn't eat just any corn, he wanted the best corn. Horses and cows can tell what's good for them. So can we if we listen to our bodies and our instincts.

But people can't follow those instincts anymore, at least individual people can't. But there was a time when tribes could, when a group living in a place for a long period of time treated food like medicine and acquired a certain amount of knowledge about this. After looking at the examples cited above, we ask ourselves again, what is Indigenous wisdom and knowledge? Indigenous wisdom and knowledge is that wisdom and knowledge that our peoples had when they were in charge of their own survival, and that they retained generation through generation.

I want to point to two pieces of work that you can look at that I find very compelling about this food story. The first is Weston Price's book on nutrition and degenerative diseases.[1] He was a doctor (dentist) who wrote in the 1930s. He noticed that when he was with primitive people, he was quite amazed that they all had pretty good teeth. He would have thought that primitive people, not having dentists, wouldn't have good teeth. It turned out it was the wealthy people who had dentists who had bad teeth and the primitive people had good teeth.

Then he went off to discover that primitive people who ate their own foods didn't have the degenerative diseases that were common to people in the cities of North America—they didn't have high blood pressure, they didn't have diabetes, they didn't get circulatory ailments, they did not die of coronary heart disease. So he wrote this up in a now classic book. If you're interested in this topic, you've got to read this book.

Price was such a quaint character. He traveled the world and he found one group of Indigenous Peoples after another, and investigated their health. He's bothering them, he takes pictures of them, he makes them show their teeth, and then he asks them questions about how they live. He finds out that their cousins who move into the city get all these bad diseases and he was the first to document that. He goes to one place after the other, from Alaska to New Zealand to Africa to all over the world. He dragged his wife all over the world to go look and see if all the Indigenous Peoples had good teeth, and he found out they did. It's a wonderful book. But, part of the reason it's so wonderful is because he doesn't have any agenda except to answer his question. He's not working for Monsanto. He's not working for any of the big drug companies. He's just trying to find out why people have good teeth and good health. How refreshing.

The next one is a new book that's just out. It's called *The China Study*; it's a 2005 book.[2] *The China Study* is a study of eighty-six counties in Northern China done over a period of twenty years. It's the largest study of the relationship between nutrition and health ever done. It was done with the cooperation of the Chinese government. There's one county at least in China where there's no recorded incident of death from coronary heart failure. No one ever died of a heart attack in this county in China. They've got records that go back forever. Nobody ever died of that.

In the other counties it's quite rare anybody dies of that. Very rare that anybody dies of cancer. Very rare that anybody dies of any circulatory disease or diabetes-related ailments. He calls the diseases that kill people in the developed world the diseases of affluence because the people who live in China have very little money to buy meat. If you've ever been to real Asia, you'll notice that their restaurants are not like Asian restaurants in America. You order a dish in America, say you have Chinese food. What is it? It's a big pile of chicken. Or it's a big pile of beef. When you go to China and order food, it's a big pile of vegetables. You've got to dig around looking for the meat. It's like there's just the one pig for one thousand meals in China.

The point being that in China they ate a lot less meat, and there is practically no processed food there; they grow most of their food themselves. So in China, you ask yourself, what's killing them? In China people die from diseases that are associated with pathogens—bugs. Here, we kill ourselves with our patterns of eating and stress.

If people have a long period of time to pay close attention to nature and they don't have any hierarchical authority figure telling them what to do, they will make choices in their diet that are based on the outcome of their choices. Did the people thrive or did they not thrive? Which of these foods did they thrive on best, and how can we take advantage of knowing this?

We get back to North America and I especially like the agricultural area of North America because I know it the best. You can look at the North American diets and you can see a real strong parallel between them and the Chinese diet; it's all rough food. If you eat real corn, beans, and squash, that is a pretty dense, heavy meal. It's not salad. You don't need a lot to keep yourself going on that.

If you study Iroquois history or the Algonquin peoples around them, they have a word in the language that means "a generation." It says that in three generations, such and such would happen. So I once asked a whole group of elder Elders, eighty-five years and older: How many years would people live? The Seneca version of that was a life span of about a hundred years.

When I first heard that, I thought that was kind of a long life span, but I also spent a lot of my time studying history. Throughout history, a lot of people lived to be a hundred years. A hundred years wasn't uncommon at all. Not only that, they were pretty vigorous in their nineties. I always liked the story about this one chief, his name was Corn Planter. He lived on the Corn Planter reservation, and he made a famous speech. Everybody looks at the speech, which he opens by talking about the Indian wars that went on in the West. He says, It's getting harder for me to get to these meetings. He says, I'm not sure I'm going to keep coming anymore.

According to my calculations he was ninety-seven or ninety-eight. He had walked from the Corn Planter reservation to Buffalo Creek, about 110 miles. No bridges. When you get to the stream, you have to swim across the stream and the next place. He didn't have a horse, according to the record. He walked. Now, a ninety-seven-year-old guy who can walk that far, we ought to be listening to what else he does.

When we talk about Indigenous Knowledge and Original Instructions, for it to mean something, we have to look at what were the behaviors that people adopted and what were the benefits of those behaviors and what can we learn from studying how they lived and what they did. In our times, with very high rates of diabetes and diseases, we're probably very motivated to embrace that kind of knowledge.

During the period of forced assimilation, Indians were strongly urged to believe that their people had no knowledge, that they couldn't think clearly, that they were savages, and so on. My experience is that the reverse is true. Today they have no knowledge and they've embraced a system of faith: faith that the grocery store food is good food, faith that the doctor says he knows what to do for you. You have a faith, but you're not encouraged to do what you need to do to avoid getting sick, and you're not encouraged to do what you need to do to stay healthy. Prevention and maintenance are not there once you're in the acculturated world.

But now we're at a time when all of us can rethink this because there's a general movement toward the idea that food is medicine. That's what the Slow Food Movement is about. A really wide community of people agrees with that. Today we can say things like: we should look at eating differently and maybe eating foods that we don't find in a grocery store; maybe we have to grow some of our own foods. Today you don't get quite the derisive looks you used to get. So, I think that's what Indigenous Knowledge means in action.

Because I spend so much time wandering around with traditional tribal peoples, there's quite a lot of that accessible to us in all these different cultures. People left stories and they left records about how they did things, what they did, what they ate, how they prepared their food, where they got their food from, and so on. They talk about how they used medicine. It's available to us, it's not lost. It's just not being used.

This presentation took place at the Bioneers Conference in 2006.

19

Re-Indigenizing Our Bodies and Minds through Native Foods

Melissa K. Nelson

There's no time like today to decolonize and re-indigenize our bodies, minds, and communities by taking back our food soveirignty. Our very survival, individually and collectively, may depend on us taking back control over the quality and production of the food we put into our bodies. "We are what we eat" the old saying goes. But we are also *where* we eat. The plants and animals that we consume become our bodies. Our food literally becomes our flesh and our flesh gives shape to our minds and spirits. After we die, our flesh then becomes the earth, the "environment," which grows food, and the whole cycle flows all over again. This is a primal and sacred cycle of birth, growth, death, and regeneration that most of us now take completely for granted. This "nutrient cycling" as western scientists call it, is the basis of our production, reproduction, and regeneration. It is one of the most basic things that we, as individuals, can control.

And yet the corporate control of our food systems is leading us down a dangerous path, one where known carcinogens and other toxic chemicals are sprayed on our foods. Additionally, we are faced with the unknown consequences of having genetically modified organisms

(GMOs) enter our bodies and possibly mutate in our DNA. Even the water that grows our food increasingly comes from dubious sources. This "Franken-food" scenario could not be further from the philosophies and practices of native food traditions.

Native food traditions honor the sanctity of food as the Creator made them and as our ancestors nurtured them. Salmon is the perfect food for many Northwest Coastal Indian Nations; buffalo is an ideal food for the northern Plains Indian Nations; corn is integral to the food and cultures of Southwest Indian Nations; acorns and abalone are the sacred staples for California Indian Coastal Nations. This list could be endless, with other examples of diverse native foods, totem foods, that have been cared for and eaten by native nations of North America and the world.

These native food traditions honor food with prayer and story, with song and dance. Eating is an intimate act that can literally nourish us, sicken us, or even kill us. We have to take responsibility for our food systems, otherwise we will end up where we are going. Will it be Fast Food nation or Slow Food nation? Will it be comprised of corporate processed food or local, native, heirloom food? The decision is up to our minds, hands, mouths, and wallets.

The earth gives us food in seed and fruit, in vegetable and in flesh, in sweetness and nectar, in salt and sour. All of our tastes, all of our smells, all of our senses are involved in this essential and blessed act of eating food. We can't get away from it. It makes us who we are, and yet we often neglect the fact that it's something we do at least three or four times a day. Native and traditional cultures have known since time immemorial that if you have healthy food, you have healthy bodies, minds, and communities. Conversely, if you pollute your land and water, you infect your food; you contaminate your bodies and negatively impact your communities. The future of our individual and collective health and vitality depends on us reclaiming and creating healthy food traditions.

But who currently owns and controls our food systems? Nestle doesn't own our water. Costco doesn't own our food. Safeway doesn't control our nutrition. We own our food, and yet we've lost control of our foods because most of us don't grow or raise or gather anymore. We let other people do that. Farmers and fisherman, ranchers and gatherers, these are the real stewards of our foods and yet through marketing, distribution, food policies, and other economic and political demands, even these food caretakers are struggling to maintain control of their food production systems. To be economically competitive, farmers put pesticides, herbicides, fungicides, and chemical fertilizers on hybrid monocrops that are only touched by machines, not human hands.

Once the food is grown and harvested it is then shipped off for processing and all kinds of additives are put in to make it last longer during the transportation process and to give it a longer shelf life. Sadly, as many have said, our dominant food system grows food for money not nutrition. Appearance and transportability have become more important than food safety. The food industry has even been experimenting with putting waste products and nanotechnology in our food. This is outrageous! Somehow, most Americans have been duped into believing that Big Macs can replace a home cooked meal of local organic foods. There's been some strange, collective forgetting of the primary source of our life and vitality.

This historical shift of going from slow food to fast food in the last fifty years has deep roots in colonial and economic processes of power and politics. As the U.S. government has slowly but consistently tried to erode Native American sovereignty, corporate powers have slowly and systematically taken away the food sovereignty of *all* Americans. For example, today it is difficult to find water that is not owned and privatized by Coca Cola, Pepsi-Co, or other corporations, who often put "additives" in the water. It's critical that we change this corporate process and decolonize our food systems through policy changes, purchasing decisions, buying at farmer's markets and Community Supported Agriculture (CSAs), and creative, nonviolent civil disobedience, protest, and activism. We can again take responsibility for knowing *where* our food comes from and at what environmental, health, and energy cost it was produced, from the carbon footprint to human impact. This knowledge is power and helps us make the right decisions about what food systems to support and what to put into our bodies. To be healthy and support the health of the planet we need to be self-determining about our own nutritional sovereignty and understand and support local and global food justice.[1]

Most cultures and ethnic groups in the United States—whether they're African American, Chicano, Hispanic, Latino, Native American, Asian American, Pacific Islander, or European—are identified with particular food traditions. Our ethnic foods help form our ethnic identities, for better or worse. For example, many Indigenous Peoples today identify with Spam, commodity foods, fry bread, and other harmful foods because these were survival foods after the devastating impacts of conquest; some would say they were also part of the conquest.

Globally, humanity often recognizes cultural diversity through food diversity. Thai food is not French food, Pueblo food is not Japanese food, Samoan food is not Ethiopian food. These place-based regional food systems are part of the beauty of cultural diversity and ethnic plurality. As the adage goes, "diversity is the spice of life" and nowhere is that more true than with the abundance and range of diverse ethnic foods and regional cuisines based on unique plants, animals, herbs, recipes, and tastes. But many of these revered food traditions have become lost, endangered, forgotten, or are no longer in use. The Fast Food Nation mentality of America is globalizing and spreading across the Four Directions of the planet. The consequences are a significant decline in human and environmental health, cultural and biological diversity, and a significant loss of a sense of place and being a part of a distinct cultural heritage. The Fast Food Nation epidemic is creating a global monoculture of low-quality consumers who have lost touch with their unique food practices. This is essentially creating a global health crisis where we have a billion people starving and a billion people obese. From a native perspective, this imbalance is creating a worldwide psycho-spiritual meltdown.

In response to these various threats to our foods, health, and the very sanctity of life, there is a growing movement—many movements actually. There is the Slow Food movement, the general organic/permaculture movement, and an Indigenous foods movement, among others. These movements are involved in both restoring and renewing food traditions from the past and creating new food traditions for the future. In the growing native foods movement Iroquois farmers are revitalizing their heirloom white corn varieties on Indian reservations while urban native youth are creating community gardens containing Incan Quinoa, Pueblo beans, and Russian kale.

As mixed-raced, urban communities, we have to create new traditions as well as keep alive and maintain traditions of health from our heritage food systems. As global citizens, we have to systematically resist dangerous experiments on our foods, our environments, our lives, our minds, and our bodies, and collaborate and create new polices, land-use plans, and food practices to address these twenty-first century health challenges. We must collectively assert our rights as human beings to live and thrive with clean water and healthy food.

Through the work of the Cultural Conservancy, a twenty-two-year-old Indigenous rights nonprofit organization based in San Francisco, California, we are involved in a whole basket of native foods and health projects designed to address these urgent issues. As has been well documented, Native Americans disproportionately suffer from major health problems. Diabetes is an epidemic for Native Americans throughout the United States and Canada, with as many as 50 percent of reservation-based adult Indian populations having "the sugar."* Cancer, obesity, and heart and kidney disease are also on the rise.

In addition to these physical illnesses and challenges, Native American also disproportionately suffer from mental health problems such as depression, substance abuse, posttraumatic stress disorder, suicide, and violence. Native American psychologist Joseph Gone and Teresa O'Nell have done research that indicates that as much as 50 percent of the adult population of many Indian reservations consider themselves depressed.[2]

---

*The Tohono O'Odham Community Action organization works to address the fact that over 50 percent of the adults on their Tohono O'Odham Indian Reservation in Arizona are afflicted with diabetes (www.tocaonline.org/Programs/Food%20System/foodsystem .htm).

Why are so many Native Americans affected by diabetes and depression? What are the root causes of these Native American health disparities and what can be done to change them today?

The Cultural Conservancy started our Indigenous Health Project in 2002 in collaboration with Native American psychologist Leslie Gray of the Woodfish Institute. We organized two health conferences to address the root causes of our health disparities and to study, consider, and create proactive, holistic solutions. We wanted to better understand and make connections between physical and mental health and educate ourselves about old and new theories and practices of mind/body medicine.

The first conference addressed mental health within American Indian communities, starting with ourselves. We convened a small, intertribal group of Native American professionals including doctors, psychologists, traditional healers, therapists, midwives, health educators, and community activists. We spent five days together at Esalen Institute in California where we engaged in daily dialogues, presentations, hands-on exercises, and retreat time in their famous mineral springs to nourish our spirits and deepen our understanding of traditional concepts of health and healing. We also spent a significant amount of time examining contemporary health disparities in Indian communities and explored and discussed various solutions including alternative and complementary medicine.

A lot of our time was spent discussing the impacts of historical traumas and the subtleties of the process of internalized oppression. Significant insights were made about how we all participate in this process every day simply by living within a society constructed and dominated by a Eurocentric ideology where hierarchy, competition, individualism, materialism, sexism, and a punitive system of education and justice are prioritized. This time was an opportunity to "heal the healers" by providing a rare, safe, beautiful retreat environment where we could focus on self-care, intimate dialogue, and collective thinking about these critical health concerns. By the end of the retreat we created a vision statement for our collective work: "Recognizing the seriously unbalanced state of

Indigenous health, we resolve to promote and disseminate a reintegrated vision and holistic practice of Native health and healing for the twenty-first century."

The second conference was a native foods think tank called "Decolonizing our Bodies, Nourishing Our Spirits." This phrase has become a central theme and focus of my work as a scholar and activist and for the health programs of the Cultural Conservancy. In partnership with the Woodfish Institute and the Occidental Arts and Ecology Center we created a five-day native foods think tank to examine the need to revitalize our Indigenous food traditions. We reviewed and discussed tribal food renewal efforts such as the work of the Taos Food Center in New Mexico, the Wild Rice Campaign of the White Earth Land Recovery Project, The Tohono O'Odham Community Action programs, the Iroquois White Corn Project, and other national-model native food programs.

We cooked together and were honored to have award-winning chefs Lois Ellen Frank (Kiowa) and Walter Whitewater (Navajo) with us to create an extraordinary Southwest meal of stuffed squash blossoms, corn, chile, beans, and buffalo. We honored the Southwest Indian Nations as master traditional farmers, food producers, and chefs and learned about many exciting projects from the Southwest. But being in northern California, we also honored the amazing food traditions of the local Coast Miwok and Pomo Nations. With Julia Parker, the remarkable and lovely Coast Miwok/Kashaya Pomo Elder and knowledge keeper extraordinaire, we processed black oak (*Quercus Kellogii*) and tan oak (*Lithocarpus densiflora*) acorns in the traditional ways.

Sadly, the local tan oak trees are being terribly affected by a disease called sudden oak death. Tanoak acorns were and are the prized acorn of the local Pomo, Coast Miwok, and Ohlone peoples because of the size, quality, and sweetness of the nut. Tragically, sudden oak death is destroying these trees at a rapid rate. If we care about California Indian food traditions, we must educate ourselves about these diseases and factors that are directly impacting our native food sources.

Even with these challenges, Julia Parker still collects, processes, leaches, and cooks acorns using a variety of traditional California Indian methods. She carefully instructed us in how to shell, peel, winnow, grind, and prepare the acorn meal for leaching out the tannic acids (all acorns have to be leeched for their tannic acids). We then made a sand bed for the leaching process. After the leaching was completed, Julia and her daughter, Lucy Parker, showed us how to cook the acorn meal using traditional baskets and hot rocks. After an afternoon process of collective learning and building community, we enjoyed the nutty, delicious, and nutritious acorn soup. Native foods prepared in these traditional manners taste different—something about their quality and flavor go right to your soul and nourish you on a deeper level.

On the following day we had another incredible Native California Indian feast from the northern tribes, the Hupa, Yurok, and Karuk Nations. Clarence Hostler and his wife, Deb Bruce, brought delicious, plank-smoked Coho salmon, seaweed, berry soup, and acorn bread. Together, we then fire roasted California bay nuts. These bay nuts, also known as pepper nuts, come from the California Laurel tree, also called Myrtle Wood. It's a member of the Lauraceae family, the same family as the avocado tree. If you look at bay nuts, they look like little avocados. You might wonder if they're edible. They are and they are delicious. You don't eat the flesh, you eat the big nut inside. You roast them. They are nutty, sweet, and chocolaty. They were a major food staple of the local coastal California Indian people. We also had Yerba Buena tea, and a berry soup mix—huckleberries, thimbleberries, salmon berries, and blackberries—for dessert. It was a delectable menu of fine California Indian cuisine.

Through hands-on work in the kitchen, in gardens, and with traditional wild food processing, this gathering inspired all of us to again reclaim our food traditions by growing and cooking with local and native ingredients. Through dialogue and presentations, we reviewed national models of native food revitalization and saw what worked and what didn't work as well. We also examined gaps in our understanding and identified areas for research, collaboration, and implementation.

It became clear that a national native foods directory would be extremely useful because even when many native people *want* to use native ingredients, they have a difficult time accessing them. So we need a central clearinghouse for where and how to obtain native foods.

Over the past three years TCC has been working with a very exciting project called Renewing America's Food Traditions (RAFT). The RAFT project is an offshoot project of Slow Food USA. One of our project goals is to restore the link between our sense of place and our sense of taste. This is a collaborative effort of the RAFT consortium, made up of seven organizations; with over more than forty-five thousand members we are still growing. We represent very diverse nonprofit organizations around the country. They are: The Center for Sustainable Environments at Northern Arizona University, whose director, the famed ethnobotanist Gary Nabhan, has been the main intellectual architect and visionary of this project; Native Seeds/SEARCH in Tucson, Arizona; Slow Food USA in New York; Seed Savers Exchange in Decorah, Iowa; Chef's Collaborative in Boston, Massachusetts; American Livestock Breeds Conservancy in Pittsboro, North Carolina; and the Cultural Conservancy from San Francisco, California.

All of our diverse organizations are working to protect heirloom seeds, conserve native ecosystems, protect endangered breeds of livestock and poultry, promote sustainable and healthy cuisine and local markets, and renew Native American foods, recipes, and practices. Together we are committed to maintaining and renewing the ecological, gastronomic, cultural, and health and nutritional benefits of native biodiversity.

RAFT is the first collaborative effort organized to accomplish four main goals. First, we are inventorying America's Indigenous edible plants and animals; this alone is a monumental project. Tomatoes, sunflowers, many beans, squash, corn, chilies—all are Indigenous foods of North America. These are some of the Indigenous foods that are in the global market, but there are hundreds, if not thousands, of other native food varieties that have fallen out of use, have become endangered, and have even become extinct. So we are actively trying to revitalize rare, heirloom varieties. The project documents the foods that have fallen into disuse and are at risk of extinction. We then determine which are capable of being restored, and we begin projects in partnership with food producers, landowners, harvesters, retailers, consumers, and chefs.

People involved in conservation biology or in the environmental movement know that when a species becomes endangered, it gets listed on the Endangered Species List. You research it. You document it. You give it special status. The first thing you do is identify what factors are causing its endangered status and what things we can do to stop those factors and create and facilitate better health for the species. A recovery plan is then created to look at ways to restore this endangered species. This is often done through an ecosystem management approach for restoration. RAFT is doing a similar thing with endangered foods of America.

As many as four thousand food varieties and species are unique to this continent. One-third of them are ecologically or culturally at risk for extinction and/or cultural or culinary abandonment, meaning they may still be growing somewhere, but the knowledge about how to gather them, process them, cook them, that knowledge has become endangered as well. This is an ongoing theme of the work of the RAFT, Cultural Conservancy, Bioneers, and others, that biological diversity and cultural diversity go hand in hand. When one becomes endangered the other becomes endangered; when one is renewed, the other is renewed. When one flourishes, so does the other.

We think that one of the most exciting ways to save our food is by eating it. We feel you need to eat your heritage. Heritage should not be clamped up or put behind glass in a museum. Heritage is a dynamic, living, changing thing. It's something that we need to eat, we need to nourish ourselves with—we need to consume, digest, and assimilate. We need to celebrate our authentic foods, and everyone can join in conserving the diversity of America's foods.

As many native communities and traditional cultures say, "If you don't use it, you lose it." That's very different from the classic preservation movement, which says, if you want to save something, lock it up, *don't* use it. Indigenous and other traditional cultures know that if you want something to continue, to be sustainable, and be a vibrant, living entity, you have to have an active reciprocal relationship with it. The exploitation and commodification that has been happening with most of our native lands and waters, our food and natural resources are a type of resource mining that is antithetical to the Original Instructions of respectful use. And yet, we cannot jump to the other extreme and lock things up in preserves, museums, seed banks, and the like without having a cultural context to sustain these resources.

RAFT wants to redefine the word *consumer* to not just mean a blind purchaser in the market-driven, capitalistic economy or an exploiter of resources but, in the ecological sense, recognizing the fact that all humans have to eat to live and all living beings have to consume food as part of the ecological web of life. We want to transform consumers into coproducers of healthy, local foods. And in fact, consumers today are already becoming coproducers of these rare, heritage foods. Sixty-five percent of those surveyed are willing to pay more for place-based heritage foods.

The Bioneers community and many others are clear that they want healthier, better foods, and they're willing to pay more for them. Of course, there's still class and race and other equity issues we need to address so these foods don't just become elite foods only for the wealthy. That's why we need to develop partnerships with philanthropists and producers and cottage industries, so that these foods are made as available as possible, especially to the communities who have suffered from imposed colonial, economic, and health inequities (unfortunately this is most of the planet).

One of the exciting things the RAFT project produced was a RAFT regional map of North America's place-based food traditions. This was a bold remapping of North America by identifying different foods as totem foods from the different regions. For example, here in northern California we are on the edge of Salmon Nation to the north and what we are calling Abalone or Acorn Nation to the south. I'm surprised to find that many people still don't know what an abalone is. It's a mollusk, a gastropod, and a fabulous food. It's a delicacy. Some Japanese and high-end restaurants serve abalone. It's about seventy to eighty dollars a plate. It sells for as much as one hundred dollars per pound, depending on certain times of year, and yet it was the staple food for the coastal California Indians. And some still dare to call their diets "primitive."

This remapping exercise is a thought experiment and is not a definitive renaming. It is meant to engender thinking and conversation about the native, regional foods we identify with. RAFT does not presume to speak for others from different regions, especially native peoples who have thousand-year-old food traditions from their different ecoregions and homelands. This map is an invitation to dialogue about the concepts of totem foods and foodsheds. It is a dynamic, changing process.

For example, at first RAFT named the Southeast area "Gator Nation," but really gators were eaten more in the Florida area. The people of Louisiana and Mississippi identify as "Gumbo Nation," so the next iteration of the map identifies the southeast area as Gumbo Nation. Also, as special and sacred as the abalone is to the California Indian Peoples and other Pacific Peoples, it was not as widely used in California as the acorn, so that was changed. Mexico should really be included as Corn Nation because it is the birthplace of that sacred food.

The new map also includes our Hawaiian brothers and sisters and identifies Hawaii as Taro Nation. This is an ongoing, dynamic, regional map that reminds us of the fact that we all come from food nations, we all come from watersheds, and we all come from foodsheds. If we start rethinking how we interact with our food and see it as an extension of our local ecoregion, we can renew our sense of place with our sense of taste.

RAFT is a versatile multiyear, multidimensional, multiorganization project. We are learning, and growing, and changing. We welcome all people to join us as members, allies, and supporters. We also welcome constructive feedback and healthy challenges. There's room for everyone in this project. It's a big RAFT.

The Cultural Conservancy's particular role in RAFT is documenting, through audio recording, oral histories of Native American culture-bearers from different food traditions. We are then creating educational materials through print and on-line profiles of "stories from the field," highlighting native food revitalization successes, challenges, and models. Our goal and role is recording and documenting these traditions, not as museum specimens but as elements of living, dynamic cultures and regional cuisines. We've conducted interviews of traditional culture bearers from the Southwest, from the Northwest, from California, Hawaii, Vermont, and Louisiana, and we plan to conduct additional interviews from people of other food nations across the country.

If you're a native farmer, food producer, chef, or are involved with collecting pine nuts or other traditional foods and herbs from your foodshed and you want to be involved with this work, please contact us. We are documenting these stories of native resilience and food recovery so they can be used to educate and inspire others.

The information will be shared through media such as print, audio, and an interactive website that will also include a national native foods directory.

TCC also helped Native Seeds/SEARCH and Slow Food USA in coordinating a Native Foods Celebration and Retreat in the spring of 2007 at the Institute of American Indian Arts (IAIA) in Santa Fe. It was a national summit of native food producers, chefs, and land stewards. For example, with my tribe, the Anishinaabe or Ojibwe, wild rice is a very important sacred food that needs to be protected and used in a good, sustainable way. Winona LaDuke has been working hard on protecting this sacred staple food and her chapter outlines the history, value, and threats to this important Ojibwe food source.

One of the reasons why native foods have fallen out of use is because we don't know where to find them. Who's gathering them? Who's producing them? Who's growing and harvesting buffalo in a healthy, traditional, sustainable way? How can we get healthy, native foods in our refrigerators, in our kitchens, in our diets, and in our bodies? A RAFT "Where to Purchase Traditional Foods of the Indigenous Peoples of North America" online and print directory has been produced to answer these questions.[3] The oral histories, coordinating the Native Foods Celebration and Retreat, and helping with the Directory are the three main ways that TCC has participated in the RAFT project.

Ultimately, we want everyone to know what foodshed and watershed we live in because that knowledge reconnects us to our local biodiversity, to the local foods and land stewards of our home regions. It also helps us understand what local foods were historically used by the native people and begs the questions, are the local Indians still using them? Why or why not? Do they need support in locating, acquiring, growing, and harvesting whatever the local native foods are? Why are they not being used? Are they being impacted by development, by disease, water pollution, or other factors? Asking and addressing these questions helps us get involved with bringing these local, native foods back into people's diets, which can help increase human and environmental health.

Thanks to Slow Food USA and the Christensen Fund, a group of approximately fifty Indigenous delegates went to Terra Madre, the world food festival in Torino, Italy, in the fall of 2006. Some delegates, like Coast Miwok/Jenner Pomo food advocate Jacquelyn Ross, presented food work there and illustrated efforts to keep Indigenous foods alive and thriving. A number of people brought their traditional foods to share with the world food community and many of us rotated in and out of volunteering at the White Earth Land Recovery booth where we educated people about wild rice, distributed information, and sold wild rice packets.

In 2006, out of all of these rich experiences, TCC developed our Renewing American Indian Nutrition, Food, and Ecological Diversity (RAIN FED) project to develop urban and rural Indian gardens and health curriculum in northern California. We have started with a fruitful partnership with the Friendship House of American Indians, Inc., Women's Lodge in Oakland, California. The Friendship House is a community-based nonprofit organization that provides residential substance abuse treatment for Native Americans. The Friendship House provides "unique, holistic treatment, recovery, and prevention programs culturally-relevant to American Indians in San Francisco since 1963."[4]

Under the leadership of TCC staff Laura Baldez, Bernadette

Zambrano, and Nicola Wagenberg, TCC has created a beautiful native foods garden filled with corn, beans, squash, sunflower, and other national Native American foods, as well as local, native California plants. The residents at the Women's Lodge have been participating in planting, tending, watering, harvesting, and cooking the garden plants. Gardening and cooking workshops have been given by traditional farmer Ed Mendoza and Kiowa chef Lois Ellen Frank. Other educational programs on nutrition, food harvesting, and cooking are being planned.

CONCLUSION

Due to the massive harmful impacts of European conquest and colonization of the Americas, Native Peoples have suffered from a terrible holocaust. This has affected every aspect of our lives and it is being felt today in the high rates of health problems in Indian country, especially the alarming prevalence of diabetes and depression. But these illnesses do not affect just Native Americans; *many* Americans of many different ethnic groups are feeling the negative consequences of the loss of heritage foods and traditional ways of health and healing.

As Native Americans remember and honor the Original Instructions that food is medicine and water is life, we are engaging in an exciting, collaborative movement—the native foods movement—to educate ourselves and each other about the need for healing and returning to the foods and medicines that sustained our people for thousands of years. Indigenous Peoples of the world are asserting their food sovereignty and this is happening on many levels, from personal food choices to political policy changes. We also realize that because of all of the cultural changes of the past five hundred years, we also need to recognize tools and medicines of Western ways and find complementary ways to utilize traditional knowledge and Western science and medicine. In partnership with the Slow Food movement and others, we are changing the way we think of, grow, eat, and celebrate food.

The Cultural Conservancy, as one of many nonprofit organizations committed to revitalizing Indigenous health and foods, has created a number of events, tools, projects, and resources to help us all decolonize our bodies and nourish our spirits. By caring for the health of each other and the beauty and bounty of the earth, we are honoring the vitality of the gift of life and helping to ensure our regeneration for the future.

This presentation took place at the Bioneers Conference in 2006.

20

Dancing for the Apus: Andean Food and Farming

Julio Valladolid Rivera

I'm going to relate to you the way in which the traditional Andean farmers grow their plants, raise their animals, grow the earth, and interact with the weather and the whole landscape. Traditional Andean agriculture is very old. Cultivation has been going on for at least ten thousand years. This agriculture is ritual, meaning a nurturing, deeply respectful way of growing. For us, everything is living. I want to share how things are in current Peruvian agriculture.

I live in an area called Ayacucho, and when the peasants there are about to go out and plant their fields they ask permission from the protecting hills, which they call *Apus* (sacred and protective hills). One of the most important Apus I work with is called *Razuwillka,* "holy snow." When the peasants of Ayacucho go to far-flung areas looking for work, for example when they go down to sea level, down to the coast, or to a dry forest, they always ask permission from *Razuwillka.*

I'm going to share with you how a peasant community called Qasanqay carries out its cultivation. There is a regional apu, *Suytu Orqo,* attendent to this community. All the farmers in this area in the month of August bring offerings to this hill. In this community, corn is grown near a river, and in this area tubers, like potatoes (*Solanum spp.*), oca (*Oxalis tuberosa*), olluco (*Ullucus tuberosus*), and mashua (*Tropaeolum tuberosum*) are planted. In the higher areas there are natural pastures for grazing animals. I'm telling you about altitudes that range from thirty-one hundred to forty-two hundred meters above sea level. At lower elevations, corn is planted, also the tubers, and uphill there are the natural grasses.

One hundred and seventy families live in this community. Each family has on an average between seven and twelve parcels of land. These small parcels are no bigger than fifteen thousand square meters. So they have three small corn parcels, four on average of potatoes and other tubers, and also other parcels with other crops.

The climate in the Andes is quite varied. There are two clearly defined seasons of the year. There is the cold dry season. It doesn't rain. The peasants call this season *Usiay uku*. The other season is the warm rainy season called *Puquy uku*. This is when the crops grow. In the community of Qasanqay one of the problems is the presence of the frosts that damage the crops. The farmers have found ways of avoiding the frosts. In the lowlands are the cornfields, but these cornfields are mixed with varieties of quinoa. During harvest season we see a variety of different kinds of corn. There are many different varieties—dark, orange, reddish. Each one of these varieties has a different use. There are corn varieties for direct eating, some for making corn beer (*chicha*), some for *mazamorras* (dessert). Others are for healing purposes.

In addition to the corn, squash is harvested out of the same field and there is quite a variety of squashes. The quinoas are also fully grown. I appreciate all of the varieties of quinoa (*Chenopodium quinoa*). Together with the corn, achita (*Amaranthus caudatus*) is grown, which is a kind of amaranth. Here also there are a number of varieties. These cultivated fields of corn are cared for, principally, by the traditional authorities from the community. These young farmers are authorities that continually go through the fields to make sure the cattle do not damage the field. They are called *Varas*, rods, which are symbols of their authority.

In growing the corn it is necessary to converse with the wild plants.

One plant we use is a cactus called *Sancay* (*Trichocerus peruvianus*). When it does not flower, that means the rainfall will be low. On the other hand, when it does flower, it tells us that there will be abundant rain. Taking into account these signals, the farmer knows which variety of corn to plant. But they always plant different varieties. Even if a rainy year is predicted by the flowers of the *Sancay* plant, farmers will throw in some seeds of drought-resistant strains. They will be in a smaller proportion, but they'll still be there.

The people of the Andes know that even the weather is living and has a personality. It's a very capricious animal. It can change at any moment. For this reason the farmer uses a mixture of varieties. As agronomists, we always tell the farmer to plant one kind of plant. If it's a good year, everything will be fine and if it's a bad year it's not going to be worth anything anyway. On the other hand, the farmer with his mixture of plants, whether it's a good year or if it's a rainy or if it's a dry year, he is still going to have some harvest, even if it's a small one.

The farmer is always respectful of nature. There is a ritual for planting corn. The farmers prepare a table where the offerings for the *Pachamama* (Mother Earth) are laid out. There are flowers, seeds, fruits, which will be respectfully and carefully buried in the ground. The community does all of the work together. This community effort is called *Ayni*. All of the fields are cultivated communally. The Ayni is performed joyfully. It is a party.

Also in this area *chaquitaqlla* are still used. They are small handheld hoes or plows. They are used to open up new ground. Often little boys, five or six years old, help to turn the earth. So they begin to work with their fathers and brothers at a very early age. But they take it like a game.

Higher up where the potato fields are found there are other crops like barley, which is an introduced crop. In the potato fields, varieties are planted together. During the flowering, it is possible to see different colors of flowers. That's telling us that it is a mixture. If we see these different kinds and colors of flowers, it means there are different varieties. In the harvest, we find different kinds of potatoes. Some varieties are resistant to excess rain. Others are drought-resistant. As I've said before, there is always a mixture planted.

Other tubers, such as oca, are also planted. It is similar to the potato, but with a sweet flavor. It is very popular in all the families. Here again, there is a variety of ocas—black, red, pink, yellow, white. So there's a great diversity, a great diversity because the Andean climate is so variable.

Also, with the planting of the potato, the wild plants are talked to. Through the flowering of the spiny bush *Taqsana* we are told whether it's going to be a wet or a dry year in the potato-growing area. This is seen through a greater or lesser amount of flowering. The stars are also consulted. We especially consult with the Pleiades, which in Quechua is called *Suchu*. At four in the morning around June 24, near the June solstice, the farmers observe when the constellation comes up in the sky. If it is very bright it is going to be a wet year. If the stars are opaque, it will be a dry year.

But it is a more subtle conversation than that. The curious farmers, those who know how to converse well with the stars, can differentiate the shine of the stars high in the sky, in the middle ranks, or closer to the horizon. When the high stars shine more you have to advance the sowing. If the low stars shine more, the sowing should be delayed. If the middle stars are the brightest, the planting is done at the accustomed time.

The farmer plants everything. He is not a specialist in anything. In the same family there are different kinds of corn, potatoes, oca, olluco, and mashua. In addition, there are different kinds of quinoa. The farmer plants principally to eat. In the highest area are the natural grasses, also containing a mixture of varieties. Here we also find llamas. Now, sheep and cows are also raised, but so are llamas. This allows the farmers to take their produce to different communities for trade. They can trade corn for llama meat. These llamas have different colored ear tags. They also have some small bells. With these bells they call the spirits of foods. When they are carrying corn from one community to another, they not only bring the corn but they also bring the corn spirit, because the spirit is what nourishes. There are also rituals for the raising of livestock. For the farmers, the llamas are on loan from the Apus.

As mentioned earlier, often a table is prepared for the Apus by placing different seeds and plants on it. Some of these cultivars are very old. They can be found on ceramics from sixteen hundred years ago. We use quinoa, olluco, mashua, and corn. Sometimes this symbolic ritual, including a cultivation of the soil, is carried out on platforms. This happens in the Colca Valley in Arequipa. (There are other ways of cultivating, for example, terracing is used in Cuzco, where the soil is used all the way from the river on up to the top of the hills.)

I was born in the Mantaro Valley. Many potatoes are grown there. While the plants are in flower the farmers adorn themselves with the flowers. Then after work the farmers rest. They are decorated with flowers and their faces are ritually painted. All of the work is done to music. When the work is over they dance around the fields, ending in a party. Andean farming is always done in conversation with the wild plants, which tell them how to have a better harvest.

A special flower for us is *cantuta* (*Cantua buxifolia*), the holy flower of the Incas. When you see this flower, it is a strong sign. Everything is always asking permission from the Apus. In this case, the apu is *Ausangati,* which is the most important apu near Cuzco. Near the June solstice forty to fifty thousand farmers gather ritually for a whole week and go up to the mountain. We don't go up the mountain to pray—we Andeans don't pray. We dance for the Apus.

This presentation took place at the Bioneers Conference in 1997.

21

On the Importance of Our Connection to Food

Jacquelyn Ross

My professional life involves creating access and communication between the Native American world and formal higher education. It is challenging, delicate work that often involves an unveiling of inequities and loss. This can be uncomfortable for all parties involved, especially when individuals face the past that their ancestors lived.

When I first started working in this field almost two decades ago, the fibers that connect traditional and contemporary education for Native Peoples soon became evident to me. Had I seen a way to live the dynamic, physical life that my great-grandpeople lived—fishing, hunting, growing, and gathering their own food—I would have chosen the same. Yet, on the cusp of the changing century, this was not an option. Indeed, our landscape is now intensely peopled and much diminished, overaltered to a degree that astonishes. It took a deliberate pause for me to understand what I was looking at, and it was in this suspended space that I realized that at least two different roads, traditional science and Western science, would have to meet to mitigate the damage.

In my personal, community life, I am an ocean-food gatherer. This is something that I was reared to do, supported by a cadre of skilled elder relatives and my parents. My family devoted considerable time to ensuring that their children knew how to do things. Our instructions included learning the basics: how to descend a cliff safely while packing fishing gear; how to walk a rocky shore and navigate the slippery intertidal zone; how to see with one's hands underwater; how to take life with care. Delivered with patience and laughter, these lessons have been a source of strength for me throughout my life. The sense memories that accompany these lessons anchor them to particular places. The connection with a specific ecosystem and the knowledge that I can provide for myself and my family is important to me.

What was at one time a commonplace seasonal food cycle for us is now something tremendously precious. My family still enjoys mussels every fall, fresh sea greens every winter, abalone every spring. The abalone, big marine snails, are sparse among the rocks now. When I was a small child they were so plentiful that they would cling atop each other under the rocks for lack of space. Out of the eight species of *Haliotis* once plentiful along the California coast, only the red abalone, *Haliotis rufescens,* survives at a level where the regulatory agency, California Department of Fish and Game, still allows human harvest of them, and then only along the northern stretch of the state.

When I'm in the water, feeling for legal abalone (seven inches from tip to tip) I am also counting the coming generation, the smaller shells. I think of all the tribal peoples along the coast who no longer have access to the abalone, one of the animals that has been on the earth for a very long time. What traditions wane when a species is lost? What words go away? What are the spiritual repercussions when someone who looms large in your earliest histories leaves your world? It seems that every day, somewhere, our relatives leave us. Human folk are treating the planet as if a better one is coming on the market soon. Some species know their place and their cycles by specific features in both land and water. These roadmaps are often altered by the folly of humans so invested in thinking big that they forget to think small.

We must remember how to think small. Food growing, gathering, and harvesting entail a level of detailed observation. Since so many of my family lessons center around food gathering, I worry when people of any culture lose touch with their foods. People responsible for food take stock of the little things. They notice the pebble in the hoof of a draft horse. Their eyes are drawn to the new plant that shoots up, seemingly out of nowhere. They know that the rock removed from the tidepool's rim causes a complete shift in that shimmering circle. The small things anchor the web of life.

When we move away from our foods, for whatever reason, we get into trouble. Reflecting on what we have available in our diets today, and how different that was from the times of our grandparents and our great-grandparents, shows us how much less healthy we are now, given the foods that are part of our daily diets. Without a conscious effort to discover the foods that are really healthy for all of us, it's easy to get sucked into a deep-fried and breaded kind of world.

The cheap cost of bad food makes it more difficult to get the foods that are truly healthful for us. We grow numb to the lives behind the food, the means of production, the cost of distribution, the cost to the land. This is one area where having a Western education can be truly helpful. One gains a new vocabulary and access to other resources that can help to comprehend the horrors borne by the land and sea in the interest of commercial food production. One gains allies in scientific communities who understand the big picture and can see the effects on their specialty species, as well as on humans. They can help frame the problems, not only in terms of science, but within the frames of health, politics, and justice.

For it is unjust for people not to be able to have their native foods. It creates stealthy, insidious genocides. The physical activity often associated with food procurement ceases. Processed foods are often ill-attuned to tribal bodies. You see the resulting effect on the Native populations now. A great many of us are afflicted with diabetes, hypertension, gall bladder disease, and other problems. Things that are happening in the United States and Canada are happening in other areas where there is severe dietary disruption. This is bigger than the problem of the children thinking that milk comes from cartons. Do we really need a "supermarket to the world?" Everywhere I've been able to visit across Native America in the last few years, I've been stunned and dismayed at how many Indigenous foods and fiber plants are gone, and when you ask the children about these foods, some may know of them but they have not always had a chance to taste them.

They may not know where they once grew and may never have been to those places. There's something profoundly sad about remembering foods that you can no longer have access to and no longer eat. I'm not interested in being dependent on somebody else for my food, and certainly not on someone who doesn't understand what fuel my body needs. My dependency is on the whole creation. Our interdependence is on the whole creation.

Slowly, in my family, we're trying to work ourselves away from the supermarket and focus more on the local co-op, fighting our way through the concrete and back into areas where we can gather our natural foods and our plants where they belong, and having that interaction with them again. We are taught that if we ignore the plants and we ignore the animals and we don't talk to them and use them (and vice versa) then one or the other of us will go away. We see that with different species being outright eradicated or just disappearing. Some of the older people are trying to go back to where a certain tea grew or a certain plant grew and it's not there anymore, or people are legally regulated out of areas where our interaction with those animals or those plants traditionally were important for the local balance.

I think particularly of our coastal area where there used to be beautiful clam beds. People would go in there and harvest and thin out the clams, which is important for their health. Certain clam beds have died when people no longer interact with them in this way, and other beds have been destroyed to make parking lots for coastal recreation. I am grateful that we still have some foods left to gather. We need to work to regain and protect whole food systems to restore the health of the land and ourselves. I think this will take Native Peoples and our allies from other communities and nations. It will take united, intergenerational efforts to acknowledge the health correlations between land and life. It will take getting fed up with the wrong foods.

Diabetes hit my family in my father's generation. My father, one of the heroes in my life, enjoyed tremendous fitness, strength, and stamina. He is a hunter, fisherman, and farmer. He suffers now from diabetes and related complications. His strong will carries him through, and we children are still learning from him and from our amazing mother as well. But it hurts to see one's elders in pain, and they both are. They carried me down the cliffs to the fishing grounds when I was just a wee babe. To descend those same cliffs in the predawn hours without their footsteps leading me feels very lonely, very strange indeed. But my family spent time with me when I was a young person to make sure that I knew how to do these things. I do. This has been a source of strength to me all of my life, having that connection and knowing that I can provide for myself and for my family when everything is in balance. Working to regain that equilibrium is important for me and for those who are yet to be born.

This presentation took place at the Bioneers Conference in 1998.

22

Protecting the Culture and Genetics of Wild Rice

Winona LaDuke

We call wild rice *manoomin* in our language, which means "the good seed." It's a grain that grows on lakes and rivers in the central part of the continent. It used to be more widespread, but as some of those areas were taken out, or they underwent recreational development or dredging, a good portion of the rice was destroyed. It's my understanding that the range once was much greater. I talked to some traditional people from Maine, and they said in their language they had a word for wild rice. But the mother lode of where wild rice exists in the world is the Great Lakes region. The variety there doesn't exist anywhere else in the world. It's unique. It's the only native North American grain. Wild rice is an immense part of an ecosystem. Remember that Minnesota is the land of ten thousand lakes. They don't all have rice on them, but many do.

For Ojibwes, or Anishinaabeg is how we call ourselves, rice is central to our history. A long time ago prophets came to us. We were instructed to move from the East, because we would perish. We were instructed to follow the shell that appeared in the sky. We stopped in seven places along the way, and the fact is that we are actually very closely related to the Wampanoags and the Abenaki and the Lenni Lenape. They speak the same languages we do. So we did originate there in our most recent migration, which may have been a thousand years ago or two thousand years ago. We moved to the place where the food grows on the water; this food was wild rice.

We were given the gift of wild rice and the knowledge of it in a month known as *Manoominike Giizis,* which is the wild rice making moon. I like to talk about that, because we also have *Namebini Giizis,* the sucker moon, and we have *Onaba Giizis,* which is the hard-crusted snow moon. This snow moon is in March when it freezes and thaws. Not everybody is on the Julius Caesar calendar.

We have an immense amount of wild rice on our lakes. The reservations in northern Minnesota were created around the rice beds. You put your tobacco out, your prayers out, and then two people launch out in a canoe. One "knocks" and the other pulls. The knockers on our boat are thirty-inch-long cedar sticks; they look kind of like large drumsticks. The pole is long, eighteen to twenty feet, with a duckbill at the bottom. This is what you use to push out on the lake. You can't paddle the canoe because for the most part the surface of the lake is quite thick with rice and plants. You have to be somewhat agile and athletic.

When you come in after the harvest, you haul in your wild rice, and you put it in gunnysacks. You then take it to your processor. We're the largest processor in the area. It is then laid out to dry before it is put into equipment that will parch it for a couple of hours. After that you let it out and then traditionally you dance on it to get the hulls off. People do still dance, but we also use a basher, which sounds quite violent. It takes the hulls off and is run by a tractor motor. Then you winnow it. You use a fanning mill if you're doing fifty thousand pounds, which is what we do. Then you sort it by size.

After that you have a feast. This is very important. You always feast your rice. We feast all of our harvests. We have a big thanksgiving feast for the first rice, and we have a big dance. We have a wild rice dance starting in August. We also have our ceremonies and our powwows.

I say that because this is kind of the intersection between traditional values and industrialization. What happened to us is these anthropologists came. First they messed us up and then they came back in the 1920s and they watched us rice. Sammy Jenks, an early anthropologist working in Ojibwe territory, had this worldview, and his commentary was, "How could so majestic a grain be given to such a primitive people? They have to work so little to get it. It's like Ojibwe Mardi Gras or a kind of an early Christmas present. Then they dance and feast. They're never going to become civilized, because they are not that productive."

So from my vantage point, Jenks had this view of what industrialized agriculture is about: it's this separation of culture from growing, as well as a bent toward colonization. "These primitive people are dancing too much and singing." These scientists set about trying to domesticate wild rice. I don't want to say they had a vendetta, but in its own way, that's what it was. They messed around with it at the University of Minnesota for about thirty years. They didn't get it domesticated until the 1950s. They started growing it in diked rice patties to domesticate it. By the 1960s, they had created the advent for the paddy rice industry and in the 1970s it really took off. The university declared that this was a fantastic accomplishment of the Green Revolution. The University of Minnesota's quite involved with the Green Revolution. This is kind of their "look what we've done in Minnesota" attitude.

Wild rice was declared the state grain in 1977. They poured all this money into it in Minnesota, and about two years later the majority of the paddy rice industry moved to California. Today three-quarters of all paddy rice that is grown is grown in diked rice paddies in northern California.

We, as Ojibwe, have been in this battle for many years, because you can't compete with a guy with a combine. They use fertilizers and fungicides. The domesticated paddy rice doesn't taste like a lake. It tastes like a paddy. It's similar to the fair trade issue in coffee, but different. It is a technology and a whole process choice.

We started battling them in the 1980s, and in 1986 my White Earth reservation sued Anheuser-Busch. They had a picture of two Indians in a canoe on a lake full of wild rice that was called Onamia wild rice, which is a band of Ojibwe. The rice was entirely from California, so we sued them. We ended up with a state labeling law in Minnesota, which requires that paddy rice producers in the state of Minnesota must label the paddy rice as "cultivated." The loophole is, of course, that you cannot drive the entire California production through that. Today millions of pounds of wild rice are produced in California without the labeling law. It's shipped into Minnesota to get processed "green." Then it's labeled "Minnesota processed" to add to the gross misrepresentation of the product.

In the late 1990s the university took up the idea of genetic work on wild rice. The researcher Ron Phillips cracked the DNA sequence in 2000 and began the mapping of it. All the Ojibwe bands and the Minnesota Chippewa tribe wrote them a letter that said, "This isn't something you can tinker with. This is an essential part of our culture. This is who we are and we reserve this, and this is part of our treaty." The treaty of 1867 between the U.S. government and the Mississippie Band Chippewa established the White Earth Reservation and discussed off-reservation treaty rights. It specifically said that we had the right to rice, and to harvest wild rice. The treaty did not say that the rice could be genetically engineered by outside parties. We started battling the university in the 1990s and we've been battling them ever since.

At all our traditional feasts and ceremonies we have wild rice. We always eat our traditional foods. I'm not a Christian, so I don't have an equivalency on this, but we have instructions, as Ojibwe people, on what it is that is essential about being Ojibwe. A lot of that is related to these foods, and foods are considered medicine.

We have a responsibility to take care of all of our foods, and to ensure their vitality. My organization, the White Earth Land Recovery Project, has a pretty wide array of food-related activities. We make maple syrup. Until about 150 years ago, most of the maple syrup came from Indian people. We were the producers. Today, that's not so. We harvest all our medicines in the woods. Wild rice is really a good food for anybody who has allergies and it has a really high nutritional content. It's high in fiber and high in vitamins.

The University of Minnesota has been engaged in analyses of various elements of wild rice. In particular, they have been looking at the effect of it on cholesterol. A study that came out last year said it had an astonishing effect on diminishing cholesterol.

So it's part of this dichotomy of worldviews. We would say, "You should eat rice," and they would say, "We can create a pill that has that essential element extracted." From our standpoint we know that it has an effect on us and so we eat it. My family eats 150 pounds of rice a year.

From our vantage point, what we notice is that, with the decline of traditional foods in our communities, because of loss of access to them, a lot of our people got sick. So today you have a really high level of diabetes. About 40 percent of the adults over forty on my reservation have diabetes. As it turns out, the best medicine for that is these traditional foods, along with exercising.

When the commercialization of wild rice happened in California, there was a huge and devastating economic impact on our rice economy and community. My family has always been involved with rice. My father met my mother selling wild rice. It was the way people made money. That's what Ojibwes *have*. It's always been a major source of trade and a major source of income for our people.

My reservation has two of the poorest counties in the state of Minnesota. The people who rice are people who do not have full-time jobs, and don't want them. They actually would prefer to harvest and live in the woods. Those people are the people who are most impacted by this loss of income. The advent of the paddy rice industry totally destroyed our market, which was a small market to start with. I'm not opposed to all paddy rice; if Uncle Ben's wants to sell that nasty old stuff, go ahead. You're going to spend eight bucks a pound, ten bucks a pound. Lake-grown wild rice is probably going for twelve bucks a pound retail.

Native people are the poorest people in the state of Minnesota and some of the poorest people in the country. What we have on my reservation is three things, as we say: we have wild rice, we have wind, and we have really smart people. So I feel like we should get the fair value.

The patenting of wild rice occurred a few years ago. NorCal Wild Rice holds the patents on a production system of creating sterile males that they created. They do this through seed selection. There's no genetically engineered wild rice anywhere. They did this seed selection, and they created this patented variety. They have two patents.

It's the beginning of outside entities owning the genetics of the plant that has been nurtured by our community for maybe thousands of years. So that occurred and then a DNA study mapping the genome of wild rice at the University of Minnesota also occurred. Around 2001 we held some meetings in our communities, including meetings with the very traditional and the religious leaders of our communities.

I brought in someone from the Center for Food Safety who worked on the basmati rice case.* I know Vandana Shiva and I asked her what to do. I told her we had a similar problem and she told me who to talk to. We held this meeting and explained to our people. The questions asked were, "Who gave them that right?" "How'd this happen?" "Did Nanabozhoo give them that right?" (Nanabozhoo is one of our half-man, half-spirit people.) The people were outraged and they asked, "What are they doing?" There was a supreme rift here.

The university continued on and was generally patronizing. (The USDA funded the university to map the genome.) The university's response to us was, "Once the Ojibwe understand, they'll be comfortable." The general argument is that basically if we were smart enough we'd be happy. The Ojibwe didn't really care for that. We feel like we're good on rice. We have a little more knowledge than the university does.

---

*In 1997 the American-based company RiceTec Inc. was granted a patent by the U.S. patent office that created a massive outcry by traditional basmatic rice growers and exporters in India and Pakistan. See recent article, "The story of the basmati rice patent battle" in *Science Business*, http://bulletin.sciencebusiness.net.

We have a two-thousand-year relationship with the rice, we get it. This is not to say that we're not open to discussions on knowledge but we have our *own* knowledge.

On some fundamental level there's this presumption on the part of these researchers at the university that the Anishinaabeg are not a vital culture; that we don't change anything. Many perceptions and analyses of our culture are shallow. Many of these scientists have no concept of who we are. Essentially, there's this divergence and this perception that we're primitive, which continues to this day.

There is also an assumption that somehow science is infallible and that science has a right. Our perspective is that they don't have all rights and our strategy is to question their assumption and say, "From our cultural perspective, you don't have all those rights."

At some point there should be a question of university ethics. They like to hide behind this cloak of academic freedom and tell us that we're limiting their academic freedom. The university people make claims like "What the Ojibwe are proposing to do would restrict our ability to combat bioterrorism." I thought that was totally cheating. We didn't say they couldn't stop anthrax or botulism. We're just talking about rice.

We also have the treaty of 1867, which backs us up. We have this legal right, which we believe is worth something. The United States may not believe that treaties are worth anything, but we actually believe that our treaties are worth something. But a larger cast of the discussion is that we believe that the mother lode of biodiversity is worth protecting. In this case, the only place where wild rice grows proximate to paddy rice is in the state of Minnesota. So what we are sure of is that they should have no right to contaminate [by cross pollination of genetically engineered rice] the natural lakes of Minnesota. The argument that I'm making is that people probably don't want ten thousand genetically engineered lakes.

It turns out that even a very conservative park rep at city council said, "We don't always agree with Winona, but she's 100 percent right on this." Our strategy is an Ojibwe-driven strategy, because that's our responsibility, but in taking a stand, I'm also calling on Minnesota loyalty to an ecosystem and pride in what it is to be a Minnesotan.

One of our deepest concerns, though, is California. California has no sense of responsibility toward the lake rice. Sometimes in the marketing of California paddy rice, they say that the Ojibwe, or the Indians, used to be involved with wild rice—they use the past tense on some of their marketing. "But now the Indians are gone." Like the Indians are gone and moved on and became Casino-owning Indians. Implying that riceing was something we used to do, but the fact is that we still do it. Millions of pounds of California paddy rice come into Minnesota. And that's live seed. It's still green. It's not processed, and there's a risk of contamination.

The University of Minnesota has said that they aren't intending to genetically engineer wild rice, but they want the right to do that. What I'm after is an ethics agreement with the university, because that's the most likely place that it would originate. But, unable to secure such an agreement with the university, we introduced legislation at the Minnesota legislature to protect wild rice and secure a moratorium on genetic engineering. The initial legislation called for a ten-year moratorium on any genetic engineering of wild rice. Over the years this was reduced to a two-year ban.

After a three-year battle at the legislature and a long set of meetings with the University of Minnesota, *manoomin,* or wild rice, finally received protection and is once again recognized—not only as the most sacred food of the Anishinaabe or Ojibwe Peoples but also as the cherished state grain. On May 8, 2007, Governor Pawlenty approved the Omnibus Environment and Natural Finance Bill (H 2410/ S 2096); protection for wild rice was included in this bill. Andrea Hanks, the Wild Rice Campaign coordinator for the White Earth Land Recovery Project expressed great relief that the bill had passed, thanking all of those who had supported it. "Protection for Wild Rice has been a long time coming for Anishinaabeg communities, many people on all levels contributed to moving this legislation, the tribes of Minnesota, tribal leaders, allied organizations, citizens and legislators, I'm thankful for the help and support that was given," she said.

My responsibility is to protect our rice. I'd like to protect all things, but right now this is my job.

This chapter is based on a 2006 interview by Arty Mangan of Bioneers and 2007 correspondence with LaDuke. It first appeared on the Bioneers website as "Protecting the Culture and Genetics of Wild Rice: An Interview with Winona LaDuke."

23

Cultural Change, Climate Change, and the Future of Civilization

John Mohawk

The most foolish thing that the United States government has ever done was to launch a centuries-long campaign to eradicate Indigenous cultures. A great deal of profound knowledge and wisdom—wisdom we could desperately use today—was lost.

About thirty years ago, I was attending a meeting at the Onondaga longhouse in New York, and the guests at that longhouse were from Hopi country in Arizona. One of them, Thomas Banyacya, who was a translator for some of the Elders who had journeyed to us, had a story from the Elders to tell. His story was that the world had more or less come to an end a few times, but that some native people had survived, and they'd come to be aware that it was an inattention to and a disrespect for nature that had been at the root of their problems. Life on earth had been threatened and certainly civilization had been threatened because people had abandoned a respect for nature. And now this was happening again.

The Elders had sent Thomas forward to try to explain this to the world, to give us all a warning. (At one point he even addressed the United Nations.) The Elders also said we should look at the white men's written records to find evidence to support what they were saying. I took on that job and began to do research. I discovered that the anthropologists who looked at the Maya civilization and its very curious collapse in the ninth century were puzzled by what had happened there.

It doesn't seem that the Maya were overwhelmed by invaders or had a devastating internal civil war. It looks as though there had been a huge population, especially living around Tikal, and that suddenly in the space of a hundred years, around 900 AD, their civilization collapsed and the people disappeared. There's no evidence that they migrated, because there's no corresponding evidence of increased populations in some surrounding area. It looks as if they simply vanished.

One intriguing hypothesis suggested that sudden climate change might have been to blame. Scientists looked at ice cores from Greenland corresponding to the period around 900 AD and discovered that that century had been extremely cold, far colder than usual. The scientists used computer simulations to look at what the global climate would likely have been under those conditions of extreme cold in the northern latitudes. Drought in Central America was one predicted outcome. It turns out that one of the symbols that comes up a lot in Maya inscriptions at this time of collapse is the symbol for drought. Core samples of deep layers of mud from lakes in Mexico confirmed that a severe drought had indeed occurred at that time.

When we come to the desert Southwest, we find a lot of evidence of civilizations there that became quite sophisticated in the use of irrigation. They dug canals, made holding ponds, and so on. But there too, several civilizations simply vanished, leaving behind impressive buildings such as the Mesa Verde complex. Something happened. The Hopi and the other pueblos indeed have stories that say something awful happened that caused their ancient ancestors to go back into the earth and emerge later in a different world.

In South America, in Bolivia and Peru, agriculture found its way into the most extreme environments in which humans ever grew plants. For some reason, those people grew food higher up the mountains, further into the desert, and deeper into the rainforests than any other human populations ever had. Not only that, but they discovered, cultivated, transformed, and changed more species of plants into cultivars [food crops] than any other complex of cultures in the history of the world. Those Andean cultures created more than three thousand varieties of cultivated plants. That is an almost mind-boggling achievement.

These agricultural innovators did amazing research and development. They took a number of plants and adapted them so that they could grow higher and higher up in the mountains in drier and colder conditions. Incan society organized itself to be able to grow food in very different ecosystems under very different conditions to make sure that in the years when food supplies failed in one place, it would grow in another. They understood that reciprocity was a survival strategy, and they carried on this practice for centuries. In fact, they were growing more and better food in the Andes at that time than they are now.

Starting around about the fourth century AD, it seems that the area we now call Central Asia—those huge steppes then populated mostly by nomadic herding cultures—also suffered severe climate changes, including droughts and extreme cold weather. These climate changes began to cause some tribes of herdsmen to move en masse, eventually pushing some groups to sweep down from Central Asia into Europe. These massive population movements and invasions ultimately pushed the tribes living north of the Roman Empire (Goths, Visigoths, and Vandals) into Italy to topple Rome. There were other factors in the decline and fall of Rome, but this climate change most likely played a crucial role. These past episodes may offer us clues about the future of our civilization. They show us, at the very least, that civilizations can be very fragile in the face of climate change.

Later, in the late Middle Ages and beyond, an overcrowded, filthy, and highly unsanitary Europe was having to contend constantly with the "Four Horsemen of the Apocalypse"—disease, war, famine, and death—while in America the problems were different. The climate kept changing and civilizations were collapsing. But the Indians were learning how to cope with it, discovering how to plant plants that survived through droughts and cold weather. They were creating a version of what some people today call "permaculture," but a permaculture for the ages that understood that climate wouldn't necessarily remain stable.

That's why I say the stupidest thing the colonists and their governments ever did was to suppress Indian culture, because guess what? Climate change is coming again, and those cultures had a lot of very practical knowledge about how to adjust and survive in the face of major climate change.

I believe that what is coming will pose a major challenge to world civilization. A high-tech civilization that depends on running water, electricity, bridges, and so on is far more fragile than we realize. I think the Hopi were right: Western civilization will face the same kind of challenges the ancient civilizations of this continent faced, but we're not ready to deal with them. The Hopi had some important messages for us, but, so far, we're not listening.

This presentation took place at the Bioneers Conference in 2004.

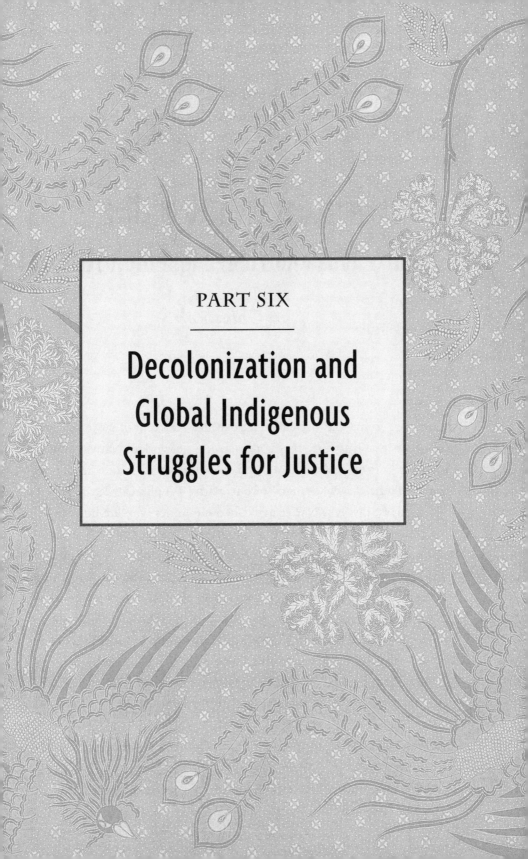

PART SIX

Decolonization and Global Indigenous Struggles for Justice

24

Protecting the Web of Life: Indigenous Knowledge and Biojustice

Tom Goldtooth

My name is Tom Goldtooth. I am the executive director of the Indigenous Environmental Network. IEN is a grassroots network of Native communities working on environmental and economic justice issues throughout North America, or what many of our Native Peoples call Turtle Island. Our network involves Native activist communities who are holding the line by resisting unsustainable development. Within the broader environmental justice movement, we often call these groups "fence line" or "frontline" communities. While most of the communities we work with are reservation-based, I want to acknowlege the fact that approximately 55 percent of our Indigenous population in the United States is actually urban, off-reservation based. Since this Bioneers Conference is in the Bay Area region of California, I also want to acknowledge that one of the biggest populations of *urban* Indians is in the San Francisco Bay area, mostly as a result of the relocation policies of the United States back in the 1950s and 1960s.

So we have rural, urban, and reservation-based communities working to protect our respective homelands, protect our treaties, our sovereignty, our culture, language, and our environment. Woven into the environment and ecosystem is what many Natives call the Web of Life. This web is part of the Circle of Life that sustains every one of us— humans, animals, fish, birds, plants, and all things within the rich biological diversity that is part of our Mother Earth. As a Native person, when we talk about biodiversity and the environment, we're talking about spiritual concepts, not only of Indigenous Peoples but all peoples throughout the world. So in my way, to discuss these concepts, I want to offer a song to bring our minds and hearts together.

All humans have two things in common: We walk on two legs and on each hand we have these five fingers and especially these thumbs. I was taught from infancy to utilize these as gifts from the Creator of this universe, gifts given to enable us to work together in solidarity, each finger, each hand, helping each other and in respect of each other. And of course, the use of this thumb plays a key role in how we use our minds and hands to build things . . . or to tear things apart. In my *Dine'* (Navajo) teachings, we call ourselves the Five Fingers Clan—which is the human people.

As two-legged creatures we also have been provided with our minds. The mind supposedly has the ability to reason and figure things out. This mind has been provided to us as a gift from the Creator, one that allows us to be creative and to be able to develop ways to live in common with each other and to live in a sustainable way on this planet, which I call Mother Earth.

We, the two-legged species, the humans, are not alone here; we share this Mother Earth with many life forms, animate and inanimate. From the waters of the great oceans to the smallest rock, and from the smallest organism to the biggest animals, we are related to each other. The relationship to the sacredness of our Mother Earth and all her children defines our spiritual, our cultural, our social, our economic, and even the political relationships that we have with each other in all life.

I just shared with you one small perspective that is the traditional knowledge of Indigenous Peoples. It's just a snapshot. The knowledge is no different from the knowledge of my *Dine'* peoples of the Southwest or my *Hunka,* the Mdewakanton Dakota Oyate people that live by the sacred lakes in an area we call the eastern doorway of the Dakota Nation located in Minnesota. This traditional knowledge is no different from either the Aborigines of Australia or the Indigenous Peoples from Africa, or the Sami from the Arctic regions of Norway, Sweden, and Finland.

This traditional knowledge has allowed our Indigenous Peoples to develop certain life ways, values, and cultural practices that have given us knowledge to live in balance and in a sustainable way for thousands of years. We are people of the land, we are people of the waters and the lakes, we are the river people, we are the desert people, we are the plateau people, we are the mountain people, and we are the people from the forests, we are also the Pacific Islanders. From the four directions of this world we are still here despite great obstacles that have challenged our survival. That is why I'm so grateful to the Creator to be able to be here and, as we say back home, to live with my relations one more day.

Back in Minnesota our world is changing right now, we are in a four-season world. And at this place in Minnesota, that is the center of our universe, all of life is preparing for winter when our Mother Earth is going to be resting, preparing herself to sleep, to be covered with a blanket of snow that will keep her warm and create the quietness that she will need to rest from a long year that starts for her in spring, and continues throughout the summer and fall. The communities have already celebrated the harvest of the sacred rice that grows on our waters. And the men are getting ready to hunt once more; this will supplement our diet instead of the processed foods of pizza, french fries, and hamburgers from border-town, fast-food restaurants.

The leaves have turned, this means that fall is here and the leaves are very colorful—brown, red, and yellow. By the time I get home maybe the wind will have come and blown the remaining leaves from the trees. At our ceremonial lodge next to the Mississippi River, one can sit and watch each of the leaves fall to the ground. Watching each leaf fall from the trees, we watch it take its journey as if it had eyes looking for an empty spot on the ground of Mother Earth to rest its body.

How many of you have ever taken the time to slow down to see that there are some things unseen—a spirit force, as in this example—guiding this individual leaf, allowing it to take that journey, floating, being carried by a breeze of wind, and suddenly whipped up to fly up into the air again? And then it finally finds its place and finds a spot to land on and then, at that proper moment and time, it lands on that one spot, the only spot around the tree where there is any bare ground. So what is this experience? What is the essence that guided this leaf to find that one spot? This is one part of this web of life and only one small part of what we call Indigenous Knowledge. Indigenous Knowledge is so beautiful.

BIOJUSTICE, BIOETHICS, AND THE PROTECTION OF EARTH MOTHER AND SKY FATHER

I now shift gears into some perspectives on biological diversity, bioethics, biopiracy, and biodemocracy. These are all part of this topic of biojustice or -injustice. I'm going to share some terms: genetic engineering, patents, human genome project, gene banking, life industry, trade secrets, cell lines, DNA, General Agreement on Tariffs and Trade (GATT), Convention and Biological Diversity (CBD), World Trade Organization, World Intellectual Property Organization (WIPO), trademarks, North American Free Trade Agreement (NAFTA), transgenic organisms, Trade Related Intellectual Property Rights (TRIPs), Intellectual Property Rights (IPR), Green Revolution, Article 8(j) In-Situ Conservation of the CBD (UN Convention on Biological Diversity) on equitable sharing of benefits arising from the utilization of Indigenous and local knowledge; the list goes on.

Here are some other terms that we have back home: Bureau of Indian Affairs, Standard Operating Procedures, Trust Status, Congress, plenary powers, treaty rights, government to government relationship, Indian Health Service, HUD, rules and regulations, federal audits, Department of Defense, U.S. Forest Service, Bureau of Land Management, Department of Interior, Development of Trust Lands, U.S. Park Service, surface mining and mineral exploration, U.S. EPA, Department of Energy, FDA, NAGPRA, BIAM, Trust Lands, and so on, and again, the word DNA. DNA, "Descendants-N-Ancestors."

John Trudell, a poet who is one of our deep thinkers, came up with the phrase "descendants and ancestors"—DNA. I like that. As Indigenous Peoples, we have to take back these terms. We have to redefine them, we have to seek new paradigms, throw out some we don't need, and move forward with some serious thinking on what we are leaving the next generations. We have to take a serious precautionary approach to what we do as a society. DNA, descendants and ancestors, that's what it's all about.

Historically, land-based cultures have always been a threat to colonial nations and states throughout the world. Land has always been the issue; whoever owns the land controls the people. Colonization, Christopher Columbus, conquest, militarization, charters, patents, ownerships, laws, copyright, trademark, property, slavery, land titles, popes, churches, lawyers, colonial governments, capital, labor, piracy, wealth, old money, new money, blue bloods, family shields of honor, kingdoms, peasants, surfs, and . . . them damn Indians.

You know the rest of the story, mining, mining, and mining the sacredness of our Mother Earth. Oil, coal, uranium, mining and extraction of minerals, mining our Indigenous minds, mining our intellectual property. Traditional medicines, traditional seeds, blue corn chips, celestial teas, and healing teas. Mining our Indigenous minds, now mining our bodies, mining our genetic information, mining ourselves, and patenting the cell lines of an Indigenous man in New Guinea, mining our bodies and now owning life, property rights. Pretty heavy stuff within all those different terms, isn't it? I could talk about any one of those different areas. There's a whole history behind them and a lot of documentation has gone on with these different issues.

Our organization, the Indigenous Environmental Network, is currently involved in national and international discussions of the rights and concerns of Indigenous Peoples, focusing on the protection of ecosystems, environmental health, climate change, natural habitats, plant and animal resources, sustainable development models, as well as Indigenous traditional knowledge, and our cultural practices. Biological diversity is the totality of plant and animal life and the ecosystems in which we live. Too many of our Indigenous Peoples call this the sacredness of our Mother Earth, the sacred natural world, our circle of life. So, biological diversity and the Indigenous concepts of the Circle of Life are one and the same.

Nowadays, scientists, governments, and research institutions are experimenting with the building blocks of life. They are manipulating the natural essence of strings that tie life together. They are splitting DNA, genetically modifying different organisms without any international ethics to guide their work. We must demand effective and measurable ethics and research protocols surrounding the protection of biological diversity worldwide. Justice demands a just and ethical international standard of code and conduct pertaining to the uses of and protection of biological resources including cells, seeds, genetic materials, plants, and other forms of life, including concerns regarding the introduction of biochemical compounds.

Bioethics encompasses a number of concerns vital to the survival of our Indigenous Peoples and our cultures. Indigenous Peoples, as caretakers, have a tremendous responsibility to protect the natural world, to prevent the exploitation of plant medicines, to oppose the patenting of our human genetic information, and to develop national and international legal mechanisms to safeguard traditional knowledge for our future generations.

Biojustice includes issues of biological testing and the experimentation of living things, including humans, bioprospecting for the appropriation of traditional plant knowledge, as well as genetic harvesting and engineering. These issues are critical concerns to our Indigenous communities worldwide, especially those directly affected by such practices: our land-based cultures and our traditional practitioners. In Minnesota we have a few families that still put out trap lines, still go out there with the canoes and harvest the rice that grows on the water; we have fence line communities such as the Prairie Island Dakota community that still go out and collect the water potato, called *bdo*.

Some of the key bioinjustice concerns of the Indigenous Environmental Network and Indigenous Peoples include intellectual and cultural property rights, encompassing the patenting of life-forms and looking at the impact of international trade regimes regarding ownership and property rights of our traditional knowledge, biological knowledge, and life forms. Biopiracy is the appropriation of traditional knowledge without consent. Human genome harvesting, patenting, and genetic engineering entail the taking of whole DNA sequences and I am sure they got a lot of this information already, despite efforts like Debra Harry at the Indigenous Peoples Council on Biocolonialism, one of our network organizations working on biocolonization issues.

The protection of culture and biological heritage from commodification and exploitation impacts on ecosystems and habitats is crucially important. We must protect against resource exploitation and environmental contamination. More discussion needs to happen about collective versus individual ownership rights. For example, when a university, industry, or pharmaceutical company wants to go out and obtain rights to our knowledge, who do they go to? Is it an individual that owns that right? Is it a medicine man or medicine woman? Does that person hold that information as an individual? Or do they hold that information from a collective perspective? Was it given to our Indigenous Nation in a sacred manner sometime long ago for all our people to have and to use? These are considerations that require discussion and resolution within our communities. As Indigenous Peoples we must assert our self-determination over traditional lands and all our resources.

The Indigenous Environmental Network maintains a perspective upholding the sacredness of life. We have opposed the sale and commodification of sacred medicinal plants used traditionally by our peoples, to biological resource brokers and pharmaceutical companies who we call biopirates. We have continued to ascertain and defend Indigenous human rights, land and water rights, culture and jurisdiction over our resources and the environment, and to present the traditional Indigenous perspectives on these issues for the well-being of all peoples, all races, all cultures, and our natural world. Within most Indigenous beliefs, no person can own living things or hold life forms as property. Our Mother Earth and our plant and animal relatives are respected sovereign liberated beings with rights of their own. Who will defend those that cannot speak?

The European concept of the natural world, which has become a dominant concept worldwide, views knowledge and culture as property, with the attitude that commodities are to be exploited freely and bought and sold at will. This has resulted in disharmony between human beings and the natural world, as well as the current environmental crisis threatening all life. This concept is totally incompatible with the traditional Indigenous worldview. Indigenous Peoples were given, by our Creator, the responsibility to protect land and natural life upon which our survival depends. Our sacred responsibility is to safeguard and protect this world.

Human beings are not separate from the rest of the natural world but were created to live in an integral relationship with it; that's what we have to offer. Understanding these Indigenous principles provides understanding of love—love for Mother Earth and Father Sky. Mother Earth and Father Sky are the creative principles that we have in this universe. All creation and compassion for each other comes from this understanding. All people must come to reidentify and realize what the relation is with the sacredness of our Mother Earth and Father Sky. This helps all people, and especially the men, understand what our relationship is to the sacred female creative principle of Mother Earth.

My prayer is for us to all resolve this global conflict, the war and violence that we have. I mentioned earlier that the common feature we all share is this human hand. As human beings we are all related to each other, we are the five-fingered clan. We are the five-fingered clan of human beings. We must learn to work together as members of the two-legged peoples. Like the five-fingers on each hand, we have different features on each finger and each finger is used differently. But they are all connected to each other and have to learn to help each other. Let us learn to work together as people of many colors, many cultures, all genders; we don't have much time.

There is an Australian Aborigine bush saying that states: "If you stay closely united, you are like a tree standing in the middle of a bush-fire sweeping through the timber; the leaves are scorched, the tough bark is scarred and burned, but inside the tree the sap still flows and under the ground the roots are still strong. Like that tree you have survived the flames and you have still the power to be born. The time for rebirth is now."

Ahe'ee, Wopida. Thank you.

This presentation took place at the Bioneers Conference in 2001.

25

Return of the Ancient Council Ways: Indigenous Survival in Chiapas

Ohki Siminé Forest

When I arrived in Chiapas in 1986 it was just before a planetary configuration of great significance to the ancient Maya. In my first year in Chiapas, it became clear to me that although nobody was talking about it, a revolution was going to happen because the oppression and racism toward the Indigenous Maya was terrible. In Chiapas, you truly feel you're back in colonial times. It felt to me there was no other choice for the people there than to create a revolution to liberate themselves from the devastating effect of the Spanish conquest and the appalling abuses of the Mexican government.

Seven years later, on January 1, 1994, I was about to give birth to my daughter. We awoke to an uprising in several towns, including San Cristóbal de las Casas where I was living. I had almost forgotten about my predicted revolution; everyone was taken by surprise. This transcendent event shook everyone, as if a huge earthquake had happened. For me, it was as if a new era had finally dawned.

Then on TV and the radio, the world learned who the Zapatistas were and about their tremendous suffering as Indigenous Maya. The world's eyes were suddenly on Chiapas, a place considered to be, only a few short minutes before, a paradise on earth. Many people left, and a new crowd of people arrived: journalists, activists, conscious people, and spies.

Chiapas was not on the map prior to this. If I told people I lived in Chiapas, very few knew where it was. Before this uprising—one of the most uplifting the world has seen—the Maya people of Chiapas had been forgotten and abandoned. We only knew them because of their incredible ancient ruins and past splendors. Yet the living Maya were an illiterate, marginalized, and extremely poor people. We learned these people also had dignity, tremendous vision, and ancient wisdom. And though they had taken up arms, they are very peaceful by nature. In the end, the Chiapas revolution shed almost no blood.

They had something of great significance to say to the world. They were making a stand against changes to Article 27 in the Mexican Constitution, which had guaranteed since the 1910 revolution that the land belonged to those who worked it. With the changes, this communal *ejido* system was becoming private property. This was a big blow to the Indigenous communal laws everywhere in Mexico. The Zapatistas also made a stand against the NAFTA treaties between Canada, the United States, and Mexico, which were going into effect that same first day of January. They were the only people in North America to risk their lives opposing this aggression against Indigenous Peoples and their way of life.

We also learned the Zapatistas were not a band of armed dreamers re-creating the Che vision, but actually millions of people organized with their own legitimate army based on the Geneva treaties; they had formed in a very coherent way to protect themselves against government abuses.

For those of us with knowledge about ancient Maya prophecies, the Zapatista uprising is also the predicted return of the Plumed Serpent. He was a high priest who created the advanced Maya civilization. Yet the Plumed Serpent was defeated by another priest named Smoking Obsidian Mirror from Tenochtitlan (now Mexico City) and forced to abandon his beautiful reign. He left as the Morning Star, saying that he would return after a planetary convergence in 1987 to bring back his governance in the Maya land. He would return as a high consciousness and take the form of a transcending serpent rising from deep within the earth, first in Palenque, Chiapas—the third eye of the Americas—and then in the world. As he rises from under the earth, he will shake from below everything and everyone along his pathway. He will shake all of the old patriarchal paradigms by bringing the people true ways of how to govern themselves and take back their freedom from the terror and corruption of Smoking Mirror.

That first day of January, I was suddenly making all these links in my mind. A few years before, a Mohawk chief in Canada shared an ancient prophecy with me: When the termination of Indians is over, the Iroquois form of government, which survived the conquest intact, will return to all the Americas. And then, apparently out of the blue, millions of people who had been enslaved by the Spaniards, then terribly exploited by the Mexican government, will suddenly organize themselves with the ancient knowledge, recalled in their blood, of Indian council ways, and they will arise to claim their autonomy. The Zapatista way of organizing is very similar to what I have observed in the ancient council ways of the Iroquois League of Peace.

Council ways are the form of government for the new times, the posttermination times, which we hope is now. The ancient council ways are based on Medicine Wheel ways. This means there's a horizontal axis composed of the eight cardinal directions. And the ninth one at the center is the vertical axis that links with the sky. Council ways are a smaller version of the great wheel of the universe, which gives us a natural form of personal and collective governance.

Natives in North America lived according to the council ways for quite some time, in huge brotherhoods and sisterhoods. There were councils for every aspect of life—peace councils, war councils, spiritual, political, economic councils, and medicine councils. One of the main characteristics of the council ways is its inclusiveness. All is included, even the "bad"—everything has its place in the larger wheel.

What makes a council a true council is its system of democracy and collectiveness at the same time. To achieve this, the people must participate and always be consulted in the decision-making process. It's the most resilient and fair form of government that exists, for it teaches people to preserve their autonomy and resources, to govern themselves, and to choose their destiny. It helps them grow responsible and conscious in promoting and protecting all forms of life.

A council, being a circle, is unbreakable. There is nothing more powerful than a circle. The system of Indian reservations was created only because our tribal circles could not be broken. It was easier to draw squares on the U.S. map around the tribes. Yet they could not break our spirit, as we've shown in 513 years of resistance. We have always been in resistance against globalization. Our chiefs had foreseen this coming.

In this same way, the Chiapas resistance is a most singular one for it has a global impact. It's not a resistance for an ethnic group, an ideology, or a class war. It's not a resistance solely for their own rights to live. It's a revolution that opened doors, not only to all the Indigenous Peoples of Mexico, but to the whole of Mexican society: mestizo people, non-Indian people, even to the anti-Zapatistas.

However, it was also not limited just to the Mexican society but is open to any one of you who wish to join with your heart and consciousness in this global resistance, this huge return of council ways. In 1994, the Zapatistas stopped their war because the civil society rose and demanded peace. They signed a cease-fire agreement, which the Mexican government has not kept. The Zapatistas said they signed that agreement at the time because they heard the drums of the civil society, the heartbeat of the common people.

What Marcos (the main spokesperson of the Zapatistas) has done is unprecedented. He made comprehensible for the common people, the terrible impacts of neoliberalism and globalization in the first and third worlds. Before that it was just intellectual talk.

If the people rose in arms—and most of them had only wooden sticks to defend themselves—it was because there were no other options. They had tried, by all means, to be heard. They always said they had weapons that aspire to be useless. Their cry, "*Ya Basta!* (That's enough)," was their claim, for themselves and their children, for decent lives, food, health care, and education.

The Zapatistas have also raised consciousness among their people about how to powerfully affect a clear line of resistance by taking practical actions. For example, they do not accept anything from their government, a government whose tactics are to buy the people with crumbs. Their resistance in this regard has made it clear to all that Zapatista dignity is not for sale.

The Zapatista people have said NO to alcohol, drugs, deforestation, and the plundering of resources, NO to the abuses of the government and their interest in the oil in the soil. This NO led them to declare their territories liberated and autonomous in 1994, a liberation from five hundred years of an unjust course in their destiny.

When you enter an autonomous community (this, ironically after you pass a federal army post) you're greeted by a large sign saying that here the people control their own land and resources. To do this more effectively they have formed the Good Government of the People, *La Junta de Buen Gobierno,* in opposition to the bad government of the financial powers. In the autonomous communities they say the Good Governments listen to everyone who visits.

Their government is situated in what is called the *Caracoles,* which means shells or snails. These are their five central meeting places for community representatives. The seashell was the traditional instrument blown by the ancient Maya to invoke their deities and to convene the people to their ceremonies. The Caracoles are a speaker to the world, to be heard and to hear everyone who comes to learn about the resistance and exchange their words. This unique communication method is an underground way of transmitting information. Like the Caracoles, this method works for those who walk close to the ground and it leaves a clear path for all to follow.

When you meet with the Zapatista men and women in one of their rustic buildings at their Caracol, they look at you through their black ski masks and you see an ancient wisdom in their eyes. The ski mask not only protects their identities but is a powerful symbol of how they were never heard despite their long and numerous efforts. The mask also says, "We would rather stay hidden for we do not want the power. This is a resistance of truths and actions." But in the end, through their masks, they see a great deal and are no fools.

In meeting with them, there is a long silence before talking, a respectful and a kind one. Then, one of the ski masks greets you in a voice that seems to have suffered for eternity yet is not complaining, but is warm and clear; that of an unarmed civil commander.

The voice starts explaining (to me) that everything here is decided by the people through referendum and it's often a long process. Starting at twelve years of age, everyone is consulted in making decisions. For eleven years the resistance has grown a great deal, but not without enormous sacrifices; they have created programs for autonomous education based on preserving the environment, as well as their ancient culture. They also have created their own health programs, trained hundreds of young men and women as health promoters all over Chiapas, and built autonomous clinics in many different areas.

As I hear this short, Indigenous man talking in a slow, deliberate fashion, I cannot stop thinking about the deeply internalized oppression the Maya carry. It's a mentality that is hard to break through, yet the ability to break free is something the Zapatista resistance has given the people. To achieve this, the native Maya kicked a huge hole in the globalization paradigms. And in this, they were the first ones to speak of globalizing resistance, for the sake of everyone, for the sake of our children.

The Chiapas resistance is also a spiritual revolution. For the Maya people, the disconnection from their own spirituality was very drastic under the Spanish Conquest. While northern Natives were marginalized in isolated reservations, many of our forefathers and foremothers did everything to keep intact the sacred link to our spiritual ways from before the conquest. In Chiapas, however, this link was destroyed by the Spaniards to such an extent that most of the Indigenous Peoples did not even know there had been a conquest and had lost touch with their spiritual traditions. However, one of the things the Zapatistas brought to the people, especially Marcos in his communiqués, is a reawakening of awareness of the ancient Maya spirituality and its deities.

I bring my attention back to the meeting when I hear the commander telling me that, in their understanding, they are not doing this huge sacrifice only for their people but for everyone. *Para todos, todo, para nosotros nada.* All for everyone, nothing for us. It is a sacrifice, for in their work as representatives they have to leave their families for many weeks, during which time they only have a few hard tortillas to eat. The representatives sleep on the hard floor of their meeting rooms—it's a very difficult life to be a Zapatista in this sense, he continues explaining. Sometimes they have no money for buses to go from one place to another and sometimes they don't sleep for days and nights. Also they risk their lives a great deal. A Zapatista life requires a lot of endurance and determination. Sometimes they get ill for lack of decent food, he says, but they keep going. They cannot give up, for the sake of their people and all humanity.

The man continues, "As Zapatistas, we have been declared terrorists for simply wanting to live, for asking for food, for health care, for education. But for us, in the eyes of the true man and true woman, terrorism is greed, racism, hate, and war. For true change, we are ready to die with dignity, in resistance, instead of waiting to die from curable diseases and hunger."

The meeting ends after a few hours and the men and women commanders tell me, very humbly, "*Muchisimas gracias* for your great sacrifice of coming to meet with us and giving a donation to help us run our clinics."

I look at them, astonished. I reply, not without difficulty in holding back my tears, "I'm not doing anything here! You're doing everything for all of us, bringing a light of hope to humanity that this is possible, that millions of people can organize at the same time to create this huge movement so the right values can return to our wounded humanity. You all talk to us about being *verdadero hombre, verdadera mujer,* the true man and the true woman. We have the same expression among the Mohawk people, *Ongwhe Onwhe,* which means the True People. It's very ancient to Native people to be true humans, true warriors of life, to fight for what we know is right and for the transformation of all darkness."

I leave "the shell" flooded with inspiration. Yes, no doubt, the Chiapas resistance is a new kind of revolution. In meeting with them I'm overwhelmed by their amazing humility and patience. It's heartbreaking, the absence of ego you see in these people. They're just right there, smiling at you under their mask, through their eyes as bright as stars.

Marcos said, "There are no recipes, no ideologies, no tactics, no laws, no regulations, no slogans—Zapatismo is but a bridge . . . a rainbow bridge among us all. . . ."

The Zapatistas have no plan; they walk one step at a time and wait to see where the next step is going to lead them, for they walk with the will and heart of the people, and with the dream of the earth. And they are shaking the world from underneath, just as the Plumed Serpent promised. It's a new kind of resistance. Their message calls us to dream with the earth and to hear her dream within us. The Chiapas resistance offers a place beyond the oppression these people have lived with for so long, one that mirrors all the oppressions we all have within. They are the new warriors.

I can go back home now with a renewed sense of hope. True changes are possible and it will come from under the earth like the Maya who sleep on her flesh. The ancient Maya prophesized that there will come a time, after a planetary convergence in 1987, when the dark times will be over, the humble will win over the arrogant. It's happening, underground, with the simple people. They barely know how to speak Spanish to defend themselves in the dominant culture. Yet in their nonviolent ways of expressing their integrity, they are now allied with hundreds of organizations and millions of people all over the world. They shine a light of integrity, while we let ourselves be contaminated by consumerist societies with the wrong values such as competition, ambition, arrogance, and offensive actions such as polluting our sacred Mother.

The Zapatistas have opened the possibility for the Maya people to break through their internalized oppression, transforming their fear of punishment. This revolution is about transforming our fears of lethargy, authority, and terror—the same fears that have created this destructive global empire. This small yet great people are teaching us to not be afraid to stand tall in our own truth. It's a deep transformation they are asking all of us to achieve in resisting oblivion together.

What I've learned from my Zapatista *compañeros* is that the seed of all true power is within us. We will all die one day, but dignity can never die because dignity is the spirit of earth within us. If humanity can learn to see through Indigenous eyes, and to hear in the land the voices of our native ancestors—which continue to speak to us of dignity—then the hearts of all people will be healed.

We are all being called to go through this lesson in courage to enter into the new times in 2013 prophesized by the Maya. For technology has brought a lot of commodities, more securities, more scientific knowledge, but life appears to have less and less meaning for humanity. Never before has humanity been so empty and bored, or made so many efforts to desperately acquire more. This desperate grasping is and has always been the only real cause of humanity's suffering and the imbalances of this earth. It creates aggression and poverty, instead of the open generosity of our natural selves. For the worst toxins are not those of external pollution but those generated by humanity's wrong thinking.

The Maya have brought to humanity a great awakening. Possessing nothing, greatly suffering from the negative impacts of globalization, they bring the lessons we most need. They strive to create true forms of organization based on the Council ways and they generously share this model with us.

We can only join our hearts with them in hoping we can also re-create, wherever we are, the underground resistance that needs to happen in a massive way. This will happen through gratitude, respect for nature, and cooperating as much as we can with the forces of life, with the like-minded people around us.

We cannot fight directly the powers of globalization that are killing us all. We can only strive to bring back the dream of the earth, her council ways, however we can. Democracy and true community mean that all of us not only speak but also take action to create a light of hope for our children—"the Coming Faces," as the Iroquois call them.

Marcos wrote in 1993 before the uprising, "Now it's time to wake up. . . . From the clash of the two winds, the storm will be born, its time has arrived, the fire of history is aroused. Now the wind from above rules, but the wind from below is arising. . . . The prophecy is here. . . . When the storm calms, when the rain and fire again leave the earth in peace, the world will no longer be the world, but something better."

I was explaining recently to my daughter that we're all connected and anything she does can affect someone else in the world. She told me she did not believe me, that she had just put her feet in the pond by our home and it did not affect me, so how could it affect a Chinese person around the globe? I explained, "You're not understanding this principle correctly. When you put your feet in the pond, because you love water so much, that makes you very happy. And here, as I am working on my presentation for the Bioneers Conference, feeling a bit stuck, your happiness inspires me; it helps me write from my heart. So who knows, maybe putting your feet in the pond here in Chiapas will affect four thousand people at Bioneers in California, and who knows where else!"

"Oh!" she said, "as much as that!" with her eyes wide open.

Later, I heard my daughter talking with a young Maya Zapatista woman while they were working "Don't drop the broom carelessly like that, you can really affect a *lot* of people!"

Yes, we all can affect, individually, a lot of people. The extermination of the Maya, a very real and present threat, would be the end of our hope for casting off the global imperialism killing us all. Let's drum to join our heartbeats with the Zapatistas in this resistance for life.

¡Viva La Revolucion!

This presentation took place at the Bioneers Conference in 2005.

26

Front Line of Resistance: Indigenous Peoples and Energy Development

Clayton Thomas-Muller

I work for the Indigenous Environmental Network. IEN has been around here in Turtle Island, what we call North America, for about fifteen years. Our sole reason for existence is to meet the outcry coming from over five hundred nations that call Turtle Island home in terms of the injustices that have been imposed on our people. Indigenous Peoples are disproportionately impacted and burdened by unsustainable development and toxic contamination. IEN was created because in America and in Canada, transnational oil companies and corporations that create toxic incinerators and waste dumps target our communities as sites to place horrible chemicals underneath or next to our children's homes and schools.

IEN has been working to protect the sacredness of Mother Earth from this toxic contamination for a little bit over a decade now. This has brought us to many different realms, from down on the Res* to band

---

* "Res" or "Rez" is a common vernacular term in Indian Country; it is shorthand for an Indian Reservation in the United States and Indian Reserve in Canada.

halls to reservation school gyms doing workshops, community education pieces, to try to help people understand the dangers of these huge corporate monsters that come into our communities, promising a better way of life through the industrialization game.

Globally there are 350 million Indigenous Peoples recognized by the United Nations. I would go as far as to say that there are 600 million, but I'll go with what the statistics say. Those 350 million Indigenous Peoples represent 86 percent of the world's cultural diversity. In other words, 86 percent of all the languages spoken on Mother Earth are spoken by that very small number that I just mentioned. Now, those 350 million Indigenous Peoples across Mother Earth are cradled in 87 percent of the world's last remaining pristine ecosystems, places where the circle of life is still strong, where you can still harvest medicines, where you can still hunt and fish without getting sick, where you can still drink from the river or the lake. These are our final stand places, and they are our sacred places—the Arctic National Wildlife Refuge, places like the protected areas in the Rocky Mountains, beautiful places like the Everglades in Florida—sacred places where life and medicine are abundant.

We are a network comprised of 250 native communities and organizations spread out across Turtle Island. IEN has been reaching out to native groups. We all have this understanding of the sacredness that we carry as Indigenous Peoples, the responsibility to protect the sacred. The fact is that 350 million people representing 86 percent of all the languages live on some of the last places left on the earth that are still healthy and we call these places "home."

Our struggle is everybody's struggle, and this is what IEN has been trying to bring out. Economic globalization, and its notion that we can have eternally expanding markets based upon consumption of finite resources, is psychotic. This process is impacting all of our nations worldwide, and we—our cultures, our languages—face extinction. By 2050, in Canada, which I call home, only three of our Indigenous languages will have survived. So diversity loss is critical.

I want to discuss the diversity of issues that we work with at IEN, but specifically I want to discuss the petroleum industry, which is what

I focus my work on. Basically, people refuse to understand or accept the fact that there are many problems that we face today, for example, climate change. Many people, especially folks living in urban centers or places where they are insulated from the true impact of what's happening right now, on the ground in our native territories across Turtle Island and worldwide, are not burdened with the same impact.

When chemical companies make toxic chemicals, persistent organic pollutants, DDT, different chemicals like that, people don't realize that these chemicals travel thousands of miles because of the nature of their composition. They travel thousands of miles through the air currents of Mother Earth, up to the Arctic and to the southern regions of the planet, and that's why many of our people that live up in the Arctic have ten times the normal PCP and dioxin levels in their breast milk. Our mothers are, of course, then feeding that to our children.

Economic globalization today has put profit before life—profit before life. And to take that statement even further, economic globalization is commodifying the very life that makes up Mother Earth—creation. One of the things that IEN tries to do is to bring awareness of the world and of the cosmic views that Indigenous Peoples have, and we fight against the commodification of what is sacred, which includes our human genes, the genes of plants, our water—and so on and so forth. We fight against the exploitation of those that cannot speak for themselves. Our work is very vast and we work on many campaigns in our organization; we have a water campaign, a mining campaign, and a persistent organic pollutants campaign. I work on the oil and gas issues.

About five years ago we had a partnership with an organization called Project Underground for the Indigenous Mining Campaign Project. This is my campaign. Transnational mining companies and oil corporations were disproportionately targeting our communities; they knew that the socio-economic conditions faced on the Res are so severe. They know that our people are reeling still from the impacts of colonization, that our people are on a day-to-day crisis mode because of the fact that we're still suffering from the highest suicide rates, the highest high school dropout rates, adolescent pregnancy rates, and incarceration rates. And so, corporations come to our communities with promises of a better life, solutions to the incredible problems that we face, trying to seduce us into the boom-bust game of big development. They target our communities, knowing that our communities are susceptible to saying yes to these harmful energy projects because of the big payoffs that come with them.

The work that I do is to try to pull together regional networks across Turtle Island, in Alaska, in Alberta, Canada, in the Montana-Wyoming region, in the Southwest, and in Oklahoma. I've been organizing our tribes, trying to provide them with popular education materials so that they can understand that this energy colonization that is happening on our lands is something we should not have any part of. It is neocolonialism.

What I commonly tell people is that where I'm from, years ago, we had Jesuit priests in black robes coming into our communities and promising a better way of life through changing the way we communicate with Creator. Of course, at that time, there was an incredible marriage between church and state. Today, the reality that Indigenous Peoples face is the new religion of the world—capitalism—and instead of Jesuit priests in black robes coming into our communities as that arm of the state to exploit us, we've got corporate CEOs in black suits coming into our communities, promising a better way of life through unsustainable development practices. These practices totally go against what people in our community of Bioneers refer to as the Precautionary Principle, but what we, where I'm from, refer to as the Seventh Generation Prophesy. In other words, the prophesy is about thinking ahead seven generations; the actions that you have today will impact your children's, children's, children's seven times over.

We've been working on the local level, what we call the front line of resistance, where our communities live, where our people live. There's something in the petroleum industry called the Hubbard Curve. This is a model that projected that the world's oil reserves would run out or would reach the halfway run-out point by 2004, and we're there. So what's happening now is that we're seeing the demand for oil continually rising, we're seeing corporations reaching out farther and farther to the most pristine and beautiful places, places that are very difficult to get to like the Arctic National Wildlife Refuge, home of the porcupine caribou and the Gwich'in nation, 86 percent of whose diet is based on the porcupine caribou herd. We're seeing oil companies trying to do everything they can to get out onto our land, what little land we have left, so that they can continue to ply the insatiable demand for this black gold, as they call it.

IEN has been fighting on the grassroots level to provide understanding to our communities that are being approached by oil refinery companies, by people that want to extract resources from the land. We're talking about climate change, about the concept of petrol politics and the fact that violence and war today on Mother Earth—in almost every single scenario—can be tied to the energy extraction industries; can be tied to the petroleum industry, and to the United States and other usual suspects like the European Union, and Canada, and their consumption of energy.

We try to educate our communities to the reality that they're not alone. Something that people have to understand is that if we continue to live beyond our ecological limits in the city environment, we're going to have to go somewhere else and get those resources. Now, whether that's Iraq or Navajo Nation, it's going to continue to happen. So what we've been doing is trying to educate our people about the real reality that this industry does to all of us. Not only does it completely destroy our land, our water quality, our animals on the land, and our ability to go out on the land, but because this is the most toxic industry next to nuclear, the chemicals and everything that they use get released into our environment and to us.

It is a dirty industry from beginning to end—from taking oil out of the ground, to the refining of that oil, to when it gets burnt up in our jets and our cars. We try to educate our people about what we call the River of Destruction. Oil industry types divide their industry into three segments: upstream, midstream, and downstream—upstream being extraction, midstream being the transport and refining of that raw crude or gas, and downstream being where they sell it to you, the consumer.

What we try to educate our communities about is the fact that at every point of that definition—upstream, midstream, downstream—there are disproportionate impacts. Whether it's Indigenous Peoples fighting against these companies, from drilling their land and destroying and polluting it, to communities of color that have to live beside huge oil refineries—for example, the Richmond oil refinery that you can see on the way to Marin from Oakland, the home of Chevron-"Toxico"—that harm them in a terrible way.

We take this work from that level, from that community grassroots organizing level, and we amplify our community-activist voices by bringing them to different forums both nationally and internationally. IEN acts as a go-between, a mediator for a lot of these big, UN gatherings like the Commission on Sustainable Development, the World Summit on Sustainable Development, the Commission on Biodiversity, and other gatherings where they make up these global, multilateral, environmental agreements. We work to bring our people up to those levels so that they can put a face to the oppression that is happening worldwide as a result of the petroleum economy, the off-ramp economy. We try to do this work with the few resources that we have. IEN is in a crisis mode consistently because of the incredible amount of requests we get for help across North America. I, myself—just one individual—work with thirty-six different tribes on oil and gas issues alone.

An important issue that people need to be aware of is the fact that there needs to be a convergence of all kinds of people working on these issues. But it's hard to achieve that because people are lacking an understanding of the disproportionate impacts that come with things like climate change. It's easy for people to negotiate conditions and terms with these evil corporations and these governments when they don't understand what's really happening. The reality is that it's an unfair negotiation process—they get taken advantage of because they don't understand the complexity of these issues and the full ramifications of these issues. As a result of that, people right now are suffering directly. We're seeing major changes in our environment from Alaska all the way down to the

Gulf of Mexico. Navajo Nation is seeing incredible changes out there, too, in their environment as a result of climate change.

We need to understand that the solutions that we trump up at these international and national debates are meaningless without Indigenous access. I say this from my heart, Indigenous Peoples need access, access, access. Access to these meetings and debates so that they have relevance and make sense to the people who are involved.

We have to come together, but how do we do that? It's impossible to do that without talking about race, without talking about privilege, without talking about gender, oppression, and the movement. Given these daunting global issues like climate change and unsustainable energy development that impact virtually every segment of humanity and all life on Mother Earth, it's going take more than just the traditional ecological knowledge base of Indigenous Peoples. It's going to take more than the hard science of the Western world. It's going take a whole lot of things because we've gone past the natural order of things.

We need to sit at the table and talk together to come up with solutions to achieve this, but this has been very difficult for people from our side to do because of that access question, because of that racism question. One of the things that I've been doing to promote access is to reach out to communities like Bioneers because it's a group with an incredible amount of diversity; with them we can talk about the disproportionate impacts that we face. Here we can bridge that gap and have dialogue.

Indigenous Peoples have made it very clear that we want to be a part of the solution. We see a lot of things happening now. For example, South Dakota is being called the Saudi Arabia of wind power. So we're seeing opportunities in the Southwest for photovoltaic, solar energy. Indigenous Peoples have been pushing and pushing for these proper solutions. We're seeing a lot of arguments about energy, arguments that posit that the development of hydrogen energy or gas energy are transitory solutions. The argument that a lot of big enviros are using in their negotiations with governments of the world on issues of energy and climate change is that gas is a transitory energy, coal bed methane. This is not true. Bottom line, the places these gas plants are going be built, the pipelines, the territories they go through and the extraction process itself, the areas where it's happening is in our neck of the woods. This is not a solution. This actually exacerbates the on-the-ground situation that our people are facing.

We have to think about that and come up with better solutions. They're already there, but we must create the political will to get them to become a reality. On top of that, Indigenous Peoples, people of color, and white people need to be able to sit down and really have a full and meaningful dialogue. Participation needs to be full and meaningful in these different debates that exist right now on this topic, because it's still a big issue for us to even have our voices heard. All of the nations of the world are represented by the United Nations, but still the Red Nation is not sitting there at the table, and you have to ask yourself why.

This presentation took place at the Bioneers Conference in 2005.

27

Speaking for the Voiceless

Richard DeerTrack

It appears that we have all fallen into a dilemma of being the total mass consciousness for what is going on in the world. Maybe we think, "Well, I'm not a part of *that* mass consciousness." I certainly could say that, but I must not forget that I had to get on America West to come to the Bioneers in San Francisco, California, where I rented a car to get to Marin, then I took the car back and rode a shuttle to get back into Marin. I am the total of the whole of what's going on in our world today. We're talking about globalization. I don't think it's surprising to know that you are a part of that slave system that has been created by the corporations of the world.

I live in an adobe house that was built by my grandfather and grandmother. The walls are about two-feet thick, the ceiling is about six-and-a-half-feet high. I have two dogs, Oogala and Tally. I live alone. I was sitting at my computer being the cyber Indian that I am, and all of a sudden I heard these little voices—"blah, blah, blah." What the heck's goin' on? My daughter's a teacher at a school next door to me. She had brought her little ones, five- and six-year-olds, probably seven years old was the oldest. They had all come into my yard because I have an apple tree there. They all wanted to pick an apple. It was a beautiful thing that happened to me. I went out there and I looked at those little ones and I thought to myself, *You are the reason I'm going to conferences and speaking. Because you are the voiceless ones, you are the ones that nobody can talk for; no one can talk for you, because, although you see what is happening, you don't yet understand it.*

Relatives, it touched me to the core. Because in a traditional society where I come from, it takes courage to break the bounds of that tradition and to come out and begin to speak about what is going on in the world outside. You can be ostracized and you can be put down for crossing that boundary. At the same time, when you come out here, the same thing happens to you. Because maybe you look a little bit different; there are still a lot of discriminatory attitudes toward people. Relatives, that has got to stop, because whether we like it or not, we live on this Mother Earth together.

Those discriminatory lines that we draw, whether they be overt, or whether they are made in silence, have to stop. If I had a choice, and this world is coming to a point where we're not going to be able to stop what is going on, if I could have taken those little ones into my house, with two-feet thick walls, and said to them, "Come in here, you're going to be safe from whatever is happening," I would have done it. But I could not guarantee those little ones that.

Right now, we're facing the most critical time, right here in the United States. It's up to us to protect those little ones that are not here yet, those that are born, those that are just growing up now, as adults.

I have a little grandson; he's eight years old. His name is Rain, that's his Indian name. The English name that we gave him is Tyler. I look at my little grandson every day, and I wonder what kind of world he is going to be living in when he's my age. I always say to the relatives that I speak to, if you go out and you borrow something from your neighbor, say you borrow a car from your neighbor, what do you do to that car when you return it? You clean it up, you wash the windows, you vacuum it out, you change the oil, you put gas in it, and you take it to your neighbor and you say, here, thank you. That is if you're a responsible person.

I hate to turn around to my grandson and say, "Grandson, here, this is what I have created for you, this world that I live in, because I'm a part of the total mass consciousness that has created what is going on." We've got to take responsibility, and that is one hell of a thing to try to do in the face of what is going on right now in our nation and in the world.

If there is anything that I bring to you, I bring a challenge, a challenge of life, and a challenge that we can make a difference. Melissa mentioned that I'm a member of the Native American Church. My grandfather and my grandmother were my greatest teachers. They told me, they said, "Grandson, when you go into that teepee and you sit in that circle, you meditate on those things that you want to change in your life. When you walk out the door, the door to that teepee, and the sun is coming up in the morning, take four steps and live just the way you were thinking and just the way you were meditating, or praying in the teepee. That is the hardest thing you are ever going to do." I didn't believe her, and I tried it. I couldn't make two steps, because other things came into my mind. I saw other things that changed my total attitude toward the way we live.

So I challenge you to walk out the door and try to live and try to think of the way that you would want our environment to be. If you can do that, and if you can convince just ten other people to do the same thing, we'll have it made. If one of you makes it, let me know, because we're going to hold you up on a pedestal.

My mother died six years ago when she was ninety-six years old. Her name was Medicine Leaf, that was her Indian name. Her given Catholic name was Santanita. But I went down to see her one time near Christmas, and she was sitting at her table and she was crying. I walked in and I said, "Mom, what's the matter?" She said, "You know, son, I want to buy a little gift for every one of my little grandchildren. But if I buy a gift for my little grandchildren, I'm not going to be able to pay for my gas to keep my house warm." And I said, "Mom, you know, all you have to do is tell me and I'll go down and pay your gas bill." She said, "Son, that's not the point. When you were growing up, you and your three brothers would each bring a load of wood home from wherever you were, put it in a wooden box, and that's how I heated my home. All I needed was a can of kerosene that costs twenty-five cents and a lamp. That was my heating bill; that was my light bill. But as a result of the many changes that have occurred in our culture, we now have modern homes with bathrooms, running water, lights, the total system has changed." We're all going through that. It doesn't make any difference who you are or where you live, corporations are digging into the shallow pockets of poor people, too. They've all got us.

You go into the cities of San Francisco or Oakland, and you'll see on the streets people who are dying of alcoholism, drugs, cancer, AIDS—you name it and they're there. We have a few organizations such as Bioneers, environmental organizations, that are trying to speak for the voiceless. In my own state, I represent one of those organizations, and that's the New Mexico Environmental Law Center. They are doing their best, through legal work, to be advocates for a strong environmental organization to operate in our state.

Time is of the essence. If there's anything that we can do together, let's do it. We can preach to one another, we can talk to one another about good things, but it's a different matter to take an action that is actually going to make a difference. If you have family, take a look at your little ones in your family, take a look at your grandchildren, your daughter, your sons, and say to them, "I'm going to do my best to make this a good place for you to grow up in." Then we have done our job.

This presentation took place at the Bioneers Conference in 2005.

PART SEVEN

Re-Indigenization

28

Re-Indigenization Defined

Greg Cajete, John Mohawk, and
Julio Valladolid Rivera

INTRODUCTION OF OUR SPEAKERS

Greg Cajete: My name is Greg Cajete. I'm from Santa Clara Pueblo and currently I'm the Director of Native American Studies at the University of New Mexico; I'm working to try and re-indigenize the University of New Mexico.

John Mohawk: I'm John Mohawk. I'm a Seneca from the Cattaraugus Reservation. A long time ago I was the editor of *Akwesasne Notes*.

Julio Valladolid Rivera: *Mi nombre es Julio Valladolid Rivera*. My name is Julio Valladolid Rivera. I was born in Huancayo in the Andes. I was a university professor for twenty-four years. I am an agronomist by profession. And I am now learning from the peasants of the Andes.

IMPLEMENTING VISIONS OF
RE-INDIGENIZATION

Greg Cajete: Each of us has come up with a perspective that we're applying in a variety of different ways, in work with plants, in work with education, in work with mothers, in work with Indigenous foods. We are collectively trying to find a vehicle to essentially re-indigenize some perspectives in mainstream thinking. In our own ways, we are trying to change perspectives with regard to individual, tribal, and collective understandings of what this thing called ecology is. We are also looking at how to re-indigenize on a practical level.

One example of a practical tool Indigenous Peoples can use to re-indigenize ourselves is finding, creating, or being a part of information clearing houses. These provide and create opportunities for Native Peoples to communicate with each other, on not only issues that deal with health, but also on issues that deal with the environment and social issues and political issues. In a sense, the clearinghouses have always been happening in Indigenous societies. They have always been evolving as responses to oppression or to various kinds of problems or crises that people have had.

With the Internet becoming more a part of Indigenous societies, or at least some Indigenous Peoples having access to that, you're going to see a kind of development of a clearinghouse kind of phenomenon. You can see that already happening. I know John Mohawk created something like that with the publication of *Akwesasne Notes*. Some of the Indian newspapers have always been, in a sense, a forum and also a kind of clearinghouse for information dealing with Indigenous issues and health. But one of the things that we lack, generally, is access. In many cases this is not only access to resources in terms of money but also accesses to other larger clearinghouses that do exist that have a track record of disseminating information on projects, nutrition, health issues, medicine, water rights, and so on.

For Indigenous Peoples, generally, we're just in the very early stages of beginning to see how we can utilize structures that are already in place, as well as begin to create our own, and also perpetuate the ones that we have always had in some form. Again, it's a struggle to do that. We're always looking for places that we can, in a sense, bring up some of these ideas or bring these perspectives into a greater audience.

We do have issues that deal with nutrition and with health, and those issues will continue and be a very important part of what we do, as Indigenous People, as we network with each other. For example, I'll be going to New Zealand next month for the first Indigenous Education Conference among the Maori Indigenous Peoples and other Indigenous groups. So we actually already have some networks that we are working with. Bioneers is certainly a part of that. It's at the edges. We participate in this, but we also have our own networks that we work with as well. So I think those things are very probable and possible.

John Mohawk: To discuss the issue of re-indigenization I would like to frame it with some context about how things are today. How in the morning newspaper the news was that not only is the Borneo rainforest being burned down but the people that gave the people the matches to burn it down got a big grant from the International Monetary Fund (IMF). Knowing that, I want to say that we're at a period now when we're seeing the end, or at least we're beginning to see the beginning of the end of five hundred years of colonization.

The five hundred years of colonization was about the grossest forms of exploitation of life on earth, human life and nonhuman life, just an incredible period. Of course it resulted in many, many extinctions—extinctions of peoples, extinctions of animals, plants—everything there is. We've been living through this very, very terrible period of conquest. This conquest is still, of course, very much alive in various parts of the world. But we also can find places in the world where the conquest has gone by. It has gone past us.

In those places there's space for re-indigenization, which I say means to rebuild that which was there before that happened, both in the form of human cultures and in the form of bringing back the biodiversity that existed prior to the colonization. At the same time, there's a possibility now of gathering consciousness among many hundreds of millions of people about how this is not only necessary but is a very good thing, a positive thing. This new consciousness will help us rethink terms like modernism and progress, and reexamine where things are going, even to rethink what capitalism can mean. If capitalism as we've known it can be a very destructive process, then we have to redefine it. We have to redefine how wealth is produced and distributed, and review all those kinds of issues.

So re-indigenization means that we're looking at a vision of the world in a postconquest, postmodernist, postprogressive era. Once we see that, we can come to ways to make that real. How we act to make that real is what the Indigenous vision is now. So it's the re-biodiversity, the recultural diversity, the rethinking of the earth as a living being. All of that is what I think re-indigenization means.

Julio Valladolid Rivera: In the Andes of Perú, the Andean culture is thriving. The *campesinos*, who seed their little acreage and scattered parcels do not need to re-indigenize themselves. We, the agricultural technicians who come from these rural areas and have gone off to university—we are the ones who need to re-indigenize ourselves. Our professional training has not allowed us to see the vast richness of agrobiodiversity possessed in the knowledge of cultivation in the Andean culture.

As technicians, we are interested in planting for maximum production. We don't notice that the campesino cultivates with care and dedication. I had to immerse myself for a long time in a period of re-indigenization, learning from them. So, the information about the cultivation of Andean plants that were grown through the application of scientific methods have been of little use to them.

So I needed to learn from the campesinos how to converse with the plants—how to attune myself to the wild plants that "tell us," with their great or little flowering, whether the growing season is going to be rainy or with few rains. This is very important in arid farming that absolutely depends on rain.

In the Andes originated one of the oldest forms of agriculture (ten thousand years old) in the world. At the postgraduate level I took a master's course in genetic improvement of plants and not one course instructed me in this type of agriculture.

Previously, when I carried out scientific experiments, I liked to weigh, measure, and photograph every part of the plant. I was interested in determining the dry weight of each one of these parts, so that afterward I could chart the "growth curves," using the most sophisticated statistical methods in such a fashion that these curves could be expressed through mathematical formulas.

Greg Cajete: The act of re-indigenization is really multiple leveled, and it's happening in many ways in Indian country today. It's a response to many of the things that we know we need and that we have to find ways to recover. My area is education and I had the opportunity of having two educations: one that was traditional and also one that was formal.

In every sense of the word, we are in the process of beginning to define an education process that is going to work for us. Not for the institutions, not for the government, but one that is going to work for us. I think that all the kinds of things that you say, especially within the last twenty years, in terms of Indian people bringing themselves up and beginning to look at themselves once again with some level of dignity and an understanding of the problems and the issues and the ethno-stress that we have all faced, and then coming to terms with that, has really been a very, very dramatic process. It's been a healing process and we're still going through that in our communities.

Among pueblo people, we are some of the most traditional people in the United States in terms of native traditions. Our situation has not been so much trying to recover what we have lost but to actually preserve and to take again a new respect for what we have. That is a different process than recovery and revitalization. It's really stepping back and valuing again something that you generally had taken for granted because you grew up with it. That has been my experience with Pueblo people—we need situations that bring us back, to reemphasize the important things that we know are part of our culture and our communities.

So Indigenous education and indigenization have many levels of meaning. It's very tribally specific. Each tribe attempts to address these issues that are involved with this re-indigenization concept in their own ways. After five hundred years of having to adapt to a colonial power, I think that we're finally in a position to begin to describe and to create a contemporary educational expression that works for us.

If you study the situations of all peoples in the world, they go through this process of struggle and of revitalization. Eventually there comes a point where people realize that we have to make an education system that works for ourselves. That's really where we're at. This includes recapturing the farming traditions among my people, the fishing traditions among my people. Among other peoples it's the tradition of again farming or hunting or fishing or protecting the forest, or protecting the deserts, or fighting for water rights. All of those types of issues come into play as you begin to come up and truly become who you are.

So these are the situations that you'll find in Indigenous society and they're all a part of this process or this idea that we call indigenization.

CULTURAL RIGHTS AND INTELLECTUAL PROPERTY

Julio Valladolid Rivera: I've acquainted myself with some plant varieties, like quinoa, of Andean origin that were patented in the United States. I wonder if it is fair that only those who patent receive privileges and not to recognize the rights in these patents that also belong to the campesinos, who have tended and maintained these varieties with care and dedication for over ten thousand years. The peasants of the Andes who were the ones that created these varieties received no compensation for this. This is a type of biopiracy.

On the other hand, the practice of claiming the "rights of intellectual property" of the campesinos with their plant varieties is a technical process—legally complicated and costly. It requires specialized scientists, which is at this time outside of the economic range of the campesinos; this is why this matter, from the point of view of the typical campesino, is "a pointless affair." The Andean culture is generous. The campesinos will always continue to offer their plants to those who ask for them. They say that if they ask for them, they need them to feed their families and it is good that they take them. It never occurs to them that those plants are taken and frequently patented for their properties, for which they claim legal rights.

In the cosmic view of the Andean campesinos, everything is alive: the hills, the clouds, the stars, the lakes, the rocks, and all of nature, to those who love them and respect them, like the mother who created them and protects them. In the native language Quechua, it's called Pachamama (Mother Earth).

Andean wisdom consists not only of nurturing Pachamama with care and respect but also of allowing for nurturance *by* Pachamama. Receiving the care and respect of Mother Earth is to reestablish a relationship of respect for nature and is the surest way to look after the continuation of life on earth.

John Mohawk: This question regarding the issue of intellectual property rights is one of those that I personally don't like to address. I was very much struck by the reaction that happened in the summer of 1997 in Germany after someone wrote the book *Hitler's Willing Executioners.* They held a whole series of meetings in Germany. The German people acknowledged that fifty-five years ago, ordinary, everyday Germans were involved in the daily activity of horrendous murder—the cold-blooded murder of women and children. They got up in the morning—ordinary, everyday Germans—and performed horrible crimes. It wasn't the Nazis, it wasn't a little group of demonized people. It was ordinary people who got up; accountants, lawyers, doctors, and they went out there and killed people. It wasn't all in the gas chambers. It was up close and personal.

What was striking to me about that is how, across history, that's happened so many times. Too many times. You think about the Spanish in the Caribbean Islands between 1492 and 1516. They got up in the morning and went out and committed torture and murder. When the first Anglos reached California they went about systematically murdering the Indians. Look at Tasmania. Look at the Banta people. You can see this process all across history.

It wasn't a bunch of crazed criminals that did these things. It was ordinary, everyday people who did them. We look back and say, well, that happened a long time ago. No it didn't. It's happening right now in the world today. Forty thousand children die in the world every single day. The major institutions of Western economic adjustments, called "restructuring," have policies in place and the purpose of these policies is to spread hunger and to create destitute people who are powerless in the world.

We do not have a system that seeks to promote life. We have a system that seeks to promote profit, and the cost of the profit is hunger and death on a day-to-day basis. Ordinary, everyday people pretend that they're blind to that. They're not outraged by that. They don't know about it. They'll talk to you about this, that, and the other thing. They're completely oblivious to it.

We give that kind of behavior names like economic globalization. Why don't we call it economic extermination? Let's be clear. You notice I'm still reacting to the morning paper. All the orangutans are now getting killed off in Borneo by fire. Essentially, fire is a product of economic globalization. It's our moment when the spotlight of world colonization and domination is pointed at some place and, of course, the victims of that place aren't always people. Sometimes the victims of that place are ecosystems. Sometimes they're orangutans.

I think that when we talk about re-indigenization, we need a much larger, bigger umbrella to understand it. It's not necessarily about the Indigenous Peoples of a specific place; *it's about re-indigenizing the peoples of the planet to the planet.* It's about us looking at the whole thing in the broadest of possible ways.

So that's how come I have a problem with intellectual property rights. What colonization was about was the commodification of everything. That's what colonization means. Today, it's the colonization of abstract things. It's the colonization in which a property right is attached to something that the person who has it didn't invent. Essentially, nature invented it, the colonist manipulated it, and now he wants to claim it for the purpose of having a profit. As I understand it, the main purpose of this is that big seed companies can sell seeds to the poorest people in the world and charge them for their food that way.

What we're looking at here is the tremendous reality of what we think of as globalization. All of these things are part of that process that concentrates the wealth of the world in the hands of the smallest number of people. This process is almost always done through the use of force, of the state, and through the use of the moral twisting of ordinary, everyday people's consciousness.

That's why I say "ordinary, everyday people." We have to reach ordinary, everyday people. Ordinary, everyday people have to have their sense of moral injustice ignited. It has to be raised a bit. They have to come to understand that they are called upon to care about what happens to the peoples and living things of this world. That's a huge job, but that's the called-upon spiritual call of the re-indigenization of the world.

Greg Cajete: I want to bring to your attention the fact that any rights are essentially about respect. One of the ways that we've dealt with this in pueblo society is that everything we do has a tradition of privacy, a tradition of secrecy. That's basically the way we've dealt with information. It's a strategy that evolved as a result of our situations as we faced the Spanish and had to go underground with our religion and with our practices. In the 1920s we also had to defend ourselves with regard to the federal government that outlawed pueblo religion.

So we have a long history of dealing with this respect issue with others. Those are the things that will begin to be continued with sovereignty and with education and certainly with cultural property rights. Essentially, we have learned from one another that we are not respected and until we begin to see that kind of respect being rekindled at the institutional level, and governmental level especially, then you'll continue to see issues that deal with property rights among Native Peoples being very dramatic in terms of their discussion or their outcome.

I want to bring your attention to the fact that it's November 1 and among pueblo peoples, this is a very sacred time. It has to do with food, incidentally. It has to do with a very special kind of ceremony that all the pueblos are doing as we speak, that deals with the sacrament of food and the paying of respects to where food comes from, and also a thing called feeding the ancestors. Every single pueblo household is doing this right now.

So as you think about your relationship to food, as you think about the Indigenous perspective, I ask that you remember that the Indigenous philosophy is really embodied in some very simple but very profound ritual activities that we perform during the whole year. In some form, in some way, we're doing different things to ensure this relationship, and this communication process that is vital to ourselves and also to the perpetuation of life on earth. If you ever see an Indigenous ceremony you're going to see that every ceremony in one way or another is tied to a central concept of seeking life and reaffirming life. This particular thing that's going on in pueblo country is a very special ceremony.

It's a very special thing because even though I'm away from that, I'm connected to that. It is nothing more than simply taking whatever you're going to eat at this dinner meal—taking a bit and piece of that—and remembering where it has come from; certainly remembering that food is life and food is sacred. Then placing it in a natural place, whether it's a tree or simply rolling it up and taking it somewhere and depositing it where the dirt is, where the water is, putting it in a special place, and saying your own special thanksgiving, if you will, for what that food means to you symbolically and otherwise. Of course, there's more to that than this, but it is a simple act of reverence.

My vision for Indigenous Peoples at this point is that we come in to our own finally as a group of people who have come through a long journey with a great struggle and have again come to find ourselves and to see ourselves once again with dignity. I think that's a very simple statement but in many cases it's a very difficult thing to do. For me education is a passion. I believe it is through the educational process, at whatever level you may choose or whatever expression you may find in it, that will ultimately make the greatest difference. Education about respect. Education about property rights. Education about colonization and decolonization. Education as it relates to plants and also our common connection as Indigenous Peoples of this earth.

So my vision is that we find a way through the process of education, through the process of interaction, to find our face, to find our heart, to find a foundation through which we may most completely express our life. I quoted that basically from a Nahuatl phrase that comes through a piece of poetry that was preserved after the burning of the many libraries in Mexico. But I think it embodies what education needs to be and can be and it certainly is the ideal vision that I have for the next generation of Indigenous Peoples.

John Mohawk: I think what happened sometime around 1450, beginning around there, is that the whole culture fell into a period of madness. It fell into a period of madness when it went on a murderous rampage against people that it perceived to be the purveyors of magic. It found those people and the ones who did the herb medicines, and most of those people that did herbal medicine they found were women, and they went on a murder and torture rampage against women in Europe that lasted three hundred years.

At the same time, they were expanding across the globe and they ran into other people who were also doing herbal medicines and were connected to nature in many other ways that were far more profound than the Europeans had remembered. They'd already lost all of that. They went on a murderous rampage against those people. And then they turned to nature itself and they went on a murderous rampage against nature. You just have to look at the origins of the thinking about that and Francis Bacon and how early science sorted itself out.

All the while that was going on, it was done at the head of their academic world, claiming that they were the purveyors of rational thought. What a lie. What society has exercised more irrational passions for more evil than this society? Yet all of us who have grown up in contact with that society, those of us who grew up within reach of its radiowaves know that, for fifty years they have been pounding a message into our brains that future utopian societies can be built on a foundation of technology and a foundation of engineering and that that's going to build a wonderful future world.

At the same moment, what's been happening is that the biological foundation of our world is being eroded by exactly those people who stood to profit from that ideology. All of us watching what was going on saw nothing but a big advertising campaign. All of us who grew up in that milieu, all of us who've been in the Western educational system, have been continuously told that on the one hand, this is rational society. On the other hand, it has diminished the fact that rationality is only a tendency in Western culture. There are a whole bunch of other tendencies and they're most of the ones in power right at this minute. At any given moment, it's those *other* tendencies that are in power. That's how come intellectuals are never in power in Western government anywhere in the world. Has anybody ever noticed that?

My final thought is that those of us who are conscious of this contradiction are recovering from Western culture. We're in recovery from that. It is that recovery that we must put our attention to—a recovery that involves the whole issue of medicine and plant life; the recovery of community, the recovery of what real, extended family can mean. In most of our cases, we can only start to think about that at this point.

We're in recovery from the effects of more than five centuries of what only can be described as cultural madness. We're identifying it. We're understanding it better. We're making it clearer and clearer to one another. We're a community of people who are not only committed to understanding it, we're committed to finding areas of practice where we can start to peel layers of it off ourselves, of the people in our family, the people in our communities, the people that we work with in our workplaces.

That, I think is a noble effort. But I have to say that I think that it's really hard to express to people the depth of the nature of the damage done to us individually and collectively. My own sense of this is that there's really a lot of hope and a lot of activity going on. You could not have had meetings like Bioneers forty years ago. You couldn't have done it. There wouldn't have been anybody there to grasp anything.

But I think now they're here and they're happy. They're energetic and people are not only talking about the theory, we've gotten to the day where we're starting to talk more and more about the practice. We still need to build the theory more. We still need to understand exactly how things came about. We have to understand how we undo those, how we unhook the major things that pull this, the energy that pulls this. But I tell you, we know the madness now, we've identified the madness now, and we're on our way to figuring out how to counter it.

Julio Valladolid Rivera: In the Andean concept of life, everything is alive—the plants, the hills, the stars, the rivers. Everything is alive. And everything is our family. Even the dead are alive. Today in the Andes, as here in the United States, there are rituals. Peasant families in the Andes prepare food that their dead ancestors like and they put this food out on table for the dead because, as I said, even the dead are alive.

The whole family, including the hills, the rivers, and the dead, with affection and respect raise their plants, their animals, and their countryside. Everything is raised. But not only do people raise the plants with affection and respect, but also the plants raise them. This wisdom is the most valuable thing they have, taken into consideration with Western thought, taking into account the survival of life on earth.

I want to finish by saying that the agriculture of the future will resemble more the agriculture of the first peoples than the commercial agriculture of today. The conception of life must be reinvigorated because it is the guarantee of maintaining life on the planet.

This discussion took place at the Bioneers Conference in 1997.

29

El Poder de la Palabra/
The Power of the Word:
Toward a Nahuatl/Mestizo Consciousness

Francisco X. Alarcón

For a Chicano, for a *Mestizo,** for a descendant of the Indigenous Nahuatl Peoples of Mesoamerica, the Day of the Dead, *el Día de los Muertos*, is a very important community celebration. I will discuss how this tradition is a manifestation of *Mestizo* syncretism of Mesoamerican cosmology. I will also share some reflections on my own journey in reclaiming an ancient Mesoamerican consciousness, which has led me to propose a new ecopoetics that advocates personal and collective empowerment for restoring global balance.

But first, I will honor the four directions and will invite all present to join me in doing a collective invocation. I will burn this small leaf of sage I hold on my hand as *una ofrenda a nuestros ancestros*—as an offering to our ancestors. Fire in the Nahuatl tradition is the symbol of life, of

---

Mestizo is a Spanish word that identifies a person of mixed racial/ethnic background. It does not have the negative connotations of its English equivalents, "half-breed" or "half-caste," and it has been increasingly accepted as a term of self-identification by Latinos both in Latin America and in the United States.

passion, of love, of remembrance, of the spirits. To Brother Smoke, out of the burning sage stick, I entrust our message, asking for permission, pleading for all blessings, as I recite aloud this ancient Nahuatl invocation to one of the oldest and most sacred powers in Mesoamerica, *Huehueteotl*, the Very Old Lord of Fire:

Prayer to Fire

can niman aman	*right here I call you now*
nomaca nehuatl	*I myself*
nOxomoco	*I, the First Man*
niCipactonal	*I, the First Woman*
nicmatiHuehueh	*I, the Old Man's friend*
nicmati Ilama	*I, the Old Woman's friend*
niMictlanmati	*I, traveler to the Underworld*
niTopanmati	*I, traveler to the Heavens*
nomatca nehuatl	*I myself*
nitlamacazqui	*I, Spirit in Flesh*
niNahualtecuhtli	*I, the Enchanter*[1]

After saying this "Prayer to Fire," I invite you to join me in calling the four main cardinal directions of the earth. We will start with the North, then turn clockwise toward the East, next face the South, and end up in the direction of the West. After completing a full circle, we will return to the center for the last invocation. As we send out sage smoke as our offering to each direction, we will repeat four times an ancient Nahuatl word that, even in the sixteenth century, eluded any clear definition but that functions as a greeting and calling to the spirits. In 1629 in colonial Mexico, Hernando Ruiz de Alarcón wrote that the Nahuatl natives would call to the four directions at the beginning of rituals by repeating, four times, the word *tahui,* an ancient expression that even he was not able to decipher: "[The natives] repeat four times this word *tahui,* which nobody understands today," he writes in his *Treatise.*[2]

In the Nahuatl tradition, North is the direction of the primordial element earth and the location of the Land of the Dead, *Mictlán*, which is ruled by a duality that is both female and male, *Mictlancihuatl* and *Mictlantecuhtli*, the Lady and the Lord of the Land of the Dead. We begin by facing North and calling on our ancestors who, it is said, came originally from the North—to grant us their wisdom. And we do so by calling out *tahui!* toward that direction four times.

We then honor the direction of the East that embodies Fire; from this direction the sun rises every day. East is the direction of our birth, of our childhood and youth, of passion, and it is ruled by another female/male duality, *Xochiquetzal*, the Precious Flower, and *Xochipilli*, the Lord of the Flowers, who are the protectors of love, of the arts and poetry, and of what is really most precious in life. So that we can continue enjoying the gifts of the arts in all our endeavors, we turn to the East and evoke that direction by saying again tahui! four times.

Next, we honor the direction of the South—of Water, of the green land of abundant rain, of corn, of *jitomatitos, frijolitos,* and *chilitos*. That's the fertile land of Mesoamerica where my *familia* and ancestors came from. The direction of the South is dedicated to honor all women and is moved by another female/male duality, *Chalchiuhtlicue*, the Lady of the Streams, and *Tláloc*, the Lord of Rain. And so that we can have the sprouting, cleansing, and healing power of Water with us, we face South and again invoke four times the word tahui!

Then we acknowledge the West. This is the direction of Wind where the sun goes down at the end of the day. In the Nahuatl tradition, the West also represents the end of our life journey. And as the sun sets in the western horizon, it is *Tlazolteotl*, the Mother of All Seasons, who waits for us at the end of our days. She is the all-forgiving Mother who makes us all again part of the earth, in the sacred cycle of life and death. This direction honors all warriors, who—like the revered Mesoamerican cultural hero *Quetzalcoatl*, the Feathered Serpent—are willing to dedicate themselves for the betterment of all humanity. When we celebrate the Day of the Dead, we are connecting with our ancestors, and so that we may have faith in ourselves and hope in the future, here we invoke

Tlazolteotl and *Quetzalcoatl*, the Lady and Lord of the West and great protectors of humanity, by chanting four times *tahui!*

In the Mesoamerican tradition there is also a fifth direction; many people seem to be unaware of it, and so, there is a lot of debate on this one. Some say that the fifth direction is up toward the sky, some say that it's down deep inside the ground. Mesoamerican *tlamantine,* wise Elders, explain that the fifth direction is really the person next to you. There is a very powerful Maya mantra that summarizes the best of human ethics: *In Lak' Ech,* which translates as *Tú eres mi otro yo* (You are my other I). In the invocation of the fifth direction, we all turn and face each other. Everyone is truly a mirror of each other: that nose, those eyes, that mouth, that person you see in front of you is in reality yourself looking at yourself. But each of us is also an irreplaceable and unique human window to the universe. That's why we now invoke the ancestors of all the people congregated here and call on the spirits of all traditions to join us as we say to each other four times the sacred call and greeting: tahui!

I have to confess that it is with some hesitation—and after literally agonizing for weeks—that I put in writing, with some detail, a ritual that, for the most part, for me and many others, is really part of an ancient oral tradition. Personally, I have facilitated or performed the ancient Mesoamerican ritual I explained above hundreds of times. I have done this in the most diverse settings, literally covering most aspects of human events, from intimate rites marking life, like weddings and funerals, to public ceremonies involving hundreds of people (some even a few thousand). Once, I even did it in the Senate Chamber of the California State Capitol, in Sacramento, during the official inauguration ceremony of a lieutenant governor.

But I have come to the conclusion that, like poetry, this is something I didn't really choose to do, rather, it's something that "has chosen" me. Let me elaborate a bit more on what I'm saying here. When many of my closest friends were dying of AIDS during the early 1980s in San Francisco—where I lived at the time—it was me, the most agnostic and least "spiritual" of the group, who, maybe out of frustration and a sense of impotence before death, dared to speak up and take up *la palabra.* I remember feeling a very painful sense of silence as I stood in a circle of friends, around a dearest friend, who lay dead in the middle of a bed inside a Mission District flat that had been mine until some years prior.

We all stood mute for a long time and then just started crying, feeling helpless, defeated, rejected, condemned to suffer the insufferable, with no words to weep our sorrow, no prayer to heal our wounds. Most of us had been raised as Catholics but did not want to relapse to that faith system that, as adults, we found very oppressive and homophobic. It was with anger and a sense of desperation that Nahuatl word formulas and prayers that I had learned from my Grandma Elvirita in Mexico and from other Elders came rushing to my mouth, and I have not stopped espousing this wisdom ever since.

RECLAIMING OUR MESOAMERICAN HERITAGE

We are now going to move to an examination of Mesoamerica. Let's go back sixty thousand years, back to the time of the first human dwellers of Mesoamerica, the cultural region (now Mexico and Central America) that existed before the arrival of the Europeans.* It is a very important place for many reasons; from this geographical area of the world some of the most original human civilizations have emerged. My family comes from the state of Jalisco. My grandmother was a Nahuatl speaker who was part of the vast cultural continuum of Mesoamerica. For me, it's truly miraculous that I'm connected to that tradition.

When I was seven years old I went to the top of the Pyramid of the Sun in *Teotihuacán*, an archaeological site located about thirty miles northeast of Mexico City. This is the largest pre-conquest urban center, a sort of a Mesoamerican New York. It's a huge and extremely well organized, multi-ethnic metropolis, one that still mesmerizes urban planners and architects. The Pyramid of the Sun is truly a man-made

---

*The date of arrival of the first "Americans" keeps moving further back in time. Many scholars hold that there is evidence that people arrived at the American continent at least 60,000 years ago; others push back this date to closer to 100,000 years ago.

mountain. You have to climb some 365 stone steps to get to the top, each step representing a day in the solar year, so when you go up the steps you go symbolically through a whole year of your life. To honor this history and this place I will share some poems with you, because poetry communicates in ways that prose cannot. Poetry allows us to travel through time and space. This is my poem, "Four Directions." Every time I read this invocation to the four directions I can see myself on top of the Pyramid of the Sun:

Four Directions

West

we are

salmon

looking for

our womb

North

eagles

flying

the Sun

in our beak

East

coyotes

calling

each other

in the Moon

South

we turn

into snakes

by eating

chile

eating chile[3]

We have been through five hundred years of silence. Today, things are happening in connection to the Mestizo consciousness. It is part of a "re-indigenization" process; I love that one, the concept of *la reindigenación*. The idea that we have to somehow connect again with the cultural continuum that America is about. America did not start in 1492, not in 1776. America goes back thousands of years. And I really believe for America to *be* America, we really have to become Americans and know the mythologies and the peoples that have been here for thousands of years. This poem has to do with silence:

Silence
I smell
silence
everywhere

clean
nice home
smell

banks
smells
so do malls

no deororant
odorizer
or perfume

can put away
this stink
of silence[4]

For many of us, our America has been taken away from us. Our America has been invaded, occupied, whitewashed, gagged, suppressed, sanitized, and at best, ignored. But against all odds, the cultural tradition of Mesoamerica has survived and is alive, well, and all around us. It cannot be reduced to just museum artifacts, bones, and stones. It can be found in the flesh and spirit of many contemporary native and Mestizo peoples. Our mere existence is a testimony of our ancestors' will to live. The realization of this basic fact is both simple and complex.

Mesoamerica as a civilization permeates all aspects of our daily lives, from the food we eat, the colors we prefer, to the ways we behave, worship, and even dream. Our nightmares and our visions are anchored in the psychodynamics of a Mesoamerican worldview. The syncretic nature of the *Virgen de Guadalupe* is a case in point— ancient Mesoamerican goddess worship continues under a Catholic disguise.*

Tonantzin

Madre	*Mother*
¿aquí estás	*are you here*
con nosotros?	*with us?*
enjuáganos	*wipe up*
el sudor	*our sweat*
las lágrimas	*our tears*
Coatlicue	*Coatlicue*
tú que reinas	*you who rule*
sobre las serpientes	*over snakes*

---

*According to tradition, the *Virgen de Guadalupe* appeared and spoke in Nahuatl to Indian Juan Diego in Tepeyac, a hill in the outskirts of Mexico City, where *Tonantzin,* "Our Mother Goddess," was worshipped. Her image has been espoused to several social movements and causes both in Mexico and the U.S. Southwest. For example, she was on the first Mexican flag of Father Miguel Hidalgo's Indian army fighting for independence from Spain in 1810, on the banner of the Mestizo popular armies of Emiliano Zapata in the Mexican Revolution of 1910, and also appeared in California along picket signs in the 1965 Delano grape strike organized by Chicano union leader César Chávez.

Calchiuhcueye	*Calchiuhcueye*
haznos	*grant us*
el favor	*our request*
Citlalcueye	*Citlalcueye*
que nos guíen	*let your stars*
tus estrellas	*guide us*
Guadalupe	*Guadalupe*
sé nuestra aurora	*be our dawn*
nuestra esperanza	*our hope*[5]

Mestizos and Mestizas have been actively engaged in a profound cultural revolution throughout this hemisphere during the span of the twentieth century. The universalist notion of the *Raza Cósmica*, proposed in the 1920s by Mexican philosopher José Vasconcelos as the fulfillment of a Western humanistic utopia in which all human races intermingle to form an all-inclusive cosmic progeny, has now been molded into the "new Mestiza consciousness" being advanced by Chicana writer Gloria Anzaldúa in her moving *Borderlands/La Frontera: The New Mestiza* (1987):

> The new Mestiza copes by developing a tolerance for contradictions, a tolerance for ambiguity. She learns to be an Indian in Mexican culture, to be Mexican from an Anglo point of view. She learns to juggle cultures. She has a plural personality, she operates in a pluralistic mode—nothing is thrust out, the good, the bad and the ugly, nothing rejected, nothing abandoned. Not only does she sustain contradictions, she turned the ambivalence into something else.[6]

This new consciousness has been shaped by the present realities that we as Mestizos and Mestizas must face in our daily lives in the United States. It also implies a common struggle against the racism, classism, sexism, homophobia, and other forms of oppression still common in our complex society. But Anzaldúa warns, "Awareness of our situation must come before inner changes, which in turn come before changes in society. Nothing happens in the 'real' world unless it first happens in the images in our heads."[7] One of the most pressing changes that needs to happen is our recognition and celebration of a cultural face of ours that has been suppressed and denied for so long—our living Mesoamerican heritage.

DIALECTICS OF *MESTICISMO*[8]

This awareness of our Mesoamerican past should be projected into our present and our future in radically new ways. Not in the nostalgic or romantic modes a la Jean-Jacques Rousseau ("the noble savage"), but as the liberating praxis of a new Mestizo/Mestiza ("mixed-bloods") consciousness. I have called this praxis, *mesticismo,* which purposely combines Mestizo/Mestiza and *misticismo* ("mysticism"), to differentiate it from *mestizaje.*

Mestizaje is a term that commonly refers to the historical mixing of the races and cultural traditions in Latin America, sometimes as a direct result of sexual abuse and downright exploitation of Native Peoples and African slaves by European colonial powers. Mesticismo comes out of the experiences that the dominant cultures have confined to the realm of the "other" and the "marginal," those condemned to live dangerously in psychological and cultural borderlands. *El Mesticismo le da vuelta a la tortilla* (Mesticismo turns things around) and sets out a fluid ontology in which any notion of "self" must include the "others," equally trespassing upon neat demarcations like subject/object, human/nature, us/them, and other similar dichotomies common of Western thought and mythologies.

Old Mesoamerican paradigms are beginning to be studied and understood within their own systematic worldviews. Mesoamerican myth and wisdom, religion and science, have often been dismissed out of ignorance or petulance. Most missionaries and modern scholars have failed to recognize this Mesoamerican world as another human totality. As a cultural universe in itself, Mesoamerica has always been a constellation of different peoples, a historic area full of contradictions and riddled by conflict and ambiguities. But until now its sheer originality has been glanced over, mostly by missionaries, archaeologists, anthropologists, and historians. It's about time for contemporary artists, poets, and writers to interpret this reality in their own terms.

America must be able to see, hear, touch, taste, and smell this America. This may well lead us to new ways of "seeing, " "reading," "feeling," "thinking," "creating," and "living." Why not envision, for example, a new ecopoetics grounded in a heritage thousands of years old that upholds that everything in the universe is sacred? Ancient native paradigms could possibly offer some viable alternatives to modern dilemmas. Old keys could open new doors.

RECLAIMING
A SYNCRETIC ECOPOETICS

For me, this new liberating Mestizo/Mestiza consciousness not only embraces "others" as equal and unique human beings but also calls for a new global awareness of the "oneness" of all living creatures and of nature as a whole. This vision of the "oneness" of all life is shared by many of the ancient earth-worshipping religions, the shamanistic spiritual traditions of Native Peoples in the Americas, Siberia, and other parts of Asia. In the Western cultural tradition, mystics (saints, visionaries, poets, and other outcasts) have left moving testimonies of their own epiphanies and encounters with this "oneness" of all creation. Some of them experienced very special intimate connections with the divine in the cosmos: achieving ecstasies (the ultimate orgasms).

In the Mesoamerican spiritual tradition, we encounter manifestations of this engrained vision of the "oneness" of all life in which the "self" is not alienated from the surrounding nature. In the Mesoamerican mythologies, humans interact with animals, plants, and the forces of nature in very close and profound ways. One of the best examples of this worldview is the Popol Vuh, a genesis book of the Maya Quiché people of Guatemala that has been acknowledged as a Mayan bible. This book was written in 1558 by an Indigenous scribe who wrote the Mayan language using the Latin alphabet. This book records the ancient oral tradition that survived the burning of most native codices by zealous Christian missionaries and Spanish colonial authorities. In 1701 a Catholic priest named Francisco Ximénez found the book in his Santo Tomás parish in Chichicastenango, Guatemala, and translated it to Spanish.

In 1854 this manuscript was snatched from the library of the University of San Carlos in Guatemala and taken to Europe by Abbot Brasseur de Bourbourg, who translated it this time to French and subsequently sold the manuscript to another collector, Alfonso Pinart. After Pinart died, his widow sold the manuscript to Edward E. Ayer, who brought it back to America, and placed it in the Newberry Library of Chicago, where it is today.[9]

Another notable example of a surviving account of the Mesoamerican spiritual tradition involving native religion, myths, beliefs, and medicine, is a colonial treatise on Nahuatl magic and curing practices. Entitled *Tratado de las supersticiones y costumbres gentílicas que hoy viven entre los indios naturales desta Nueva España, 1629* ("Treatise on the Superstitions and Heathen Customs That Today Live Live Among The Indians Native to This New Spain, 1629"), it was written by Hernando Ruiz de Alarcón (1587–1646), a Catholic parish priest born in Mexico.

De Alarcón had been commissioned by the Spanish Inquisition to record the Nahuatl magical spells and healing practices a hundred years after the conquest of Mexico. Hernando Ruiz de Alarcón was a younger brother of the more famous Juan Ruiz de Alarcón (1581–1639), also a native of Mexico who spent most of his life in the Spanish royal court in Madrid and is considered one of the greatest playwrights of the Golden Age of Spanish literature. Hernando Ruiz de Alarcón, based in his parish of Atenango, a small town in the present state of Guerrero, spent ten years compiling, translating, and interpreting the Nahuatl spells and invocations collected from fifty different Nahuatl informants living in communities in the states of Guerrero and Morelos, in the central part of Mexico.

In a long interview with me done by Kenny Ausubel and later published in his book *Restoring the Earth: Visionary Solutions from the*

Bioneers (1997),[10] I explained in detail how mostly by chance I came across Ruiz de Alarcón's *Tratado* in the National Museum of Anthropology and History located in Mexico City. After studying Nahuatl and reflecting on the *Tratado* written by another Alarcón who could also be a distant relative of mine, I decided to write a poetic response to his *Tratado*. The end result of this process was *Snake Poems: An Aztec Invocation*, a book of 104 poems published in 1992, the same year of the Columbus Quincentennial.[11]

As part of *Snake Poems* I decided to include thirty Nahuatl invocations and spells from the *Tratado* in their original language, alongside my English versions of the same spells. *Snake Poems* is a syncretic poetic text in which ancient Nahuatl spells converge with postmodern verses, with irony functioning at different levels. If Hernando Ruiz de Alarcón's main objective in recording this magical tradition was to suppress and eradicate native beliefs and heathen healing practices based on ancient Mesoamerican spirituality and religion, by writing down in scrutinizing details the Nahuatl spells in their original language and then translating them into Spanish, he ironically ended up preserving for posterity the same magical heathen tradition he wanted to destroy. The ultimate irony is that a Chicano poet also named Alarcón, some four hundred years later, using the colonial Alarcón's "writings" learns "to undo what is done" by writing a postmodern *Tonalamatl* (Spirit Book) with a diametrically inverse sense of urgency: the reclaiming of an ancient Mesoamerican ecopoetics.

Tonalamatl/Spirit Book

> *pages*
> *whisper*
> *sigh*
> *sing*
>
> *glyphs*
> *dance*
> *left*
> *to right*

I follow
the drums
the scent
the stairs

mountain
mist
sprays
my hair

I learn
to undo
what is
done

an ancient
jaguar
roars at
my face

I start
singing
all kinds
of flowers[12]

Songs
xochitl
flower
flor[13]

This process of cultural reclamation calls for the retrieval of a syncretic poetic praxis that I have called ecopoetics to stress the deep sense
of interconnection linking the poetic self and nature. Ultimately this

poetic self dwells in the collective consciousness and/or sense of "oneness" with the surrounding ecosystems. When doing public readings of *Snake Poems,* I usually start with the invocation to the four directions—as I explained at the beginning of this essay—and burn some sage and copal (tree resin). Since this ecopoetics is eclectic, I believe it should also appeal to all the senses. The main purpose of this ecopoetics is to reconcile and heal the internal split experienced by any Mestizo (also felt by most people currently living on the planet), which is a direct result of the relentless world expansion of the West at the expense of conquering, colonizing, and exploiting Indigenous Peoples, their cultures, and their lands. And to make sure that Hernando Ruiz de Alarcón listens, I read—in both Spanish and English—the following poem addressed to him:

Hernando Ruiz de Alarcón (1587–1646)

eras tú	*it was you*
al que buscabas	*you were looking for*
Hernando	*Hernando*
hurgando	*searching*
en los rincones	*every house*
de las casas	*corner*
semillas	*for some*
empolvadas	*dusty seeds*
de ololiuhqui	*of ololiuhqui*
eras tú	*it was you*
al que engañabas	*whom you tricked*
y aprehendías	*and apprehended*
eras tú	*it was you*
el que preguntaba	*who both questioned*
y respondía	*and responded*

dondequiera	*everywhere*
mirabas moros	*you saw Moors*
con trinchete	*with long knives*
y ante	*and in front of*
tanto dolor	*so much sorrow*
tanta muerte	*so much death*
un conquistador	*you became*
conquistado	*a conquered*
fuiste	*conqueror*
sacerdote	*priest*
soñador	*dreamer*
cruz parlante	*speaking cross*
condenando	*condemning*
te salvaste	*you saved yourself*
al transcribir	*by transcribing*
acaso	*maybe*
sin saber	*without knowing*
el cielo	*the heavens*
soy yo	*I am*
el de tu cepa	*from your tree*
el de tu sueño	*from your dream*
este cenzontle	*this mocking bird*
del monte:	*in the wilderness:*
tu mañana	*your tomorrow*[14]

Most of the Nahuatl spells in the *Tratado* include a phrase, *nomatca nehuatl*, in which *nomatca* means "myself" and *nehuatl*, "I." This phrase could be translated into English as "I myself." I believe this phrase establishes the position of the speaker in a shamanistic incantation in which the subject and the universe are one. Nahuatl is a compound language in which new nouns can be formed by bringing together different words. In Nahuatl we could link the word *nehuatl*, meaning "I," with *amatl*, which means "paper, book," to form a new compound noun, *namatl*. This really defies the Western logic of English since it would mean "I-am-the-book," which in English doesn't make much sense, but in Nahuatl, *namatl* makes perfect sense. In the invocation used for planting corn in the *Tratado*, the shamanistic phrase appears at the beginning:

For Planting Corn

Ruiz de Alarcón (III:4)

nomatca nehuatl	*I myself*
nitlamacazqui	*Spirit in Flesh:*
tla xihualhuian	*hear me, Tonacacihuatl*
nohueltiuh	*elder sister*
Tonacacihuatl	*Lady of Our Flesh*
tla xihualhuian	*hear me, Tlalteuctli*
Tlalteuctli	*Mother Earth*
ye momacpalco	*on your open hand*
nocontlalia	*I am setting down*
nohueltiuh	*my elder sister*
Tonacacihuatl	*Tonacacihuatl*
ahmo timopinauhtiz	*don't shame yourself*
ahmo tihuexcapehuaz	*don't grumble*
ahmo tihuexcatlatlacoz	*don't laugh at us*
cuix quin moztla	*tomorrow*
cuix quin huiptla	*or the day after*
in ixco icpac nitlachiaz	*I want to see again*

in nohueltiuh	*the face of my elder sister*
Tonacacihuatl	*Tonacacihuatl*
niman iciuhca	*let her stand*
in tlalticpac hualquizaz	*on the ground*
in nicmahuizoz	*I shall greet*
in nictlapaloz	*I shall honor*
in nohueltiuh	*my elder sister*
Tonacacihuatl	*Tonacacihuatl*[15]

This was not just a metaphor; corn *is* your sister—made of corn. *Nomatca nehuatl* for me is sort of the "abracadabra" in this spiritual tradition. We recognize ourselves as part of the universe. There's no separation between the self and the universe.

This next poem, I believe, should really be danced. I've actually done this with friends of mine, Aztec dancers. One of my friends, Gina Pacaldo, was nine months pregnant when she performed this poem at MACLA, a Latino cultural center in San Jose, California. And she was so wonderful when she did it; it was a true magical experience:

Nomatca Nehuatl
I myself:
the mountain
the ocean
the breeze
the flame

the thorn
the serpent
the feather
the Moon
the Sun

the sister
the brother
the mother
the father
the other

the ground
the seed
the chant
the cloud
the flower

the deer
the hunter
the arrow
the neck
the blood

the dead
the dancing
the house
the quake
the lizard[16]

There is a wheel of twenty days in the Mesoamerican solar calendar, and there's another wheel of thirteen days. So for those two wheels to reconnect again at the same sign, they have to go on for twenty days, fifty-two times. That's why we have fifty-two years in a Mesoamerican century. In the year 2011, there's going to be a big celebration, because that's the year we will be entering a new cycle of time in the Mesoamerican tradition. We have come through five suns or human eras. The first one was the Sun of Earth, the second was the Sun of Water, the third was the Sun of Fire, the fourth one was actually the Sun of Air, and now we are in the fifth era or Sun of Movement. The current one is basically the new sun, the Sun of the Flower, the final blossoming of humanity.

Chicano poets and artists since the 1960s have been involved in the process of reclaiming a sense of a group identity, connecting themselves with the Indigenous cultures of the Americas. Cultural celebrations known as *Floricantos* have been organized from time to time in Chicano communities throughout the United Sates. *Floricanto* is a Spanish compound noun formed by bringing together "flower" and "song," a translation of the phrase *in xochitl in cuicatl,* which in Nahuatl means "poetry." The last poem of *Snake Poems* is a celebration of this ancient ecopoetics:

In Xochitl In Cuicatl

cada árbol	*every tree*
un hermano	*a brother*
cada monte	*every hill*
una pirámide	*a pyramid*
un oratorio	*a holy spot*
cada valle	*every valley*
un poema	*a poem*
in xochitl	*in xochitl*
in cuicatl	*in cuicatl*
flor y canto	*flower and song*
cada nube	*every cloud*
una plegaria	*a prayer*
cada gota	*every rain*
de lluvia	*drop*
un milagro	*a miracle*
cada cuerpo	*every body*
una orilla	*a seashore*
al mar	*a memory*

un olvido   at once lost
encontrado   and found

todos juntos: we all together:
luciérnagas   fireflies
de la noche   in the night
soñando   dreaming up
el cosmos   the cosmos[17]

An important celebration in the Chicano/Latino communities in the United States, one that brings about a heightened awareness of a personal and collective connection with the Mesoamerican tradition, takes place around *Los Días de los Muertos* (The Days of the Dead) on the first and second day of November. Some people mistakenly refer to it as the "Mexican Halloween." But this is a syncretic celebration that, on the surface, is a Catholic feast but in reality is a commemoration of Mesoamerican spirituality.

Instead of the fear of death and the cover of disguises pretending to trick death, there is a celebration and acceptance of the cycle of life that *includes* death. It involves all aspects of the human drama, the sublime as well as the humorous ways. In San Francisco, California, since the mid-1970s, this celebration involves a community procession with the participation of thousands of residents and visitors, with colorful paper banners, and Aztec dancers. This procession ends in a neighborhood park where community altars honoring the dead are built.

For many years I have been involved in this community celebration by calling the four directions at the beginning of the procession and in each of the four focal points during the procession. In 1996, as part of the ritual ending the procession, I read an invocation I had written dedicated to our friends, family members, acquaintances, and all people who have died of AIDS. This invocation could well summarize the healing purposes of an ecopoetics that reclaims the past to forge a better future.

Tlazolteotl!
Goddess of Love
Goddess of Death
Eater of Filth
Mother of All Seasons:

Mother of the Rivers
cleanse your son
with waters flowing
from the Fountain of Youth

Mother of the hummingbirds
dry off his last tears
kiss each aching bone
dress him in morning flowers

Mother of the Mountains
caress him with murmurs
take him into your bosom
the dream of your deepest canyon

Mother of the Night
weep with us
light his path with the stars
of the Milky Way

Mother of the Sea
embrace his ashes
turn him into bright red coral
amidst schools of laughing fish

Mother of all Seasons
Eater of Filth
Goddess of Death
Goddess of Love

Tlazolteotl![18]

This presentation took place at the Bioneers Conference in 1997.

30

Mending the Split-Head Society with Trickster Consciousness

Melissa K. Nelson

The complex realities of Indigenous life and *all* life today requires us to study the resistance, survivance, and persistence of over five hundred Native American Nations over the past five hundred years. It is truly amazing how many of our ancestors were able to adapt to and accommodate all of the colonial efforts at removal, relocation, assimilation, and extermination by different European, then U.S., powers. It is also remarkable that Indigenous Peoples survived and thrived for tens of thousands of years before the era of imperialism. Historically, no other group of people has that record. They witnessed and outlived numerous floods, fires, climatic shifts, and other major ecological cycles of change. Our cultural survivance from colonialism and our physical viability over millennia are testaments to the power and strength of our Indigenous Knowledge and lifeways.

Today all of humanity faces unprecedented ecological and social crises. These crises are having a dramatic impact on Native Peoples around the world. These global challenges only confirm our understanding of the destructive patterns of colonial systems on lands and people. Every day the negative impact of capitalistic industrialism is seen on our planet's life support systems. This should cause all people who are concerned with a viable future to rethink the dominant paradigm that is causing such ecological damage. Are there healthier ways for the land and water and our children to live?

Even with all of these complexities and challenges, Native American elders and leaders like Ohlone chairwoman Ann Marie Sayers say, "Today is the best time to be a California Indian since the time of contact." What does she mean by this? I understand her meaning to be that these days Native Peoples are finally being recognized as human beings who have rights. This was not the case even thirty years ago. I think she may also be referring to the extraordinary Indigenous cultural movement occurring across the earth—native groups are renewing so-called extinct languages, recovering ancestral lands, and are actively maintaining and revitalizing traditional knowledge systems and cultural practices. Despite opposition, Indigenous Peoples are restoring their Original Instructions in a modern context.

Since 1993 I have directed a nonprofit organization called The Cultural Conservancy (TCC). In 2005 we celebrated our twentieth anniversary, giving us over two decades of experience working with Indigenous Peoples on cultural revitalization and environmental protection. We've learned a lot, received a lot, and have given a lot. This organization and the experiences it has facilitated have been a profound teacher of intercultural synergy and reciprocity with the land. We've been working with and on behalf of Indigenous communities on many interrelated issues such as sacred site protection, environmental restoration, resource management, language preservation, audio recording and media-making, indigenous health, and native foods. We are proud to have assisted in the preservation of many cultural treasures including the Southern Paiute Salt Songs, the Mojave Creation Songs, the Mother Earth Songs of the late Shoshone spiritual leader Corbin Harney, and the Kongpo Songs of Tibet. Each of these tribes and native communities has full control of these audio recordings and use them for their own revitalization and educational purposes. We have worked with many native groups on the protection of sacred sites and ancestral lands, including the Winnemem

Wintu of Mount Shasta, the Kogi of Colombia, the Hawaiians on Maui and O'ahu, the Ohlone of the San Francisco Bay Area, and an intertribal group of California Indians in their efforts to protect a rare native plant-gathering site in Sonoma County, California.

The central question that I address in my professional work as an Indigenous rights activist and American Indian Studies professor, and personally as a mixed blood person is, how do we decolonize and re-indigenize our native communities, starting with ourselves? Related questions are: how do we halt and reverse the erosion of traditional cultural practices and the degradation of the environment? How do we renew our connection to and care of the land? How do we renew our Indigenous Knowledge systems and resist what Vandana Shiva calls "monocultures of the mind?" How do we revitalize ourselves from the inside out? A Tongan Elder friend Emile Wolfgramm always asks the question, "Are we worthy of the conspiracy of our ancestors?" These questions help me reflect on my thoughts and actions, and how I answer them lets me know if I'm being part of the problem or part of the solution.

Paraphrasing what Albert Einstein and many visionaries after him have stated, we cannot solve our global crisis with the same thought process that created it. Indigenous Peoples have sustainable, time-tested practices that go back thousands of years. Profound experiences and connections to nature are inculcated in spiritual and other practices. These place-specific "Original Instructions" are blueprints for how to live sustainably within our home ecosystems. Not only do they guide us on how to positively interact with the environment—plants, animals, trees, winds, fire, clouds, rain, soils, stars, and other life-forms—but they also describe how to interact with "all our relations"—people within clans, villages, tribes, nations, and other peoples of the world. Whether a neighboring tribe, an insect nation, an island people, or an unseen relative, the Original Instructions give us ethics and protocols for how to honor and respect this gift of life in its many manifestations. It's very important that we recognize these special teachings within our own traditional knowledge system and respect the diversity of "instructions" given to other cultures. By honoring who we are as Native Peoples we are able to understand other cultures' struggles. This understanding enables us to stand in solidarity with other Indigenous Nations and ethnic communities. Together we can support each other's efforts to heal, and to restore ourselves from the storm of colonization.

There are many different ways that we can revitalize our cultures and decolonize our lives. Indigenous Peoples are responding differently and creatively all over the world. I want to offer two specific ways that we do this work. First of all, to decolonize our minds, we need to embrace a type of trickster consciousness to break out of the binary thinking imposed on us by Eurocentric thinking. Cultural arts and Indigenous languages are two of the best ways to support this mental decolonial process. But what do I mean by trickster consciousness? It's a term coined by Anishinaabe scholar, Gerald Vizenor, who writes about the importance of different ways of thinking and how to free the mind of the limits of the Western intellectual paradigm. Trickster consciousness helps facilitate a paradigm shift in our thinking. As Vizenor articulates, "Trickster consciousness is a comic liberator that craves chance, surprise, difference. The trickster is a healer in a fragmented world. The trickster denies singularity, monocultures, and completion. The trickster is communal, sensuous, erotic. The trickster is going to help us get us to our next place."[1] And trickster mediates between supposedly contradictory forces or elements by retaining aspects of both, something that our Western paradigm often has a difficult time with. Ojibwe artist Carl Beam has called this process "trickster shift."[2] Canadian scholar Allen Ryan explains this meaning, "What Beam calls the 'trickster shift' is perhaps best understood as serious play, the ultimate goal of which is a radical shift in viewer perspective and even political positioning by imagining and imaging alternative viewpoints."[3]

We see in the dominant Western world that decisions are often based on "either/or" thinking—it's either this or that, black or white, Republican or Democrat, in or out, for us or against us. This binary thinking has so thoroughly pervaded our minds that it has become an unconscious reflex in thought. Historically, through a multiplicity of languages and lifeways, Indigenous Peoples have honored differences in thinking and being. The trickster, the coyote, as an archetype, as a person, as a cultural hero in our oral traditions and stories, is a teacher and reminder of plurality, diversity, paradox, humor, surprise, and humility. Trickster forces us to retain an understanding of all sides of a story by revealing them to be coexisting parts of one greater whole—interconnected and indistinguishable. There are numerous native ceremonies, rituals, and practices, such as the role of the Hopi Clown, the Okanagan Four Societies process, and the Lakota Condolence ceremony that encourage the understanding of diverse points of view. It is thought that this flexibility in thinking and the embracing of humor also helps us overcome pain and hardship.

One of the ways we can invite this trickster consciousness or coyote way into our lives and decolonize our minds is through traditional cultural arts: music, dance, weaving, carving, beading, regalia-making, sculpting, painting, and other mediums. By engaging the hands with natural materials—wood, plants, stone, pigments, leather—or engaging the mind with song, music, and sonic imagination, we can disrupt our Eurocentric conditioning. There is something about the rhythm of using our whole bodies and other parts of our minds that opens up a more fluid way of knowing and being. All artists know that when you are "in the groove" or "in the flow"—using your hands, bodies, and minds in creative ways—that the trappings of Cartesian logic fall away. We are not thinking of the past or concerned with the future. We are present in the moment as an integral part of creation. This creative liberation is a foundation and form of cultural sovereignty.

We are re-indigenizing ourselves by using our native languages, which is no small feat when a language has been in the oral tradition with no written record, when it was beaten out of you in boarding school, when it was forbidden by the government who would withhold food rations if you didn't speak English. The brutal legacy of colonization is felt in every aspect of life, and language is one of the core places where identity and traditional ways of knowing spring from. Consequently, native languages were targeted by the U.S. government, which focused on eradicating Indigenous languages through assimilation programs, including the infamous American Indian boarding schools. But even this systematic attempt at colonizing Indigenous minds was not completely successful.

I am just a beginner in learning *Ojibwemowin,* my Ojibwe language, but even the little bit I have learned has already shifted my fundamental perceptions of space and time, energy and matter, and the essence of reality. For example, in the older, more advanced Oijbwemowin there are four past tenses, four present tenses, and four future tenses. This fact alone opens up a new way of thinking about time and reality. Ojibwemowin, like many native languages, is verb-based, so actions and doings become more important than nouns or things.

If we want to embrace trickster consciousness and disrupt colonial patterns of thought, then we have to learn our native languages, our mother tongues. By learning and supporting the syntax, grammar, vocabulary, and the sounds of native languages, we are gaining intellectual flexibility and cognitive prowess—skills that are necessary to decolonize the mind. Learning our Indigenous languages is a way to recover intellectual sovereignty. Thankfully, there are dozens of major national Indian organizations focused on the revitalization of Indigenous languages and there have been two major national laws passed to stop the erosion and support the recovery of Native American languages (P.L. 101–477, the Native American Languages Act of 1990 and H.R. 4766, the Esther Martinez Native American Languages Preservation Act of 2006).

There's a vigorous cultural revitalization and renaissance happening today with Indigenous artists, culture bearers, and language keepers all around the world. With every native word we learn, every wooden drum we build, every new song we create, every heirloom corn we grow, we are reconnecting to our cultural heritage and our native imagination. This is re-indigenization. Today, due to technology and some of the benefits of the western world, Native Peoples are using film, computers, recording equipment, and other technical tools to create modern Indigenous art—digital storytelling, mixed-media paintings, websites, TV shows, DVDs, and other exciting new media.

If you're lucky enough to live in the San Francisco Bay Area, we have the American Indian Film Festival every fall, where our modern-day storytellers use the film medium to tell stories of survival, tragedy, family, youth, and humor. These modern Indian stories remind us of trickster's teachings and help educate nonnatives that Indian people are still alive today and involved in their cultures, heritage, and lands.

The Cultural Conservancy has had the privilege and honor of working with the Southern Paiute Nation on a major project, the Salt Song Trail Project. It is part of a decolonizing and healing process. We co-produced a film, *The Salt Song Trail: Bringing Creation Back Together*, which addresses the colonial impacts of the boarding school experience and provides proactive tribal solutions for how to heal from it. Indian boarding schools were absolutely devastating for the loss of traditional culture—they were the most significant assimilation tool used by the U.S. government and Christian churches. So much has been lost as a result of that experience.

This same assimilation-through-boarding-school colonial process has occurred in other Indigenous territories around the world, including all of the Americas, Canada, New Zealand, Australia, and other Pacific Islands. In Australia they call the young Aborigines who were taken to these schools, the "stolen generations." Chickasaw law expert James Sakej Henderson and others call this group the "Split-Head Society," those who were taken to boarding school and assimilated into Euro-centric ways. He says they have retained their aboriginal souls but have been colonized with Eurocentric heads. In many ways, most of us modern mixed-blood native people are members of this Split-Head Society.

So how do we re-member and heal and put ourselves back together again? Native Elders and leaders are saying that we need to reclaim our traditions and we need to do this by going back to places like boarding schools and have healing ceremonies there. We need truth and recon-ciliation to be able to move forward as whole people. In environmental circles we hear a lot about ecological restoration, which is absolutely critical. But at Bioneers and at Indigenous gatherings we also talk about cultural restoration and spiritual renewal. If we are going to reharmonize nature and culture in a modern context then we need to talk about how all of us are going to heal and learn from these destructive legacies of colonization.

In 2005, our Cultural Conservancy team went to the Sherman Indian Boarding School in Riverside, California, with members of the Southern Paiute Nation. There we participated in and documented a healing ceremony as a much needed rite of passage for all of the children who died there and never went home. The singing of the Salt Songs are a traditional way the Southern Paiute honor their dead, in this case those children who didn't go back to their homelands and have a proper ceremonial transition to the next world.

These Salt Songs are the sacred songs of the Paiute people and they are used at funerals, memorials, and wakes. They are also traveling songs, some would say that they are similar to the songlines of the Australian aborigines in the sense that they describe both physical and metaphysical geographic sites and places on their cultural landscape. The Salt Songs travel through Utah, Nevada, Arizona, California, and along the Colorado River. The songs also aid in peoples' travel and serve as orienting devices. When a loved one departs from the physical world they travel on a spiritual journey; the songs describe that journey on a spiritual trail. So these songs are healing for the person who passes on, but they're also a healing for the family members who are left behind.

We went to the Sherman Indian Boarding School cemetery and we were honored to be invited to participate in and film the ceremony that was held there. There are sensitive issues involved with filming ceremonies, and this invitation indicated great trust and friendship. But we still had to debate it and talk to Elders and sit in council for many hours to work through the concerns. Ultimately, Salt Song singers felt that it was necessary to bless these children with the Salt Songs and make a visual document to recognize the truth of what had happened there. It was critical to have this intergenerational healing ceremony for those children and their families. Afterward, the singers and family members said they felt like a weight had been lifted from them and tears of joy were shared.

It is crucial to recognize that both Canada and Australia have had official truth and reconciliation processes, reports, and laws passed that have recognized the horrible history of boarding schools and their negative intergenerational impact on the Indigenous populations. Both countries have issued apologies and have approved settlement agreements to provide financial reparations to Aboriginal people who were forced into boarding schools (called residential schools in Canada).[4] As of 2007, the U.S. government has not had any similar process or recognition of the negative impact of the American Indian boarding school experience. It is still a dark, hidden secret of this country, especially with the government and many churches.

Our project and film were done collaboratively with a group of Paiute Salt Song singers and tribal members, most notably the two Salt Song Project codirectors and visionaries, Kaibab Elder Vivienne Jake and Chemehuevi leader Matthew Leivas. They see the Salt Song Trail project as having many dimensions. It is a decolonization and healing project because they are decolonizing what happened to their people from the boarding school experience. They also see it as revitalization project because they are maintaining and restoring their Salt Song Trail tradition—their songs, the stories within the songs, the trail the songs describe, and the languages and the knowledge that are encoded in those songs. Through the beauty, depth, and power of this ancient Salt Song cycle, the Southern Paiute and those touched by the project are experiencing a "trickster shift." We are transforming the tragedy of the boarding school experience into one of empowerment and intergenerational healing. We are changing poison into medicine, mending our split-heads, and recognizing our wholeness.

This is a project that's very near and dear to my heart and I have learned many important life lessons from Vivienne Jake, Matt Leivas, and the other Salt Song singers. We have created a model of a tribally based healing and revitalization project using modern technology. We are helping to document all of this so the Paiute have new tools (CDs, DVDs) to teach their youth. It involves spiritual, cultural, and ecological restoration and shows how all of these are intimately related. The next phase includes expanding the DVD with more interviews with Salt Song singers, boarding school alumni, historic photographs and audio recordings, and a remapping of the trail. We plan to continue to locate historic and sacred sites along the Trail and go to them for healing ceremonies and teachings. Hopefully, through our collaborative efforts, we will be able to regain access and care for some sites so Paiute people can again gather their salt and their medicinal plants as they used to do for thousands of years.

For Indigenous Peoples, when you lose languages, you lose land-based practices; when you lose natural resources and biodiversity, you lose cultural knowledge. Conversely, when we recover Indigenous languages and affirm cultural arts, we restore the native landscapes, habitats, and ecological relations that support those voices and creative expressions. These cultural revitalization actions open up trickster consciousness and aid us in decolonizing our minds.

Nature and culture are intimately entwined, not only for Native Peoples, but for *all* peoples. Many nonnative peoples have just forgotten that. Some native peoples have too. But many today, across the globe, are waking up to this fundamental relationship and are simultaneously dropping harmful patterns and embracing healthful behaviors, reharmonize our cultural lifestyles and practices with the gifts and limits of nature.

All peoples who have experienced some trauma can benefit from the gift of Indigenous survivance. Humanity and the earth are in places of trauma now—and we all can learn from the native experience, from trickster consciousness, to heal the earth and ourselves.

This presentation took place at the Bioneers Conference in 2005.

31

Re-Nativization in North and South America

Tirso Gonzales

Today the colonizer mentality, in one way or another, dwells in more than 90 percent of the total human population on Earth (including Indigenous Peoples)—an outcome of imperialist expansion, globalization, and modernization à la Western mechanistic style. Underlying the clash between the European colonizer (their descendants included), and the Indigenous Peoples' cultures, there is the clash of entirely different worldviews, ways of knowing, and ways of being. Throughout the last five hundred years, the colonizers' modern, mechanistic, postenlightenment, Cartesian worldview has pervaded Indigenous societies around the world. First Nation scholars Marie Battiste and James Youngblood Henderson comment, in the following way, on Eurocentrism: "It is the imaginative and institutional context that informs contemporary scholarship, opinion, and law. As a theory, it postulates the superiority of Europeans over non-Europeans. It is built on a set of assumptions and beliefs that educated and usually unprejudiced Europeans and North Americans habitually accept as true. As supported by the 'facts,' or as 'reality.'"[1]

The current, global, environmental, ecological, societal, moral, and spiritual crises inform us about the fundamental past and present flaws of the colonizer's Euro-American worldview. Perhaps this can be expressed as the result of navigating in the widespread, shallow, and, as Karl Marx noted, "frosty waters of egotist calculation." Some of the main characteristics of this Euro-American worldview are that it is anthropocentric and grounded in the Judeo-Christian and Cartesian cosmovision. This vision places man above nature, considers the earth as dead and inert—something to manipulate from outside, and exploitable for profits.

This Euro-North American worldview emphasizes the importance of the individual: life moves around men's material needs; innovation is protected by individual property rights; truth is only possible through science; only what is tangible is real; materialism is the only thing that matters; spirituality is irrelevant, and nature is an endless source of resources. This approach to life is obviously flawed and fragmented. This worldview practiced at home, school, and work is the most important factor in this global crisis. It has been and persists in being a recipe for disaster. It is the template of unsustainable development practices that have impacted Mother Earth, life as a whole, and communities, rural and urban, all over the world in a very erosive manner, for the last five hundred years.

Today, the colonizer mentality not only continues to threaten and undermine Indigenous Peoples' communities, languages, cultures, lands, territories and places but it threatens the descendants of the colonizer as well. Place, in Quechua and Aymara, is called *Pacha,* the representation of the cosmos at the local level. The local *Pacha* is the fundamental base for long-term communities: the community of nature, the community of human beings, and the community of gods and deities. These are the basic elements of life's sovereignty. Water, air, land, energy, and the seed are facing serious challenges in their cycles to sustain the regeneration of life. The loss of respect for life and its sacredness are reflected in the unsustainable type of development carried out by the colonizers and neo-colonizers throughout the last five hundred years. What is called for is a paradigm shift, from the Eurocentric paradigm to Indigenous/ecocentric ones. We can respond to that call for this transition by becoming natives to this land, by *re-nativizing* ourselves.

Indigenism (*Indigenismo* in Spanish) in Latin America is strongly associated with assimilation. This type of policy has been proposed by the state and a conspicuous group of urban middle-class intellectuals—some of them Marxists. In the context of Latin American colonized erudite intellectuals, the term "re-indigenization" can easily be interpreted as part of a process of neo-indigenism, in the same way that processes of cultural affirmation and decolonization in the Andean-Amazonian region of Peru have been termed "Neo-narodnism" or "Neo-campesinismo" or "Neo/re-peasantization" or simply "a return to the past."

Such facile, fancy conceptualizations are, in fact, to be understood as misinterpretations stemming from Eurocentric, positivistic disciplines. They are pronounced by very disciplined scholars who are more than ready to forcefully adapt reality to their non-Indigenous approaches, responding to their own interests in self-serving ways. In the end, they serve the needs of their disciplines, not the needs of communities.

I would like to suggest some ideas in regard to the issue of re-indigenization/re-nativization or becoming native to this land and its relation to the decolonization of land-territory-body-mind-spirituality. The proposition means different things to different people. We have different stories, different histories—precolonial, colonial, and neocolonial—different experiences, different pasts, different presents, and different futures. The situation involves different agendas but re-indigenization/re-nativization is critically important for peoples in the North and for peoples in the South, as well as for native peoples from the Americas, and ultimately for all the peoples of this earth.

Sacredness, reciprocity, nurturing, and respect are key concepts embedded in ancient Indigenous Peoples' worldviews. They are the pillars in procuring dialogue and balance among all the communities: nature, human beings, and deities/gods. This is an undervalued currency in modern societies around the globe. Two serious issues facing the Indigenous world are due to development and its insatiable exploitation of nature where scarcity becomes the rule and the pollution of the basic elements of life are a direct consequence. The second major issue is Indigenous language erosion and/or disappearance. This is a permanent threat to Indigenous ways of knowing.

Through language we not only express our view of the world; language connects us deeply *with* the world, with "all my (our) relations." Place and language revitalization as part of a process of cultural affirmation and decolonization is central. Many Indigenous communities and individuals are rapidly losing their languages. I have experienced losing the language of my mother, the Aymara language. This, in the (neo) colonizer's dominant Eurocentric view, is part of a no-return process of hybridity, assimilation, a dilution of identity. In the (neo) colonizer's point of view this way is a positive signal of modernization: acculturation is to become who you are not.

In the past, the conscious efforts of the colonizer to marry native women from the native elites to colonizers was not based on sexual attraction or love necessarily; it was also part of a hungry and self-interested strategy to secure power and control of resources. Of course, sexual violence took place, in the past and even today. The racist Eurocentric nomenclature for this genetic mixture and outcome in the Americas was and still is: the mixed-blood, half-breed, the Mestizo, the Métis, the cholo, the ladino.

In the context of Peru, it means *ni chicha, ni limonada* (wishy-washy). The paradox is that the colonizer coined the term *mestizo* but never used it in Europe. Despite the great historical mixture of races that has taken place and still does, nobody in Europe, in particular in Spain, calls him or herself Mestizo. And there are strong reasons, as Native American scholar Jack Forbes has noted a long time ago, for the European people today to call themselves Mestizos.[2] The racist term mestizo, has dismembered the identity, hopefully temporarily, of a vast sector of Latin American people.

Due to insidious racism—subtle/veiled/unveiled—today this sector does not acknowledge and/or claim their Indigenous background, much less the worldview and languages associated with it. Today, as well as during the colonial past, being Indian or having an Indian background is a stain; for that reason many in Latin America feel forced to forget their Indigenous background or call themselves "peasants." Being Indian in Latin America is equated with being primitive, ignorant, reluctant to change, and basically stupid. It is something very bad. For that reason many people in South America prefer to put their Indian Andean-Amazonian ancestors "under the carpet." These racist processes, however, are now going into retreat due to the new development in re-ethnicization. Re-ethnicization simply means to acknowledge our ancestors, our identity, where we come from, and what our deepest roots are. It is to re-engage with an Indigenous-ecocentric worldview.

Modernization/development theories in connection with Indigenous Peoples have an almost natural assimilationist component. According to modernization theories and governments, Indians in Latin America were supposed to become *campesinos* (peasants) and later small conventional agricultural entrepreneurs. Thus, in the best-case scenario, they would become modern. In the worse case scenario Indians would simply vanish.

The fact is, however, that the Indigenous population has not disappeared. It is growing. In fact as some critics of past Latin American Census have noted, a new Indian census in Latin America would show that the Indian population could be as high as 100 million. So the Indian population is not only growing, but there is also an ongoing process of digesting different forms of modernity. This peculiar process of digesting colonization and neo-colonization can be observed in countries like Mexico, Peru, Ecuador, Bolivia, and Guatemala. As Eduardo Grillo[3] has noted, the old colonial hacienda and the republican hacienda are gone, and some cities are being reshaped from an Indigenous view.

Re-nativization means to regain the strength of who you are and how you want to be connected to this world and to your specific community. Re-nativization may mean for non-Indian people who I have met in the North, a beginning to reconnect themselves to Mother Earth and revisiting the past, their histories, their family stories, and how they want to procure balance and harmony among all living beings in the world. This is a process in the making. Just take a look at youth movements such as Slow Food in Europe, Canada, and the United States, the organic agriculture/permaculture movement, Pesticide Action Network, Youth for Environmental Sanity (YES), and Native Movement, among many others.

These are issues that we should pay close attention to. Re-nativization doesn't mean the same thing for everybody. For at least 45 million people in the Americas—North, Central, and South America—re-nativization involves different agendas, because we have been impacted in different ways by the historical process of colonization and neocolonization. In more recent times, we are affected by the economic globalization process that is basically handled by major international development agencies and the industrial world.

For Indigenous Peoples around the globe, in particular those in the Americas, re-nativization implies, for once and for all, fulfilling self-determination; with this comes respect for their lands, territories and the communities embedded within—nature, human beings, and deities/gods. As the British Columbia Assembly of Nations and the Union of British Columbian Chiefs have expressed this at the First Nations Summit: "Indigenous Peoples have the right of self-determination, and the right to survival, dignity and well-being."

This presentation took place at the Bioneers Conference in 1997.

32

Taro Roots Run Deep: Hawaiian Restoration of Sacred Foods and Communities

Mark Paikuli-Stride,
Eric Enos, and Nalani Minton

Three Hawaiian (*Kanaka Maoli*) leaders share their profound native philosophy of *Aloha 'Aina*, "to love that which nourishes you," and provide on-the-ground examples of the relationship between spiritual revitalization and ecological restoration in Hawaii. Through the lessons of their sacred food, Taro (*Kalo*) and related cultural practices, these stories of re-indigenization inspire a truly holistic approach to healing humanity's relationship with the land.

Nalani Minton: As cosmic peoples, the Indigenous Peoples of the earth realize that the problems of genocide and planetocide that have been generated over the last couple thousand years need to be healed from a profound level, from a cosmic and spiritual level. It's good to hear the voices of our ancestors to remind us how to live. In the ancient languages of our traditions, we believe that our people love the land so much that when we "die" or transition, we merely enter another dimension . . . so we can always call upon our ancestors, who are always with us . . . for their guidance, wisdom, and help.

Mark Paikuli-Stride: My name is Mark Paikuli-Stride, and I'm the co-founder of an organization called Aloha 'Aina Health Center. We're located on the windward side of the island of Oahu. *Aloha 'Aina* is an old term in Hawaiian. It means "to love that which nourishes you." *'Aina* in Hawaiian means land. The reason we named it that is because we feel the land and our environment gives us all that we need to sustain ourselves. The problems that we're facing are problems that [people] are facing all over the world. These projects that we're being introduced to [at Bioneers] and even our projects in Hawaii give us hope for a better future, and we need this to move forward.

Another thing that really sticks in my mind is the webbing of the community—people starting with the spiritual revitalization of themselves, their communities, and their families. We are facing some challenges today and if we don't deal with them now, our children are definitely going to be facing these challenges. It's best we start preparing for them.

Kalo [taro plant] is the main staple of the Hawaiian people. As we face the loss of our agricultural land in Hawaii, a big part of the culture is being taken away. The health of the people is declining, our water is becoming contaminated, and cancer is on the rise. Hawaii is one of the leading states for prostate and colon cancer in men. For women, we're one of the leading states for breast cancer. These problems continue to rise, as well as ADD and autism.

We know that being taken away from the traditional diet is a big part of this problem, and being taken away from the land to grow this food is really the source of the problem. Part of the spiritual revitalization starts with our connection back to the land; that's how we spiritually revive ourselves.

We bring a lot of the kids and families to the wetland terraces that are up in the back of Maunawill Valley. They range anywhere from five hundred to one thousand years old. We've reopened an old archaeological complex that had been abandoned for hundreds of years and was in an area of agriculture that is in question right now. I am part of a co-op of banana farmers and that's how we were fortunate to get into this valley. When we came into it, we prayed, talked to the *Kupuna* (Elders), and we decided to reopen the taro patches that were on these banana lands.

One of the things we are facing in this valley, is that the State has required that we only grow bananas on these lands, so this was an issue that we had to really pray upon and find guidance about with regard to the right time to make the move onto the land and how to do it. Fortunately, we've been able to restore around twenty-six taro patches in this area. The valley is loaded with taro patches, which is a sign of how many people this land used to sustain at one time. There are springs coming out of the valley, out of the rocks, that feed these taro patches.

I can't say enough about this plant. Reconnecting to the land and to this plant has changed my life. It's really this spiritual and physical nourishment that people need in Hawaii.

Three generations of people are on the land. That is our focus right now and it really starts with community and family, trying to reach out to families, bring them back to the land, let them reconnect to the land and the culture, and let the land inspire in them in what they need to do. It's very healing and bonding for the parents and their children.

Access to these kinds of lands is very hard. There are not a whole lot of taro farmers left in Hawaii. Our access to the mountains, our access to gathering foods and medicines, is being taken away very quickly. The average cost of a single-family home in Hawaii right now is $600,000. This is frightening for me because I have five children, and I just can't even fathom how we're going to be forced to live in a system to even survive on our own lands in Hawaii. An acre of agricultural land is going for around $80,000. That is a low-end price now.

We are trying to reach out to the community and bring back awareness, not only to the Hawaiian community, but to all the people who are living within our community. We need to live and work together, and we need to preserve our resources for future generations.

You're going to hear the word *ahupua'a* throughout all of our stories. It is a division of land that runs from the mountain to the ocean, and within this area are all our resources—food, shelter, water, clothing, and medicine. It's a management system of these resources. Each family that lives within each of these ahupua'a has a responsibility to maintain this ahupua'a. We're trying to reach out to the families and help them to understand that we need their help.

We try to tie health into everything. Everybody's smiling in the taro patch. It's a wonderful thing. The kids love to get into the taro patches and into the mud. It's very healing and reconnecting. You can eat the taro plant from the top to the bottom. You can eat the leaf, which is high in calcium, like a dark, leafy green; you can eat the stem. They are finding medicinal properties that aid in digestion, so I've heard that pharmaceutical companies are actually capsulizing it and using it as an aid for digestion. Then, of course, taro is a starch.

Being that we're in Hawaii, in such an isolated place, around 80 percent of our food is imported and access to healthy food is very hard. There are a few health stores on the island of Oahu, maybe a handful, but you rarely see local people going into these places. The access to healthy foods is almost impossible, and then we're forced to eat a diet that's not of our genetics.

Our goal is to educate and bring awareness to these lands, and while we're cultivating and revitalizing these lands, we're putting them into protection. We really have to educate around that food production and make these foods available. We partner with some very family-oriented schools. We work with foster families and issues of drug and alcohol addiction and the same thing happens every time: when they're able to make this reconnection back to the land, you see their spirits soften and their hearts soften, and they're able to be receptive to things that are being told to them through the land to heal themselves and heal their family.

We're partnering with several organizations whose goal is to save and preserve the sacred sites and also to revitalize and restore these food production areas, and to be ecological stewards of our ahupua'a. We find that reaching the child isn't the only way. It has to be a holistic and whole family movement. These traditions that were held within the ahupua'a were morals, values, and traditions that held the family together. We need those values today.

One of the things we're facing now working with the youth is that families are broken. They're facing so many problems that the mother is sometimes no longer the caregiver. Both of the parents are out of the house, the children are roaming free and getting involved in things that they shouldn't get involved in. Ice (methamphetamine) is an epidemic on our island right now and it's devastating families.

I'm a recovered ice addict, cocaine addict, and alcoholic. The land was a major healing part in my life, and I know that the land can heal. I know that the land provides if we can only listen and give back what it asks for.

Traditional farming is organic farming, and that is give and take. You don't take, take, take and deplete and deplete, where nobody will have it after you. This is the mentality that we have to get into to make sure that our children are going to have something in the future.

In our community, houses are selling for over a million dollars. My parents moved into Kailua and they bought their house for $70,000. These houses now are going for $500,000–$800,000. Houses along the ocean where our access used to be open—we could go camp down at the ocean, make bonfires, fish—we no longer have that right anymore. Our access to the ocean is narrow strips, and we're not blaming the people, but we need to soften their hearts in some way. We need to find a way. One of the ways is also bringing them and giving them a cultural experience and letting them see what we're talking about, that this is something that can help everybody. Indigenous Knowledge is key. Science is a big part of it, but the Indigenous Knowledge is something that's been passed on from generation to generation. There's so much that we can learn from it.

It softens my heart to see children in the taro patch with big smiles. It's sad, sometimes, that we have Native Hawaiian children come to the taro patches, maybe seniors in high school, and they've never been in a taro patch before, never been in a stream and caught the little marine life that's in the stream. Storytelling happens when kids come to the land. The genealogy goes directly back to the kalo plant. There's around 226 acres in our co-operative of farmers and there are four farmers actively farming right now. The rest have faded out. This is a situation we're dealing with now, to revitalize our co-operative of farmers.

In the valley that I'm farming in, which is under a state lease, if our organization or our co-op wanted to deal with the state on renegotiating our leases, our lease lands would go to open-auction bid. The head of the DNLR, the Department of Natural Land and Resources, already told us that you would not see any Hawaiians in that valley if this were to go back to the state. The highest bidder would come in and they would get control of that valley. This is happening all across the state of Hawaii. Foreigners are coming in and buying up whole ahupua'a. They're turning them into million dollar houses. They're not farming these lands like they were meant to be.

We're working with other organizations to try and get our food back into the schools, which is very important. It's unfortunate that we're finding the youth losing their taste for our traditional foods, which is going to be a problem. We need to give them these foods so that they understand.

When we came to this land, it was all trees and bushes. This really is where my heart is—to reach out to the families, reconnect them, help them, and work together with them in restoring these places. My children are the motivators driving me, because I know that if my wife and I don't make these changes and we wait for other people to make these changes, we're going to be sorry. It's for the future generations, our kids, and our grandkids. If we don't do something now, we'll be watching from the other side and we won't be happy with what's happening.

Eric Enos: Aloha. The faster we become citizens of the world, the better this world will be.

One thing that really makes me sort of sad is when I see people say, God Bless America. I think why only America? God loves everybody and we should see everybody as auntie, every person as uncle, every person as grandmother, every person as grandfather, and every child you see should be our child, too. That's a responsibility we have to the world, the world citizenship. We truly believe, as Indigenous Peoples, that everyone is Indigenous. We all come from the earth. We all share her breath and her life.

Where I am from, we're in the back of the valley of Wai'anae on the island of Oahu. The idea of Hawaii being for someone else is the reality that we are facing. All of the people I work with do not have a chance to live in their own homeland. Native people in Hawaii have very few chances. The only chances they have are these reservations called Department of Hawaiian Homelands, and they're just like the reservations in the United States. They are the lands that nobody wanted. We can take those lands and we can still reaffirm our values, but it's a struggle every single day.

We all came from the sea. If someone were to say, what is a Hawaiian, I would begin with the ocean and the things that cling to the rock that come out of the ocean itself. Because in all our cultures a Hawaiian was not a person that walked with two feet—it's the wind, the rain, the clouds, the animals, the plants. Those were our first ancestors. What's really interesting is that all Indigenous Peoples understand this—that our creation came from the turning of the heavens. In our creation chants we talk about that: the beginning of life was the swirling and the turning and the movement of the universe itself. Then it talks about the sea. It told us that these are the things that we came from, and that human beings are way, way, way down the line. Before that it was all these things that nature gave us.

Our community is a very rural, dry community. I can tell you a story about when all of our valleys were taken away. Eighty percent of our people ended up as "squatters" on the outskirts of Honolulu. We were all uprooted from our lands, and that's our history. It's the same history that you all know, you've heard the story, but it happened in Hawaii also—the illegal overthrow of Hawaii by U.S. forces.

We went up into the only valley on the coast of Wai'anae. Many magnificent valleys are owned by the military or private landowners. We have no access to our mountains or watersheds. The only places we have are little strips along the ocean.

We've had no identity to the mountains for the last three generations. We only got into this land through a fluke because state lands and leases are political plums of those that supported the government leadership. One of the political leaders in the community went to jail, so his lease to this land was up for grabs. Under the model cities program, Lyndon Johnson's great war on poverty, community action and legal aid programs came about, but the social programs came out of the burning of Watts. The country said, Whoa, we need to start paying attention to what's happening to the inner cities. At this time, the community was organized and they had a nonprofit board that could go after this lease, and they got it. The landed gentry in our community were very upset about this.

I was with a youth program and we went up into the valley and found no water. As we walked on the land, we cleared the trees on it and found that these were abandoned taro terraces. We looked at these things and tried to figure out how to get them back. We were looking at the land and clearing it with the youth programs, but we needed water. About a mile up into the valley, there is a place where they planted sugar plantations at the turn of the century, dammed the streams, and took the water out of the valley for sugar. We went up there in the exact place where they had dammed it, and there was a little bit of surface running water. I tried to get permission to use this surface runoff water for our project, and I found out how many different ways government can say no. In the summer of 1978, we said yes, and we did it. This was an illegal act.

One coconspirator was the mayor of the summer youth program. One was a social agency in our community that stuck out its neck to help us get a little loan so we could buy two-inch PVC pipe. Another coconspirator was a University of Hawaii waste systems engineer who showed us how to stick this pipe into the abandoned sugar cane ditch, put in a little dam and a screen and bring the water down. We brought it down during the summer.

I knew nothing about taro. I went to a private school for Hawaiians—

one of the richest schools in the country. We ate our traditional food one day a year. I knew nothing about Hawaiian history. The whole purpose of that school, and it was all done with the best of intentions, was to make good, industrious white men and women out of Hawaiians. I don't think these people had evil intentions, they just felt that everybody needed to be like them. We said, well, maybe we need to look at what's positive about *our* culture.

We learned about taro and I learned how to grow taro from Russians in Wai'ahole—they're wonderful people, they brought the state to the Supreme Court in water rights—but it's really curious where we learn, where the knowledge comes from, because a lot of our knowledge was lost, but not totally. I think there are First Nation stories of a fragment of their ancestor, and that fragment, that little bone, brought back life again to that person.

There are very poetic chants that talk about where water is found. There's such beauty in the thinking of people who have worked with the land and the water for thousands of years, and their stories, their myths, are in the songs and the chants. The poetry in these songs is incredible, powerful poetry.

The color of our land up there has changed. When you first went up there, it was dry, barren, brown, yellow, and it's just through bringing this water down that it turned green, a beautiful green, and life came back. This is where we reconnected with our Elders; we reconnected against tremendous odds. We are bringing back the traditional fishing canoes. All of these exciting things are about the healthy watershed, from the rain-fed mountains out into the deepest, bluest part of the sea, and it has to be healthy. We're developing curricula in the schools, taking Indigenous Knowledge and matching it up with the Department of Education standards.

People do not have access to healthy food. If you go to families in the markets and check out what they're buying, it's canned goods, canned soda. We are growing our own fish now in our programs with a hatchery in our community.

Public housing is another reality in Hawaii, the poor man's Hilton.

There is no place to farm or fish, but plenty of places to buy drugs. It's loaded. The meth epidemic in Hawaii is incredible. Lualualei, the largest valley in the state of Hawaii, is a naval ammunition storage facility. One resort offers artificial reefs, the best fishing grounds with no public access. It's land for the wealthy, and all our communities are being faced with this.

Homelessness is another issue.

How are we going to go back to our own communities and build communities around these values, values that we all share as uncle, as auntie? Because when we look at somebody, we look for family and bringing people into the family, because racism is a tool that they've used against us to divide us. And the idea is one world, one nation.

We gathered people in the valleys and talked about the cultural sites. We are reviewing the process of community organizing, and we are doing that kind of cultural archaeology so we can learn how to transform these sites. We want to achieve reforestation in the mountains, bring back the traditional foods, bring back the cultural anchors, and bring back a connection to youth, in part by creating programs in the schools to help us achieve these aims.

Nalani Minton: As "Hawaiian people," we are a Pacific Island people. We're the Maoli of Hawaii. We're related to the Maohi of Tahiti and to the Maori of Aotearoa or what's called New Zealand in colonial terms.

When I came home from college, I spent about ten years living with Kupuna in different valleys on different islands learning our medicine and healing traditions. For the next fifteen years, I was involved with the voyaging canoe Hokule'a, that reconnected us to different parts of the Pacific and to our Pacific identity. Our culture is an antidote to a lot of the duality of living in foreigner-controlled, contemporary life. Our culture has helped us to find our spiritual identity in the face of many problems, including the huge population collapse of our people and many of the disparities that we all still live with. We are trying to remedy this by planting the seed in each generation to go to the source of life itself, and to learn to protect those natural relationships that allow us to be self-determined people.

As *Kanaka Maoli* we believe not only in self-mastery of all the things we need to know to survive and help our families and community and culture survive, we believe in being self-correcting. We work in the natural ahupua'a settings, where you have the cloud zones where the moisture comes and the high forests that bring that moisture down to an elevation where you can cultivate your food and all the things that you need. We have the *kahakai*, the shoreline area, which is so rich with all different kinds of life, and on out beyond the fish ponds into the deepest ocean. That is a model of peace, because each area itself has all that is needed to sustain life.

We have to look at the natural systems that predate the monetary and colonial systems imposed on earth and the peoples of the earth for the past couple of thousand years. How did people live when they were relating to the cosmic nature of life, to the movement of stars and the ability to be whole beings? In the long voyaging canoes, we felt different parts of ourselves come alive and integrate. We hadn't felt that for a long time, because we hadn't voyaged for a long time.

When you look at all the migratory patterns of butterflies and lobsters and crabs and all the birds and different animals that create an electromagnetic field of energy and of life around our planet, you realize that human beings used to be part of that, and that part of whole-being experience is part of the antidote to some of the terrible alienation, contamination, and poverty that has been created by the destruction of nature. That nature is within us as well. We say as Maoli, Maohi, and Maori, we're genetically related in relationships as families, where the soul is placed in the body, the three *piko*: the piko at the top of our heads that connects us with our ancestors and the cosmos; the umbilical piko that connects us with our mother, our family and the earth; and the genital piko of creation that connects us with our children, the future, and future generations. That knowledge, identity, and *kuleana* (responsibilities and relationships) are not only in our present time, but that past, present, and future are actually all one space/time continuum.

When I went to the United Nations, Geneva, for the Decade of Indigenous Peoples (1992–2002) to report on Indigenous rights and on the health conditions of our Maoli people, I listened to over eight hundred speakers a year. Often they were discussing genocide and war and the terrible effects of destruction. But there was also a level of relanguaging that came from Indigenous cultures, where the collective memory is much, much longer than the last few decades or even the last couple of thousand years. That is the part that renewed a sense in me of who we really are as Indigenous Peoples, as whole beings in the universe—there is this connection to everything as family.

When we say that we're related to all life forms as family, part of what we mean by that is *kino lau*. As Kanaka Maoli, we believe that when we leave the body at "death" or at a transition period, that our spirit can take any form. In Hawaii we believe that the love of the land of Hawaii itself is so strong that we never leave, that there are layers of ancestors who are around us who we can call upon or who we can recognize and whose mana we can connect with for protection and support.

One of my cousins in Hawaii is a noninstrumental, navigator, Nainoa. He has trained over a hundred navigators in the last twenty-five years during the time of the long canoe voyages. One of the things he noticed was that the information in the sky was telling him a whole story about how to place ourselves within the right star line so that the land we are seeking in a canoe actually comes to us, too. We are connected by that star line because we're under the same star line and when we move toward each other, we will meet. His teacher Mau from Satawal, taught him in silence for the first year, guiding him to connect with his own personal, cosmic relationship with the universe. Once connected, the universe continued to teach him through his own observations and contemporary, practical, and spiritual experiences.

In the ancient world, there are many, many stories of the spiritual guidance of people by being completely connected. This idea of being related to all life-forms as family is not a fantasy to us. There is one pervading consciousness that unites and connects us all, and that's because our ancestors spiritually take different forms of life to reconnect with us. In truth, we really are related to *all* life forms as family.

Part of our spiritual preparation as Kanaka Maoli is as ancestors. It's the challenge that all of us face who are alive on earth today. How do we prepare to be the ancestors of future people? How do we make the decisions that carry the consciousness to have clean water for future generations, to put into place all of the necessary things for survival that are needed and that were given to our generation to best help us survive?

On a spiritual level, we believe that the awakening that's happening all over the world today is showing us a greater power. Even though we've been pushed to the limit and almost to extinction and many species have, in fact, become extinct, we see how these events—as we saw in times of natural disasters like the Indonesian tidal waves and hurricane Katrina—enliven the capacity of goodness in people to connect with each other and collectively to realize a much greater power.

The revitalization of Kanaka Maoli culture is very profoundly part of the effect of change and transformation in my life. I made five films on ahupua'a knowledge and sadly, many of the films document places that don't exist anymore. The last film I made is a film with kupuna John Ka'imikaua, called *A Mau A Mau,* which means to continue forever. Our Elders teach us to look beyond the democracy of majority rule, because in our ancient traditions, we had councils of people who represented every area of spiritual and cultural life. The principle of the decisions that are made by *'aha* councils is that the people who have to live with those decisions must be part of making the decisions. There are over seven thousand languages with peoples who speak them living on earth . . . why then should only the G8 superpowers make the decisions of economic globalization/gobble-ization over property, ownership, control, exploitation, and war—decisions that the rest of us must live with? Without nature and the expressions and wisdom of cultural integrity insanity rules our lives and ruins our earth.

A lot of the time our culture is commercialized and seems to exist only as the music or the background for tourism. But this part of the film *A Mau A Mau* presents a ceremony that has to do with Kanaka Maoli expressing our connection to life; our deep gratitude and profound recognition of all that is given to us as cosmic people who awake in whatever time we live in, to consciously communicate with the cosmos and to understand what are the right ways to heal ourselves and the earth. We will give our best to this collective endeavor, placed as we are all over the earth in cosmic connection with our parents *Papa* and *Wakea*, Earth and Sky, to carry light and to help light up the consciousness of human beings and all the life systems that protect our existence and our world.

E Mau Ke Ea I Ka 'Aina I Ka Pono. . . . The very life of the land and all that nourishes life is protected by the right intentions, the right actions, and the right outcomes of the people.

This discussion took place at the Bioneers Conference in 2005.

33

The Power of Being a Human Being

John Trudell

I'm not sure if I think of things in terms of Original Instructions, I just know that there's the original knowledge. I'm a part of that native community that's been involved in the relocation process. On my reservation we were being punished for things that happened in Minnesota in the 1860s.* We had our ceremonies suppressed and all of the Christian church information imposed upon us. We were taken from our land and isolated in the industrial training schools, the boarding schools. By the time I came around and my generation came around, the ceremonies weren't there anymore and the language was kept amongst the old because they were afraid to pass it on because of what had happened to them.

---

*In Minnesota in 1862 there was a Sioux Uprising (also known as the Dakota War of 1862) after the United States had broken their treaty promises to Dakota leaders. Several bands of Dakota people revolted and waged war on the United States and white settler groups. Several hundred white settlers and Native Americans died in the warfare. Over three hundred Sioux men were taken as prisoners and sentenced to death for the uprising. President Lincoln reviewed the trial records and approved the mass execution of thirty-nine Sioux men. On December 26, 1862, thirty-eight Sioux men were hanged in Mankato, Minnesota. This is still the largest mass execution in United States history. See the *Dakota War of 1862* by Kenneth Carley (Minnesota Historical Society Press, 2001) and *Through Dakota Eyes—Narrative Accounts of the Minnesota Indian War of 1862* (Minnesota Historical Society Press, 1988).

Yet in terms of traditions, the Elders told me what they told me and I learned from them what I learned from them. Once I became taller and had to take responsibility for being out on my own, I thought, well, do I want to go back and learn my language, do I want to go find this tradition the way that everybody perceives we're supposed to be? I thought, no, there's a reason for my generation, there's a reason we are here. There's a reason we are who we are. And a part of that reason is that you can look at what's lost and you can look at what's here, and I thought, well, maybe one of the reasons for our generation is that we are an interpretive generation. We understand the predator mindset better; each generation understands it better than the previous generation.

I looked at the language and I decided that I was not going to go back and learn my language. I'm going to use this one, English. I'll use it as my act of revenge for fuckin' teaching it to me in the first place! See, to me, *that's* "traditional"—to take and use the resource that's there, because that's the way it is. You use the resource that's there. I rely on the ancient knowledge because when I look at tradition, after having the experiences I've had, I understand that they can take the ceremonies away and they can take the rituals away and they can take certain things away, but tradition is based upon respect. Somehow, though, in the brutalization and the trauma of genocide, we lose that perspective. We see so many things that are being taken from us and this creates all of the traumas.

From the very beginning, I had to go back and understand the original knowledge. To me this is the fact that we're all human beings. Every one of us, we are the descendants of a tribe. Every one of us has a tribal ancestry and we have a genetic memory. Encoded in that genetic memory is the experience of our individual and collective evolution. You can follow it through the ancestry. The information is there, because we're human beings—the knowledge of all those experiences are with us.

The human is temporary but being just is. Being is being. So it's like we're on an e-ticket ride to Disneyland. It's a terrible ride, but we're on the ride, in the human form. But when the ride's over, we go back to being. It's not really about the ride because everything is about energy.

As beings, we are energy; we are spirits in the form of humans. In the ancestral genetic memory we understood that this is a spiritual reality that we're in. It's not a physical reality, it is a spiritual reality because it's the reality of being, with physical things in it. It is the evolution of being. That's what's going on. It's the evolution of being, not humankind; the evolution of being is what reality is about.

We have these experiences as humans. We are put into this mix of physical and spiritual, however we're put into it. But it is the individual experience of *being* and how that being evolves as we go through the human experience; *this* is what's connected to the realities of what power really is. Power is not a man-made device or structure. Power is not a political, religious, or social system. That's not power. Those are systems of authority. The reality of power is an entirely different reality, and that reality is us—human beings; the power of the human being.

But they diminished the power of the human being because we don't think like human beings anymore, we don't identify as human beings. We are citizens or Republicans or Democrats or liberals or leftists or Indians or women or men or victims; we're everything but a human being. We do not perceive and participate in this reality from the consciousness of human beings. We participate in this reality from the consciousness of different labels and victimizations. But those are only parts and we can't achieve what it is we're looking for unless we understand how to be a human being. To be a human being we have to connect to the reality of our relationship to power and these are Original Instructions.

An original instruction is that we have intelligence so we need to use it clearly and coherently. We need to take responsibility for our lives and think. We must use our intelligence to think, to create the reality that must be created, because there are no existing solutions. I guarantee it. There is no answer to the problem that is here and now. That solution does not exist.

Your democracy, your religions, none of it works. Actually, all of it is the *cause* of the problems. For there to be any real solution, we must create it. It is one thing to say I respect tradition and I respect the Creator and I respect life and all those things. But we have the responsibility to use our intelligence clearly and coherently so we can manifest that respect into a coherent, balanced reality.

How bad can you make yourself feel through your fears, your doubts, and your insecurities? You can sit around feeling powerless. How bad can you make yourself feel through your fears, your doubts, and your insecurities and how does that affect the people around you? If you have the ability to do that, that's your power.

So this deal about being powerless or feeling powerless is all a lie. We have power. It is perpetual. We constantly have power, and we're constantly using it or it's being misused. We're not using it in the way all the spiritual holy holies want us to use it. So let's take our clear, coherent minds and use our power and show respect to the Creator. To show respect to the Creator and the creation, we should value the gifts and take responsibility for the tools that we were given. This is the power of a human being.

The thing about hope is it was the last thing in Pandora's box of evil. I was a little kid and they said, the gods gave Pandora the box of evil and they told her not to open it. She opened it anyway, because she was a woman, right? So she opened it anyway and the seven evils of the world came out. Incidentally, hope came out. But hope is there to help us cope with the evil, right? I was in the sixth or seventh grade when I first heard this, but I got it even then. Hold it. It's the box of evil, fool. Hope's lying. Hope is the biggest evil of all. They didn't say the box of evil "plus hope." I know there was no shortage of boxes because they'd been putting our thought and consciousness in boxes forever, so I know it wasn't about that.

But the subtleties of this is when we take certain sounds and words like hope, we think it is good for us. Hope is waiting to be served. I think it's better to pray, to activate our intelligence. It is all a matter of how we use our intelligence and our thinking process. Part of the reason for the situation that we're in is because almost everything we're doing is a contradiction to the responsibility of being. Our intelligence and the power of our intelligence have been put into a box. We've been programmed to believe, we have not been taught to think. We've not been encouraged to think. We've been programmed to believe.

What happened to us, to the Native Peoples on this hemisphere, happened to your tribes, all peoples. You're descendants of tribes and it happened to your tribes, it just happened to your tribes before you got here. And then when you got here, you did to us what they had done to you. All of that was done to change your tribal perception of reality; to change and alter the spiritual perception of reality and turn it into a religious perception of reality, because there's a difference between spiritual and religious. Religious is about submission and obedience and authoritarianism. Spiritual is about taking responsibility.

We have to look at this, submission is not taking responsibility. It is an easy, convenient out that they programmed into us that's acceptable. "Well, I submit to them because this is good." I may be crazy, but *they* are insane. Think about it. We're born, there's something wrong with us for being born. We commit the original sin for being born. Think about that coherently. You are the descendant of a tribe. We are *all* the descendants of tribes.

In the real reality, when we are born into this reality it's like a giving of gifts. The gift of life is given to the gift of life. When we leave, it's still continuing because it's about being. So it's always about the giving of life.

But here we are now, put into a reality where we believe we committed a crime for being born. Then you never see yourself ever again the way you really were put here because you see yourself through judgment. All of these are Original Instructions in someone's religion. Our responsibility is to recognize life, not to judge it. We have to recognize life and not judge it because judgment is blinding. You cannot judge and recognize simultaneously. You cannot believe and think simultaneously. Maybe occasionally because there's always an aberration, but you cannot believe and think simultaneously all the time because belief limits thinking. Believing puts thinking in a box. So all thinking that goes on is limited by the definitions of the belief.

We need to have an understanding of this process because everything that ever happened, happened to make us believe what they wanted us to believe. They wanted us to believe that there was something wrong with us and that we had to obey them. This was the gig they ran on the tribes of Europe and the descendants of the tribes of Europe and they ran it here. But it was about altering our perception of reality from a spiritual perception of reality into a mining perception of reality. The mining tools became religion and government and politics and racism and sexism and all of these other divisive things.

Mining tools are not who we are. We are human beings—our bone, flesh, and blood is made up the metals, minerals, and liquids of the earth. We have being that is our spirit, our energy, and our essence. All things of the earth are made up of the same thing. All things of the earth have being. They can take the being out of the earth, that's uranium. They put it through a mining process and convert it to being a form of powerful energy. They do it with fossils. They do it with us. They take the being part of humanity and mine the being part of humanity through how they program us to perceive reality. They then take that and they turn that into fuel to run this system that we're in. This is the gig that goes on all the time. But to be a human being, we have to connect to the reality of our relationship to power and this is an original instruction.

This presentation took place at the Bioneers Conference in 2006.

Indigenous Resources

PART ONE

UNCOVERING THE ECO-SPIRITUAL VALUES OF THE ORIGINAL INSTRUCTIONS

Organizations

The Cultural Conservancy (TCC)
P.O. Box 29044, Presidio of San Francisco, CA 94129
Phone: (415) 561-6594 • Fax: (415) 561-6482
E-mail: mknelson@igc.org
Website: www.nativeland.org

First Nations Development Institute (FNDI)
703 Third Avenue, Suite B, Longmont, CO 80501
Phone: (303) 774-7836 • Fax: (303) 774-7841
E-mail: info@firstnations.org
Website: www.firstnations.org

First Peoples Worldwide (FPW)
3307 Bourbon Street, Fredericksburg, VA 22408
Phone: (540) 899-6545 • Fax: (540) 899-6501
E-mail: info@firstpeoplesworldwide.org
Website: www.firstpeoplesworldwide.org

Native American Science Academy
E-mail: vnthater@silverbuffalo.org
Website: www.silverbuffalo.org/NativeScienceAcademy.html

Books and Periodicals

Deloria Jr., Vine. *Red Earth, White Lies—Native Americans and the Myth of Scientific Fact.* New York: Scribner, 1995.

Grim, John. *Indigenous Traditions and Ecology—The Interbeing of Cosmology and Community.* Cambridge: Harvard University Press, 2001.

Harney, Corbin. *The Way It Is—One Water, One Air, One Mother Earth.* Nevada City, CA: Blue Dolphin Publishing, 1995.

Mohawk, John. *Utopian Legacies—A History of Conquest and Oppression in the Western World.* Santa Fe: Clear Light Publishers, 2000.

Peat, David F. *Blackfoot Physics—A Journey into the Native American Universe.* San Francisco: Weiser Books, 2006.

PART TWO
INDIGENOUS DEMOCRACIES

Organizations

Center for World Indigenous Studies (CWIS)
1001 Cooper Point Road, SW, Suite 140, Olympia, WA 98502
Phone: (360) 586-0656 • Fax: (253) 276-0084
Website: www.cwis.org

En'owkin Centre
Lot #45, Green Mountain Road, RR #2, Site 50 Comp 8, Penticton, BC, V2A 6J7 Canada
Phone: (250) 493-7181 • Fax: (250) 493-5302
E-mail: pr@enowkincentre.ca; enowkin@vip.net
Website: http://enowkin.tripod.com

Kalahari Peoples Fund (KPF)

P.O. Box 7855, University Station, Austin, TX 78713–7855

Phone: (512) 453-8935 • Fax: (512) 459-1159

E-mail: meganbie@io.com

Website: www.kalaharipeoples.org

Indigenous Resource Center of the Americas (IRCA)

Department of Native American Studies, University of California at Davis, CA 95616

Phone: (530) 752-0357 • Fax: (530) 752-7097

E-mail: svarese@ucdavis.edu

Website: http://repositories.cdlib.org/irca

Books and Periodicals

Barker, Joanne. *Sovereignty Matters—Locations of Contestation and Possibility in Indigenous Struggles for Self-Determination.* Lincoln, NE: University of Nebraska Press, 2005.

Deloria Jr., Vine, and Clifford Lytle. *The Nations Within: The Past and Future of American Indian Sovereignty.* Austin, TX: University of Texas Press, 1998.

Mohawk, John, and Oren Lyons, eds. *Exiled in the Land of the Free: Democracy, Indian Nations & the U.S. Constitution.* Santa Fe: Clear Light Publishers, 1992.

Wilkins, David E. *American Indian Politics and the American Political System.* Portland, OR: Rowman and Littlefield Publishers, Inc., 2006.

Wilkins, David E., and K. Tsianina Lomawaima. *Uneven Ground: American Indian Sovereignty and Federal Law.* Norman, OK: University of Oklahoma Press, 2002.

PART THREE
THE ART AND SCIENCE OF KINSHIP

Organizations

California Indian Basketweavers Association
P.O. Box 1348, Woodland, CA 95776–1348
Phone: (530) 668-1332 • Fax: (530) 668-1386
E-mail: ciba@ciba.org
Website: www.ciba.org

Indigenous Peoples Restoration Network (IPRN)
P.O. Box 495, Douglas City, CA 96024
Phone: (530) 222-7576 (msg)
E-mail: iprn@ser.org; iprn@ser.org
Website: www.ser.org/iprn/default.asp

Native American Land Conservancy
P.O. Box 1829, Indio, CA 92202
Phone: (760) 775-2204; (800) 670-6252
Fax: (760) 775-5137
E-mail: rherrera@spotlight29.net

Terralingua—Partnerships for Biocultural Diversity
217 Baker Road, Salt Spring Island, BC V8K 2N6, Canada
E-mail: info@terralingua.org
Website: www.terralingua.org/index.htm

Woodfish Institute
Phone: (415) 263-0423
E-mail: lgray@woodfish.org
Website: www.woodfish.org

Books and Periodicals

Anderson, M. Kat. *Tending the Wild—Native American Knowledge and the Management of California's Natural Resources.* Los Angeles: University of California Press, 2005.

Blackburn, Thomas, and Kat Anderson, eds. *Before the Wilderness—Environmental Management by Native Californians.* Banning, CA: Ballena Press, 1993.

Cajete, Gregory. *Native Science—Natural Laws of Interdependence.* Santa Fe: Clear Light Publishers, 2000.

Cajete, Gregory, ed. *A People's Ecology.* Santa Fe: Clear Light Publishers, 1999.

LaDuke, Winona. *Recovering the Sacred—The Power of Naming and Claiming.* Cambridge, MA: South End Press, 2005.

Nabhan, Gary. *Cultures of Habitat—On Nature, Culture, and Story.* Berkeley, CA: Counterpoint Press, 1998.

PART FOUR
INDIGENOUS FEMININE POWER:
IN HONOR OF SKY WOMAN

Organizations

Indigenous Women's Network
227 Congress Avenue, Austin, TX 78701
Phone: (512) 258-3880
Website: www.Indigenouswomen.org

International Council of Thirteen Indigenous Grandmothers
P.O. Box 745, Sonora, CA 95370
Phone: (209) 532-9048
E-mail: info@grandmotherscouncil.com
Website: www.grandmotherscouncil.com

Kembatta Women's Self-Help Center-Ethiopia/Kembatti Mentti Gezzimma-Tope (KMG)
KMG Administrative Office, P.O. Box 13438, Addis Ababa, Ethiopia
Phone: (251) 167-0791 (office); (251) 940-3651 (cell)
E-mail: kmg.selfhelp@ethionet.et
Website: www.kmgselfhelp.org/index.html

Native Women's Association of Canada (NWAC)
Six Nations of the Grand River, P.O. Box 331, Ohsweken, ON N0A 1M0, Canada
Phone: (905) 765-9737
Fax: (905) 765-0173
E-mail: reception@nwac-hq.org
Website: www.nwac-hq.org/en/index.html

Books and Periodicals

Allen, Paula Gunn. *The Sacred Hoop—Recovering the Feminine in American Indian Traditions.* Boston: Beacon Press, 1992.

Harjo, Joy, and Gloria Bird. *Reinventing the Enemy's Language: Contemporary Native American Women's Writings of North America.* New York: W. W. Norton & Company, 1998.

Mehusuah, Devon Abbott. *Indigenous American Women—Decolonization, Empowerment, Activism.* Lincoln, NE: University of Nebraska Press, 2003.

Silko, Leslie Marmon. *Yellow Woman and a Beauty of the Spirit.* New York: Simon and Schuster, 1997.

PART FIVE
YOU ARE WHERE YOU EAT:
NATIVE FOODS AND TRADITIONAL AGRICULTURE

Organizations

New Mexico Acequia Association (NMAA)
607 Cerrillos Road, Suite F., Santa Fe, NM 87505
Phone: (505) 995-9644
E-mail: info@lasacequias.org
Website: www.lasacequias.org

Proyecto Andino de Tecnologias Campesinas/Andean Project of Peasant Technologies (PRATEC)
Martin Perez 866, Lima 17, Peru
Phone and Fax: 51-1-2612825
E-mail: pratec@pratec.org.pe
Website: www.pratec.org.pe

Taos Food Center of the Taos County Economic Development Corporation (TCEDC)
P.O. Box 1389, Taos, NM 87571
Phone: (505) 758-8731 • Fax: (505) 758-3201
E-mail: tcedc@tcedc.org
Website: www.tcedc.org

Traditional Native American Farmers Association (TNAFA)
P.O. Box 31267, Santa Fe, New Mexico 87594
Phone: (505) 983-4047
E-mail: cbrascoupe@yahoo.com
Website: www.7genfund.org/aff-tra-nat-ame.html

Tohono O'Odham Community Action (TOCA)
Address: P.O. BOX 1790, Sells, AZ 85634
Phone: (520) 383-4966 • Fax: (520) 383-5286
Website: www.tocaonline.org

White Earth Land Recovery Project (WELRP)
607 Main Avenue, P.O. Box 97, Callaway, MN 56521
Phone: (800) 973-9870 (toll-free); (218) 375-2600 (local)
Fax: (218) 375-2603
E-mail: info@welrp.org
Website: www.nativeharvest.com; www.savewildrice.org

Books and Periodicals

Barlow, Maude, and Tony Clark. *Blue Gold—The Fight to Stop the Corporate Theft of the World's Water.* New York: New Press, 2003.

Campbell, Colin T., and Thomas M. Campbell II. *The China Study— The Most Comprehensive Study of Nutrition Ever Conducted and the Startling Implications for Diet, Weight Loss, and Long-Term Health.* Dallas, TX: Benbella Books, 2006.

Ferreira, Mariana, and Gretchen Lang. *Indigenous Peoples and Diabetes— Community Empowerment and Wellness.* Durham, NC: Carolina Academic Press, 2005.

Frank, Lois Ellen. *Foods of the Southwest Indian Nations.* Berkeley, CA: Ten Speed Press, 2002.

Mihesuah, Devon Abbott. *Recovering Our Ancestors' Gardens— Indigenous Recipes and Guide to Diet and Fitness.* Lincoln, NE: University of Nebraska Press, 2005.

Price, Weston A. *Nutrition and Physical Degeneration,* 6th ed. Washington, DC: Price Nutrition Foundation, 2004.

Shiva, Vandana. *Stolen Harvest—The Hijacking of the World's Food Supply.* Cambridge, MA: South End Press, 1999.

PART SIX
DECOLONIZATION AND GLOBAL INDIGENOUS STRUGGLES FOR JUSTICE

Organizations

Cultural Survival
215 Prospect St., Cambridge, MA 02139
Phone: (617) 441-5400 • Fax: (617) 441-5417
E-mail: culturalsurvival@cs.org
Website: www.culturalsurvival.org

Indigenous Environmental Network (IEN)
P.O. Box 485, Bemidji, MN 56619
Phone: (218) 751-4967 • Fax: (218) 751-0561
E-mail: ien@igc.org
Website: www.ienearth.org

International Indian Treaty Council (IITC)
2390 Mission St., Suite 301, San Francisco, CA 94110
Phone: (415) 641-4482 • Fax: (415) 641-1298
E-mail: iitc@treatycouncil.org
Website: www.treatycouncil.org

International Forum on Globalization (IFG)
1009 General Kennedy Avenue #2, San Francisco, CA 94129
Phone: (415) 561-7650 • Fax: (415) 561-7651
E-mail: ifg@ifg.org
Website: www.ifg.org

Red Wind Councils
P.O. Box 15, Maynard, MA 01754
E-mail: pathways@redwindcouncils.org
Website: www.redwindcouncils.org

Books and Periodicals

Gedicks, Al. *The New Resource Wars—Native and Environmental Struggles against Multinational Corporations.* Cambridge, MA: South End Press, 1993.

———. *Resource Rebels.* Cambridge, MA: South End Press, 2001.

LaDuke, Winona. *All Our Relations—Native Struggles for Land and Life.* Cambridge, MA: South End Press, 1999.

Mander, Jerry, and Victoria Tauli-Corpuz. *Paradigm Wars—Indigenous Resistance to Economic Globalization.* San Francisco: Sierra Club Books, 2006.

Zarsky, Lyuba. *Is Nothing Sacred? Corporate Responsibility for the Protection of Native American Sacred Sites.* San Francisco: Sacred Land Film Project, 2006.

PART SEVEN
RE-INDIGENIZATION

Organizations

Aboriginal Healing Foundation
75 Albert Street, Suite 801, Ottawa, ON K1P 5E7, Canada
Phone: (613) 237-4441
Fax: (613) 237-4442; (888) 725-8886
Website: www.ahf.ca

Advocates for Indigenous California Language Survival
221 Idora Ave., Vallejo, CA 94591
Phone: (707) 644-6575
Website: www.aicls.org

Aloha Aina Health Center
45-559 Luluku Rd., Suite 5-A3, Kane'ohe, HI 96744
Phone: (808) 234-1171

Cultural Learning Center, Ka'ala Farm, Inc.
P.O. Box 630, Waianae, HI 96792
Phone: (808) 696-4954 • Fax: (808) 696-9411

Indigenous Language Institute
1601 Cerrillas Road, Santa Fe, NM 87505
Phone: (505) 820-0311 • Fax: (505) 820-0316
E-mail: ili@indigenous-language.org
Website: www.indigenous-language.org

Native American Health Center
3124 International Blvd., Oakland, CA 94601
Phone: (510) 747-3030 • Fax: (510) 748-0116
Website: www.nativehealth.org

John Trudell
P.O. Box 6655, Minneapolis, MN 55406
Phone: (612) 729-5995 (Speaking engagements and performances)
E-mail: info@johntrudell.com (for speaking engagements and perfor-
mances); contact@johntrudell.com (E-mail list)
Website: www.johntrudell.com

Organizations: Native Studies Educational Programs

En'owkin Centre
Lot #45, Green Mountain Road, RR #2 Site 50 Comp 8, Penticton, BC
    V2A 6J7, Canada
Phone: (250) 493-7181 • Fax: (250) 493-5302
E-mail: pr@enowkincentre.ca; enowkin@vip.net
Website: http://enowkin.tripod.com

Northern Arizona University (NAU) Department of Applied
Indigenous Studies (College of Social Behavioral Studies)
P.O. Box 15020, Flagstaff, AZ 86011
Phone: (928) 523-6624 • Fax: (928) 523-5560
E-mail: d-ais@jan.ucc.nau.edu
Website: www.ais.nau.edu/AISweb05.htm

Northern Arizona University (NAU)
Center for Sustainable Environments (CSE)
P.O. Box 5765, Flagstaff, AZ 86011–5765
Phone: (928) 523-0637 • Fax: (928) 523-8223
E-mail: Heather.Farley@nau.edu
Website: http://home.nau.edu/environment

San Francisco State University (SFSU) American Indian Studies
Department
1600 Holloway Avenue, San Francisco, CA 94132
Phone: (415) 338-1054/405-3928 • Fax: (415) 405-0496
E-mail: aismain@sfsu.edu
Website: www.sfsu.edu/~ais

University at Buffalo (UB)
Department of American Studies & the Center for the Americas
1010 Clemens Hall, SUNY at Buffalo, Buffalo, NY 14260-4630
Phone: (716) 645-2546 • Fax: (716) 645-5977
Website: http://cas.buffalo.edu/americanstudies

University of British Columbia, Okanagan (UBC) Indigenous Studies
(Community, Culture and Global Studies)
ART270, 3333 University Way, Kelowna, BC V1V 1V7, Canada
Phone: (250) 807-9337 • Fax: (250) 807-8001
E-mail: sherry.dyck@ubc.ca
Website: http://web.ubc.ca/okanagan/ikbarberschool/options/
  Indigenousstudies.html

University of New Mexico (UNM) Native American Studies
Address: MSC 06 3740, 1 University of New Mexico, Albuquerque,
   NM 87131
Phone: (505) 277-3917 • Fax: (505) 277-1818
E-mail: nasinfo@unm.edu
Website: www.unm.edu/~nasinfo

University of Saskatchewan (US)
Department of Native Studies
Address: Room 134 Kirk Hall, Saskatoon, SK, Canada S7N 5C8
Phone: (306) 966-5556 • Fax: (306) 966-6242
Website: www.usask.ca/nativestudies

Books and Periodicals

Duran, Eduardo. *Healing the Soul Wound—Counseling with American Indians and Other Native Peoples.* New York: Teachers College Press, 2006.

Duran, Eduardo, and Bonnie Duran. *Native American Postcolonial Psychology.* New York: SUNY, 1995.

Jolivette, Andrew. *Cultural Representation in Native America.* Walnut Creek, CA: AltaMira Press, 2006.

Wilson, Angela Waziyatawin, and Michael Yellow Bird. *For Indigenous Eyes Only: A Decolonization Handbook.* Santa Fe: School of American Research Press, 2005.

Journals, Newspapers, and Additional Periodicals (Websites)

Akwesasne Notes
www.ratical.org/AkwesasneNs.html
http://pages.slic.com/mohawkna/mnnotes.htm

American Indian Culture and Research Journal
www.books.aisc.ucla.edu/aicrj.html

American Indian Quarterly
http://muse.jhu.edu/journals/american_indian_quarterly

Cultural Survival Quarterly
www.culturalsurvival.org/publications/csq/index.cfm

Indian Country Today
www.indiancountry.com

Native Peoples Magazine
www.nativepeoples.com

News from Indian Country
www.indiancountrynews.com

News from Native California
www.heydaybooks.com/news

Wicaso Sa Review
http://muse.jhu.edu/journals/wicazo_sa_review

Notes

Introduction: Lighting the Sun of Our Future

1. www.iwgia.org/sw155.asp. Indigenous Issues. International Work Group on Indigenous Affairs (IWGIA).

2. U.S. Census Bureau, 2002.

3. David E. Wilkins, *American Indian Politics and the American Political System* (Portland, OR: Rowman and Littlefield Publishers, 2002), 41.

4. Alan Leventhal, Les Field, Hank Alvarez, and Rosemary Cambra, "The Ohlone: Back From Extinction" in Lowell Bean's *The Ohlone Past and Present: Native Americans of the San Francisco Bay Region* (Banning, CA: Ballena Press, 1994).

5. Vine Deloria Jr., *Red Earth, White Lies—Native Americans and the Myth of Scientific Fact* (New York: Scribner Press, 1995), 37.

6. Rodney Frey, ed., *Stories That Make the World—Oral Literature of the Indian Peoples of the Inland Northwest* (Norman, OK: University of Oklahoma Press, 1995).

7. Rose von Thater-Braan, *Science of Learning: Traditional Knowledge and Native Science in the 21st Century,* Native Science Academy, www.silverbuffalo.org/NSA-ScienceOfLearning.html.

8. Gregory Cajete, *Ignite the Sparkle—An Indigenous Science Education Curriculum* (Asheville, NC: Kivaki Press, 1999).

9. Gregory Cajete, *Native Science—Natural Laws of Interdependence* (Santa Fe, NM: Clear Light Publishers, 2000), 28.

10. "The Hopi Message: An Address by Thomas Banyacya, Kykotsmovi, Arizona. December 11, 1992."

11. Brenda Norrell, "Hopi Warnings to the World," *Indian Country Today* (Mar. 29, 2005).

12. From an interview with Vivienne Jake, Kaibab Paiute Reservation, September 21, 2003.

13. Lawrence Gross, "Cultural Sovereignty and Native American Hermeneutics in the Interpretation of the Sacred Stories of the Anishinaabe," *Wicaso Sa Review* (Fall 2003).

14. Ibid., 129.

15. Brave Heart, Maria Yellow Horse, and L. M. DeBruyn, "The Historical Trauma Response among Natives and Its Relationship with Substance Abuse: A Lakota Illustration," *Journal of Psychoactive Drugs* 35(1), (Jan.–Mar. 2003).

16. Eduardo Duran, *Wounding Seeking Wounding: The Psychology of Internalized Oppression,* unpublished manuscript, 2002.

17. Betty Bastien, J. W. Kremer, J. Norton, J. Rivers-Norton, and P. Victors, "The Genocide of Native Americans," *Revision* 22, no. 1:13–20.

Chapter 5. Indigenous Knowledge as the Basis for Our Future

1. Julian Burger, "Indigenous Peoples and the United Nations," in *The Human Rights of Indigenous Peoples,* edited by Cynthia Price Cohen (Ardsley, NY: Transnational Publisher, 1998), 3–16.

2. Indigenous Knowledge document. Canadian International Development Agency, 2002.

3. Harold Cardinal and Walter Hildebrandt, *Treaty Elders of Saskatchewan* (Calgary, Alberta, Canada: University of Calgary Press, 2000), 16.

Chapter 18. From the First to the Last Bite

1. Weston A. Price, *Nutrition and Physical Degeneration,* 6th ed. (Washington, DC: Price Nutrition Foundation, 2004).

2. Colin Campbell and Thomas M. Campbell III, *The China Study—The Most Comprehensive Study of Nutrition Ever Conducted and the Startling Implications for Diet, Weight Loss, and Long-Term Health* (Dallas, TX: Benbella Books, 2006).

Chapter 19. Re-Indigenizing Our Bodies and Minds through Native Foods

1. Vandana Shiva, *Stolen Harvest—The Hijacking of the World's Food Supply* (Cambridge: MA: South End Press, 1999); Maude Barlow and Tony Clark, *Blue Gold—The Fight to Stop the Corporate Theft of the World's Water* (New York: New Press, 2003).

2. Teresa O'Nell, *Disciplined Hearts—History, Identity, and Depression in an American Indian Community* (Berkeley: University of California Press, 1996); also see the numerous excellent publications by Joseph Gone at http://sitemaker.umich.edu/joseph.p.gone/publications.

3. The RAFT website: www.slowfoodusa.org/raft/index.html.

4. From the Friendship House website: www.friendshiphousesf.org.

Chapter 29. El Poder de la Palabra/The Power of the Word

1. Francisco X. Alarcón, "Prayer to Fire," in *Snake Poems: An Aztec Invocation* (San Francisco, CA: Chronicle Books, 1992), 103.

2. The most complete and scholarly edition of Ruiz de Alarcón's *Tratado*, which includes the original spells in Nahuatl and their English translations as well as versions only in English of Ruiz de Alarcón's introductions and commentaries written in Spanish, was edited by J. Richard Andrews and Ross Hassig as *Treatise on the Heathen Superstitions That Today Live among the Indians Native to This New Spain* (Norman, OK: University of Oklahoma Press, 1984), 162.

3. Alarcón, "Four Directions," in *Snake Poems*, 6.

4. Alarcón, "Silence," in *Snake Poems*, 7.

5. Alarcón, "Tonatzin," in *Snake Poems*, 125.

6. Gloria Anzaldúa, *Borderlands/La Frontera: The New Mestiza* (San Francisco: Spinsters/Aunt Lute, 1987), 79.

7. Anzaldúa, *Borderlands/La Frontera*, 87.

8. A previous version of a discussion of "Mesticismo" was published by Francisco X. Alarcón, "Reclaiming Ourselves. Reclaiming America," in *The Colors of Nature: Culture, Identity, and the Natural World*, edited by Alison H. Deming and Lauret E. Savoy (Minneapolis: Milkweed Editions, 2002).

9. Victor Montejo (illustrated by Luis Garay), *Popol Vuj: libro sagrado de los mayas* (Mexico City: Artes de Mexico, 1999), 7–8.

10. Kenny Ausubel, "Francisco X. Alarcón Rediscovers the Americas," in *Restoring the Earth: Visionary Solutions from the Bioneers* (Tiburon, CA: H. J. Kramer, 1997), 65–84.

11. Francisco X. Alarcón, *Snake Poems: An Aztec Invocation* (San Francisco, CA: Chronical Books, 1992). Some of these poems have also been included in Francisco X. Alarcón, *From the Other Side of Night/Del Otro lado de la noche: New and Selected Poems* (University of Arizona Press, 2002).

12. Alarcón, "Tonalamatl/Spirit Book," in *Snake Poems*, 18.

13. Alarcón, "Song," in *Snake Poems*, 19.

14. Alarcón, "Hernando Ruiz de Alarcon," in *Snake Poems*, 8–9.

15. Alarcón, "Alarcon, For Planting Corn," in *Snake Poems*, 74.

16. Alarcón, "Nomatca Nehuatl," in *Snake Poems*, 150.

17. Alarcón, "In Xochitl in Cuicatl," in *Snake Poems*, 150.

18. Alarcón, "Tlazolteotl," in *Goddess of the Americas/La Diosa de laws Americas: Writings on the Virgin of Guadalupe*, edited by Ana Castillo (New York: Riverhead Books, 1996), 309.

Chapter 30. Mending the Split-Head Society with Trickster Consciousness

1. Gerald Vizenor, "Trickster Discourse," *American Indian Quarterly* 14, no. 3 (Summer, 1990), 277–87.

2. Allan Ryan, *The Trickster Shift—Humour and Irony in Contemporary Native Art* (Vancouver: UBC Press, 1999).

3. Ibid., 5.

4. See the 2006 Canadian Indian Residential Schools Settlement Agreement at www.irsr-rqpi.gc.ca/english/irssa.html and www.residentialschoolsettlement .ca/English.html and the 1997 Australian "Bringing Them Home: The 'Stolen Children Report'" at www.hreoc.gov./au/social_justice/stolen_children.

Chapter 31. Re-Nativization in North and South America

1. Marie Battiste and James Youngblood Henderson [Sa'ke'j], "Eurocentrism and the European Ethnographic Tradition," in *Protecting Indigenous Knowledge and Heritage, A Global Challenge*, Purich's Aboriginal Issues Series (2000), 21.

2. Jack Forbes, "El concepto de mestizo-metis," in *Plural Segunda Epoca* XIII-Ino. 145 (Oct. 1983).

3. Eduardo Grillo, "Development or Cultural Affirmation in the Andes?" and "Development or Decolonization," in *The Spirit of Regeneration: Andean Culture Confronting Western Notions of Development,* edited by Frédérique Apffel-Marglin with PRATEC (London: Zed Books, 1998).

Bibliography

Alarcón, Francisco X. *From the Other Side of Night/Del Otro lado de la noche: New and Selected Poems.* Tucson, AZ: University of Arizona Press, 2002.

———. "Reclaiming Ourselves. Reclaiming America." In *The Colors of Nature: Culture, Identity, and the Natural World,* edited by Alison H. Deming and Lauret E. Savoy. Minneapolis, MN: Milkweed Editions, 2002.

———. *Snake Poems: An Aztec Invocation.* San Francisco: Chronicle Books, 1992.

Andrews, J. Richard, and Ross Hassig. *Treatise on the Heathen Superstitions That Today Live among the Indians Native to This New Spain.* Norman OK: University of Oklahoma Press, 1984.

Anzaldúa, Gloria. *Borderlands/La Frontera: The New Mestiza.* San Francisco: Spinsters/Aunt Lute, 1987.

Ausubel, Kenny. "Francisco X. Alarcón Rediscovers the Americas." In *Restoring the Earth: Visionary Solutions from the Bioneers.* Tiburon, CA: H. J. Kramer, 1997.

Banyacya, Thomas. "The Hopi Message to the UN General Assembly." December 11, 1992. http://nativenet.uthscsa.edu/archive/nl/9301/0164.html.

Barlow, Maude, and Tony Clark. *Blue Gold—The Fight to Stop the Corporate Theft of the World's Water.* New York: The New Press, 2003.

Bastien, Betty, J. W. Kremer, J. Norton, J. Rivers-Norton, and P. Vickers. "The Genocide of Native Americans." In *ReVision: A Journal of Consciousness and Transformation* 22, no. 1, 1999.

Brave Heart, Maria Yellow Horse, and L. M. DeBruyn. "The Historical Trauma Response among Natives and Its Relationship with Substance Abuse: A Lakota Illustration." *Journal of Psychoactive Drugs 35*, no. 1 (January–March 2003).

"Bringing Them Home: The 'Stolen Children' Report 1997." Reconciliation and Social Justice Library. www.austlii.edu.au/au/special/rsjproject /rsjlibrary /hreoc/stolen/.

Cajete, Gregory. *Ignite the Sparkle—An Indigenous Science Education Curriculum.* Durango, CO: Kivaki Press 1999.

———. *Native Science—Natural Laws of Interdependence.* Santa Fe: Clear Light Publishing, 2000.

Canadian Indian Residential Schools Settlement Agreement 2006. www. irsr-rqpi.gc.ca/english/irssa.html and www.residentialschoolsettlement. ca/English.html.

Campbell, T. Colin, and Thomas M. Campbell II. *The China Study—The Most Comprehensive Study of Nutrition Ever Conducted and the Startling Implications for Diet, Weight Loss, and Long-Term Health.* Dallas: Benbella Books, 2006.

Castillo, Ana. *Goddess of the Americas/La Diosa de las Américas: Writings on the Virgen of Guadalupe.* New York: Riverhead Books, 1996.

Deloria Jr., Vine. *Red Earth, White Lies—Native Americans and the Myth of Scientific Fact.* New York: Scribner, 1995.

Duran, Eduardo. *Healing the Soul Wound—Counseling with American Indians and Other Native Peoples.* New York: Teachers College Press, 2006.

———. *Wounding Seeking Wounding: The Psychology of Internalized Oppression.* Unpublished manuscript, 2002.

Duran, Eduardo, and Bonnie Duran. *Native American Postcolonial Psychology.* New York: SUNY, 1995.

Frey, Rodney. *Stories That Make the World—Oral Literature of the Indian Peoples of the Inland Northwest as Told by Lawrence Aripa, Tom Yellowtail, and Other Elders.* Norman, OK: University of Oklahoma Press, 1995.

Gross, Lawrence. "Cultural Sovereignty and Native American Hermeneutics in the Interpretation of the Sacred Stories of the Anishinaabe." *Wicaso Sa Review* 18, no. 2 (2003): 127–34.

Indigenous Issues. International Work Group on Indigenous Affairs (IWGIA). www.iwgia.org/sw155.asp.

Jolivette, Andrew. *Cultural Representation in Native America*. Walnut Creek, CA: AltaMira Press, 2006.

LaDuke, Winona. *All Our Relations—Native Struggles for Land and Life*. Cambridge, MA: South End Press, 1999.

Leventhal, Alan, Les Field, Hank Alvarez, and Rosemary Cambra. "The Ohlone: Back From Extinction." In *Ohlone Past and Present: Native Americans of the San Francisco Bay Region*, edited by Lowell Bean. Banning, CA: Ballena Press, 1994.

Mander, Jerry, and Victoria Tauli-Corpuz. *Paradigm Wars—Indigenous Resistance to Economic Globalization*. San Francisco: Sierra Club Books, 2006.

Montejo, Víctor. *Popol Vuj: libro sagrado de los mayas*. Mexico City: Artes de México, 1999.

Norrell, Brenda. "Hopi Warnings to the World." *Indian Country Today*, March 29, 2005.

O'Nell, Teresa. *Disciplined Hearts—History, Identity, and Depression in an American Indian Community*. Berkeley: University of California Press, 1996.

Pratt, Scott. *Native American Pragmatism—Rethinking the Roots of American Philosophy*. Bloomington, IN: Indiana University Press, 2002.

Price, Weston A. *Nutrition and Physical Degeneration*, 6th ed. Washington, D.C.: Price Nutrition Foundation, 2004.

Reed, Bill, and Robert Bringhurst. *The Raven Steals the Light—Native American Tales*. Boston: Shambhala, 1996.

Ryan, Allan. *The Trickster Shift—Humour and Irony in Contemporary Native Art*. Vancouver: UBC Press, 1999.

Shiva, Vandana. *Stolen Harvest—The Hijacking of the World's Food Supply*. Cambridge, MA: South End Press, 1999.

Steingraber, Sandra. *Living Downstream: An Ecologist Looks at Cancer and the Environment*. New York: Addison-Wesley Publishing Company, 1997.

Von Thater-Braan, Rose. "Science of Learning: Traditional Knowledge and Native Science in the 21st Century." Native Science Academy. www.silberbuffalo.org/NSA-ScienceOfLearning.html.

"We the People: American Indian and Alaska Natives in the United States." U.S. Census Special Reports, 2002.

Wilkins, David E. *American Indian Politics and the American Political System*. Portland, OR: Rowman and Littlefield Publishers, Inc., 2002.

Wilson, Waziyatawin Angela, and Michael Yellow Bird. *For Indigenous Eyes Only: A Decolonization Handbook*. Santa Fe: School of American Research Press, 2005.

Contributors

Rebecca Adamson, a Cherokee, is the founder of the First Nations Development Institute (1980) and founder/president of First Peoples Worldwide (1997). She has worked with many grassroots tribal communities and nationally as an advocate for tribal issues since 1970. Her work helped to establish the first reservation-based micro-enterprise loan fund in the United States and a national movement for reservation land reform. On the international front, First Peoples Worldwide has worked on land tenure and Indigenous rights issues in Australia, Botswana, and Namibia and led the World Bank to create the First Global Indigenous Peoples' Facility Fund in 2003. She has also been active in the nonprofit sector, serving on many boards, advisory councils, and commissions, for groups ranging from major philanthropic institutions to governmental, UN bodies. She is on the National Editorial Advisory Committee for *Indian Country Today* and the Editorial Advisory Board for *Native Americas* and was a founding member of Native Americans in Philanthropy and International Funders for Indigenous Peoples. Adamson has won many prestigious awards for her leadership and innovative grant making, published numerous papers, and is a coauthor of *The Color of Wealth—The Story Behind the U.S. Racial Wealth Divide.* She holds a master of science degree in Economic Development from the University of Southern New Hampshire, where she also taught a graduate course on Indigenous Economics.

Francisco X. Alarcón is a visionary Chicano poet and educator who explores the Mestizo experience of the Americas. Poems from his book *Snake Poems: An Aztec Invocation* (Chronicle Books, 1992) expressing the Nahuatl heritage of Mexico were incorporated into a *Seeds for Change* catalog some years ago. He is also the author of *From the Other Side of Night/Del otro lado de la noche: New and Selected Poems* (University of Arizona Press, 2002), ten other volumes of poetry, and numerous bilingual children's books. Francisco was one of the three finalists nominated for the state poet laureate of California few years ago. He teaches at the University of California, Davis.

Paula Gunn Allen, Ph.D., a poet, writer, and scholar in Native American Studies and an expert on Native American women's writing, was born in New Mexico in 1939, of Lebanese-American and Laguna-Sioux-Scotch ancestry. She grew up immersed in pueblo culture. Allen's writing career began in 1974 with the publication of *Blind Lion Poems*. She edited the MLA's landmark *Studies of American Indian Literature: Critical Essays and Course Designs*, published in 1983. During her academic career, Allen taught at Fort Lewis College, the College of San Mateo, San Diego State, and San Francisco State. Following that, she taught at the University of New Mexico, UC Berkeley, and, lastly, at UCLA, until her retirement in 1999.

/'Angn!ao /'Un (known informally as "Kiewiet") is a Ju/'hoan (Ju-twan) San leader and traditional healer from Namibia. The second Chairman of the Nyae Nyae Conservancy (NNC) in Namibia, Mr. /'Un also heads its Education Committee. The NNC was the first conservancy for natural resources established in Namibia after its independence in 1990. The NNC is accepted by the Namibian government as the Traditional Authority for the Nyae Nyae region, in which approximately two thousand Ju/'hoan San people retain some control over their traditional hunting and gathering territories. His work for the NNC consists of representing his community with decision-making on the regional, national, and international levels. He grew up with, and still practices, traditional skills of the Ju/'hoan San. Along with his skills as a politician and orator, he is both a hunter and a healer. /'Angn!ao speaks six African languages.

Jeannette Armstrong (www.enowkincentre.ca) is an award-winning Okanagan-Canadian author and artist whose works include children's books, novels, poetry, video and TV productions, and a collaboration with architect Douglas Cardinal on a book entitled *Native Creative Process*. A renowned leader in Indigenous and environmental education, she is the executive director of the En'owkin International School of Writing and Arts, a council member of the Okanagan Nation, and an advocate of Indigenous rights, serving on many international councils. In 2003, she was the recipient of the Ecotrust, Howard and Peter Buffet Award for Indigenous Leadership.

Megan Biesele (www.kalaharipeoples.org) cofounded one of the first U.S. anthropological advocacy organizations, the Kalahari Peoples Fund, in 1973 and currently serves as its coordinator. For nearly three decades, Megan worked with Ju/'hoan San (Bushmen) communities in Botswana and Namibia as an advocate and documentarian and was director of the Nyae Nyae Development Foundation of Namibia (NNDFN) from 1987 to 1992. Currently she is preparing her collected folklore and other texts in the Ju/'hoan language for use by linguists and other scholars and working on Ju/'hoan community education projects and archives.

Gregory Cajete, Ph.D., a Tewa from Santa Clara Pueblo, New Mexico, is a groundbreaking educator and scholar renowned for honoring Indigenous Knowledge; he has lectured at colleges and universities around the world. He is also a noted artist (ceramics, pastel, and metal), herbalist, holistic health practitioner, and ethnobotanist. Affiliated with the Institute of American Indian Arts in Santa Fe for twenty-five years, he served there in many capacities, including as chair of Native American Studies. Currently he is a director of Native American Studies in the College of Education at the University of New Mexico. Dr. Cajete has authored four books: *Look to the Mountain: An Ecology of Indigenous*

Education; Ignite the Sparkle: An Indigenous Science Education Curriculum Model; A People's Ecology: Explorations in Sustainable Living; and *Native Science: Natural Laws of Interdependence.*

Katsi Cook, a Wolf Clan Mohawk, mother of six, grandmother of seven, is a maternal and child health consultant whose mission is to restore traditional birth and reproductive health knowledge to Native American families through the development of community-led and culture-based research, outreach, education, and clinical practice models. The founding aboriginal midwife of the Tsi *Non:we Ionnakeratstha* (the place where they will be born) *Ona:grahsta'* (a birthing place) Six Nations Maternal and Child Centre in Hagersville, Ontario, Katsi's work integrates environmental health research, aboriginal midwifery, and the democratization of scientific knowledge and systems of Indigenous Knowledge. A key figure in a campaign to evaluate and monitor the effects of PCB and other organo-chlorines on breastfeeding Mohawk women in the St. Lawrence River and Great Lakes Basin ecosystem, Katsi was also a professional member of the Interim Regulatory Council of the College of Midwives of Ontario and is writing curriculum to assist in the training of a new generation of aboriginal midwives, doulas, and other birth-workers.

Richard DeerTrack, a decorated Korean War veteran with forty years' federal government experience in senior management, budgeting, and policy work, has been a public servant at the highest levels of tribal government at Taos Pueblo for over twenty years and active in founding countless social, cultural, artistic, and entrepreneurial initiatives, including the Blue Corn Trading Company (1981–1989). The Blue Corn Trading Company marketed Native American products including organic foods and herbal remedies under a philosophy of returning benefits to the Native American community. Richard is the founder and current director of the Cross-Cultural Communication Project and of DeerTrack and Associates, a consulting firm on Indian affairs. He sits on many boards and is president of the board of the New Mexico Environmental Law Center.

Eric Enos is the cofounder and program director of the Cultural Learning Center at Ka'ala in Hawaii's Wai'anae Valley, which serves over four thousand school children, community groups, university scholars, international groups, and substance abuse treatment programs annually. Students learn the art and science of pounding *kalo* into *poi*, traditional *kapa* making, native plant use/ethnobotany, and the making of traditional dyes, baskets, mats, and foods. Ka'ala's projects include the archaeological mapping of sacred sites and the restoration of rare and endangered native plants and streams.

Ohki Siminé Forest (www.ohkisimineforest.com), born in Quebec of Mohawk descent, began a spiritual journey at an early age, traveled to Asia to study with Mongolian shamans, and was admitted into the Wolf Clan at the Long House of Kahnawake/Iroquois League of Peace in 1984. For twenty years, she has made her home in Chiapas, Mexico, where she was initiated into the world of Maya healers and where she founded a spiritual center. Ohki's nonprofit organization, Red Wind Councils, provides humanitarian assistance to help Maya Indigenous communities achieve self-sufficiency and achieve social stability. Its projects include health care, farming, women's collectives, cultural preservation, construction, and education. She is the author of *Dreaming the Council Ways: True Native Teachings from the Red Lodge.* She visits the United States regularly to speak and lead retreats.

Bogaletch Gebre, Ph.D. (www.kmgselfhelp.org), is the executive director of Kembatta Women's Self-Help Center in Ethiopia, which she founded in 1997 to help eliminate female genital mutilation (FGM), nearly universal in the Kembatta region until recently. Herself a victim of female genital excision, she was the first girl in her village to be educated beyond the fourth grade. She later attended Hebrew University in Jerusalem on a full scholarship, became the first woman invited to join the science faculty at Addis Ababa University, was a Fulbright Scholar at the University of Massachusetts, and earned a Ph.D. in epidemiology from UCLA (where she ran five marathon races to raise money for Ethiopian famine victims). Since her return home, Dr. Gebre has been instrumental in spreading awareness throughout Ethiopia. Empowering women at the individual and community level, her center has helped train community health workers, peer educators, and village leaders about the dangers of FGM and HIV. The center has introduced health curricula into local schools, constructed maternity and HIV/AIDS testing clinics, and created women's vocational trainings and environmental restoration projects.

Petuuche Gilbert lives at the Pueblo of Acoma and works for the Acoma Realty and Natural Resources Office. He served in tribal governmental service for eleven years and considers himself a civil servant dedicated to the Pueblo of Acoma. He also works with the Indigenous World Association, a United Nations Non-Governmental Organization, to advocate the human rights of Indigenous Peoples. Mr. Gilbert graduated from the University of New Mexico with a Bachelor of Arts degree and from the University of Arizona with a Master of Arts degree, both in Political Science.

Tom Goldtooth is the national coordinator of the Indigenous Environmental Network, an alliance of native grassroots groups and communities working on environmental issues. He has been a leader in native social, economic, and environmental justice movements for over twenty years and is a founding board member of the Washington Office on Environmental Justice; the Environmental Justice Fund Initiative; and the Great Lakes Regional Indigenous Environmental Network. He is an advisor to the staff of the Greenpeace U.S. Native Lands Campaign and recently completed a three-year term on the U.S. EPA Environmental Justice Advisory Council Sub-Committee on Waste Facility and Siting.

Tirso Gonzales, Ph.D., a Peruvian of Aymara descent, is a scholar, international consultant, and activist who works closely with Indigenous Peoples throughout the Americas. Currently an assistant professor of Indigenous Studies at the University of British Columbia in Okanagan, Gonzales was formerly a postdoctoral fellow at the University of California at Davis and Berkeley. In the recent past he worked as a member of the Peruvian National Commission of Indigenous Andean, Amazonian, and Afro Peruvian People. Gonzales explores the use of participatory methodologies and techniques on issues central to Indigenous community development, "agri-*cultures*," strategic visions, and the local management of natural resources. He is committed to supporting the agenda of Indigenous Peoples as well as processes related to ecological knowledge, food and seed sovereignty, cultural affirmation, and decolonization.

Leslie Gray, Ph.D., conducts a psychotherapy practice in San Francisco while teaching ecopsychology and Native American studies locally and internationally. Her innovative work blending Indigenous healing methods with Euro-American therapeutic practices has been featured in numerous publications including the Sierra Club Books anthology, *Ecological Medicine: Healing the Earth, Healing Ourselves.* Leslie is a member of the Society of Indian Psychologists and director of Woodfish Institute (www.woodfish.org), which she founded in 1998 to promote traditional knowledge in original ways.

Kxao =Oma is an English-Ju/'hoan translator and education advisor on San dropout rates for Jennifer Hays (a U.S. anthropologist). In early 2004 Kxao started work for the Nyae Nyae Conservancy as a Programmes Manager. The purpose of the Nyae Nyae Conservancy is to control and sustainably manage the Nyae Nyae land and natural resources to ensure the long-term improvement of the quality of life of members and the maintenance of culture of the Ju/'hoansi people. Mr. =Oma attended the annual meeting of the Permanent Forum on Indigenous Issues at the United Nations in New York in May 2005. There he represented both the Nyae Nyae Conservancy and the larger San community of southern Africa.

Winona LaDuke, from the White Earth reservation in Minnesota, is a two-time Green Party U.S. vice-presidential candidate, a mother of five, and program director of Honor the Earth, a Native American foundation working on environmental and energy issues. Founding director of the White Earth Land Recovery Project, Winona has worked for over twenty years on Indigenous land issues and is the recipient of a wide array of prestigious awards, including, most recently, the International Slow Food Award. She has written extensively on Native American and environmental issues and is the author of five books, including: *Last Standing Woman, All Our Relations,* and most recently, *Recovering the Sacred.*

Chief Oren R. Lyons, Onondaga Council of Chiefs, Onondaga Nation, Haudenosaunee, a leading advocate for American Indian and Indigenous causes, led the first Indigenous delegation to the UN, helped establish the Working Group for Indigenous Populations and other international bodies, cofounded the Traditional Circle of Indian Elders and Youth, the Haudenosaunee Environmental Task Force, and many other groups. Oren is also a widely exhibited artist, the author/illustrator of *Dog Story* and coauthor/editor of *Exiled in the Land of the Free: Democracy, Indian Nations and the U.S. Constitution,* and a major figure in world lacrosse (an Iroquois invention).

Dennis Martinez, of O'odham\Chicano\Anglo heritage, has worked in ecological restoration and forestry for thirty-four years as a contractor, nurseryman, consultant, teacher, writer, speaker, and university lecturer throughout North America and in Hawaii, working to integrate traditional Indigenous ecological knowledge and modern science. Currently chair of the Indigenous Peoples' Restoration Network (IPRN) and codirector of the Takelma Intertribal Project in southwest Oregon, Dennis serves on many councils and steering committees of major tribal restoration and sustainable forestry groups. He has authored countless restoration, forestry, and ethnographic reports and assessments for a wide variety of clients, including the World Wildlife Fund, the U.S. Forest Service and BLM, and tribes and NGOs throughout North America.

Nalani Minton is an activist, educator, and filmmaker whose primary focus is on Hawaiian cultural and spiritual traditions. She is also a therapist in the field of recovery from intergenerational trauma, serves as an advisor to the University of Hawaii for its *Ike Ao Pono* program, is on the advisory board of the Aloha 'Aina Health Center, and was a representative at the UN's Indigenous Peoples' Forum over the last decade, which culminated in the Hague Peace Appeals.

John Mohawk, Ph.D. (1945–2006), a Turtle Clan Seneca was, in the late 1960s and early 1970s, the editor of *Akwesasne Notes*, the largest Indian publication in the United States at that time and a crucially important, groundbreaking forum for North American Indigenous struggles during that heated period. John was an assistant professor of American Studies at the State University of New York at Buffalo and on the board of the Collective Heritage Institute (CHI), the parent organization of the renowned annual Bioneers Conference, until his untimely death in December of 2006. John was also a farmer who worked to revive traditional Iroquois foods and helped develop a number of food products based on white corn. The author of several books (his most recent was *Utopian Legacies*—a fascinating look at some of Western thought's problematic dimensions), John was a uniquely original thinker on a wide range of topics and—as a font of great wisdom, humor, and joy—he was a mentor and a great inspiration to many.

Melissa K. Nelson, Ph.D. (www.earthdiver.org.), is a mixed-blood cultural ecologist, writer, educator, media-maker, and activist whose work is dedicated to Indigenous revitalization, environmental protection and restoration, and cross-cultural reconciliation. She is a professor of American Indian Studies at San Francisco State University and president of the Cultural Conservancy, a nonprofit Indigenous rights organization. Melissa has worked with many tribes and native communities throughout North America and the Pacific on community-based applied research projects regarding language and oral traditions, health, foods, and sacred sites. She coproduced the award-winning documentary film

The Salt Song Trail: Bringing Creation Back Together. Of Anishinaabe/ Métis/Norwegian heritage, she is an enrolled member of the Turtle Mountain Band of Chippewa Indians and lives in the San Francisco Bay Area.

Mark Paikuli-Stride is (with his wife Kamakanoe) the cofounder of the nonprofit Aloha 'Aina Health Center, which helps Hawaiian families achieve better health through nutrition and wellness education. Mark and Kamakanoe are also restoring ancient *lo'i kalo* (taro patches) in Maunawili Valley and bringing back the ahupua'a system of sustainable agriculture to help restore traditional Hawaiian values and to reintroduce traditional foods in school lunch programs and the larger society.

Julio Valladolid Rivera is a key figure in PRATEC, an NGO dedicated to preserving and spreading Andean perspectives on peasant agriculture and culture. PRATEC also seeks alternatives to modern approaches to development in the Peruvian Andes to counter socially and ecologically destructive effects of such development. PRATEC draws from the traditions and agricultural practices of rural, native peasants who have been organizing themselves locally, and re-appropriating land through direct action campaigns since the 1950s. In 1990, Julio and his comrades began teaching a course on Andean culture and agriculture for native peasants and soon incorporated the Andean practice of "ritual agriculture" that embraces kinship-oriented visions of the land and encourages respect for all living entities through ritual actions and offerings that express both a deep respect for *Pachamama* (Mother Earth) and local communities.

Jacquelyn Ross is from the Pomo and Coast Miwok people of Sonoma and Marin counties and is an enrolled member of the Federated Indians of Graton Rancheria. She is a traditional fisherwoman, food gatherer, and basketry student. Jacquelyn works in the University of California system, working on tribally focused education efforts. She also serves as a policy consultant to nonprofit organizations. Her articles on health and environmental concerns have appeared in *News from Native Cali-*

fornia, News from Indian Country, and the U.S. Environmental Protection Agency website.

Enrique Salmón, Ph.D., of Rarámuri heritage and raised in the Sierra Tarahumara of Mexico and in the United States, is an ethnoecologist specializing in the Indigenous cultures, plants, and lands of the Southwest. Dr. Salmón has undertaken a variety of applied research programs with Native American Peoples of the Colorado Plateau, including the Havasupai, Hopi, Navajo, Mayo, and Yaqui, and has worked with a number of environmental and Native American organizations in the region. He currently teaches American Indian Studies at San Francisco State University and is writing a book on native food ways. He is also an accomplished jazz musician and avid whitewater canoeist and backcountry skier.

Marlowe Sam, a member of the Colville Confederated Tribe, is a co-facilitator of the Four Societies Process Method, an Okanagan traditional form of community conflict resolution and collective transformation that he has helped lead with a variety of social change organizations. Marlowe has served as an advisory board member for the Pacific Cultural Conservancy and has acted as a primary mediator in several tribal conflicts. Over the past three decades, Marlowe has been a frontline activist against social injustices against the Indigenous Peoples of North America. He is currently completing a Master of Arts degree at the University of British Columbia-Okanagan.

Priscilla Settee, Ph.D. (Cree), is an associate professor in the department of Native Studies at the University of Saskatchewan. She has coedited and is a contributor of the *Expressions in Canadian Native Studies,* Canada's first native studies textbook. Settee has chaired and coordinated four international conferences on Indigenous Knowledge. She coestablished and teaches with the Canadian Indigenous Languages and Literacy Development Institute, which is presently in its seventh year of operation. In that capacity she has developed graduate courses on the topics of Indigenous languages, community sovereignty, and intellectual property. Settee is presently chair of Saskatoon's Aboriginal high school (Oskayak High School). She has a master's degree (University of Manitoba); a bachelor of education degree (University of Saskatchewan); a bachelor of arts degree (University of Guelph); and an interdisciplinary doctoral degree in education and agriculture.

Clayton Thomas-Muller, of the Mathais Colomb Cree Nation (Pukatawagan) in Manitoba, is an activist for Indigenous self-determination and environmental justice with ten years' organizing experience. His many achievements include helping create the Urban Aboriginal Youth Multi-Purpose Center Initiative (UMAYC). The UMAYC is a fund that sponsors aboriginal youth initiatives across Canada, representing Indigenous groups at many major UN conferences and international summits, and serving as native energy organizer for the Indigenous Environmental Network (IEN). He is currently a health human resource research officer with Canada's National Aboriginal Health Organization. Clayton is also a gifted poet and spoken-word performer.

John Trudell (www.johntrudell.com), a famous AIM activist in the 1970s, became a world-renowned spoken word performer in the early 1980s. Born of mixed tribal blood, he grew up in and around the Santee Sioux reservation near Omaha, served in Vietnam, and in 1969 participated in the historic occupation of Alcatraz by Indians of All Tribes. In 1971, he joined the American Indian Movement (AIM) and was its national chairman from 1973–1979. In 1979, Trudell's mother-in-law, pregnant wife, and three children were killed in a fire of unknown origin. Through this horrific tragedy, he began to find his voice as an artist and poet. A meeting with Jackson Browne in 1979 introduced him to the musical world. His first album with legendary Kiowa guitarist Jesse Ed Davis was *A.K.A. Graffiti Man*. More recent endeavors include *Blue Indians* and *Bone Days* (produced by Angelina Jolie). Trudell has also worked as an actor in such films as *Thunderheart, On Deadly Ground,* and *Smoke Signals,* and as a consultant to *Incident at Oglala,* a Robert

Redford–produced documentary about the infamous shootout at Pine Ridge. Trudell is the subject of filmmaker Heather Rae's documentary, *Trudell* (2005).

Verna Williamson-Teller, the Governor of the Isleta Pueblo in New Mexico from 1986 to 1996, was the first woman to be elected governor of an American Indian pueblo. An environmental activist and educator in New Mexico and nationally, she served on the board of the New Mexico Environmental Law Center until 2004 and was a recipient of the prestigious Alston/Bannerman Fellowship. She is currently serving as chief judge of the Isleta Pueblo Tribal Court.

BOOKS OF RELATED INTEREST

Moonrise
The Power of Women Leading from the Heart
Edited by Nina Simons with Anneke Campbell

Planetary Healing
Spirit Medicine for Global Transformation
by Nicki Scully and Mark Hallert

Original Wisdom
Stories of an Ancient Way of Knowing
by Robert Wolff

The Secret Teachings of Plants
The Intelligence of the Heart
in the Direct Perception of Nature
by Stephen Harrod Buhner

Plant Spirit Healing
A Guide to Working with Plant Consciousness
by Pam Montgomery

Walking on the Wind
Cherokee Teachings for Harmony and Balance
by Michael Garrett

Weather Shamanism
Harmonizing Our Connection with the Elements
by Nan Moss with David Corbin

The Universe Is a Green Dragon
A Cosmic Creation Story
by Brian Swimme, Ph.D.

Inner Traditions • Bear & Company
P.O. Box 388
Rochester, VT 05767
1-800-246-8648
www.InnerTraditions.com

Or contact your local bookseller